ROBERT CLARKE
To "B" or Not To "B"—
A Film Actor's Odyssey

ROBERT CLARKE

To "B" or Not To "B"— A Film Actor's Odyssey

**By Robert Clarke
and Tom Weaver**

MIDNIGHT MARQUEE PRESS, INC.
BALTIMORE, MARYLAND

ISBN 1-887664-02-5
Library of Congress Catalog Card Number: 95-081887
Manufactured in the United States of America
Printed by Kirby Lithography Company, Arlington, VA
First Printing by Midnight Marquee Press, Inc., February 1996
Front Cover Design by Susan Svehla

Acknowledgments: John Antosiewicz Photo Archives, Ronald V. Borst/ Hollywood Movie Posters, Eric Caidin/Hollywood Book and Poster, John Goodier, Steve Hammett

To Tom Weaver, who spent many of his Sunday afternoons for several months taping our long-distance telephone conversations, transcribing them and helping me turn it all into this book. He has no peer when it comes to the excellence of his writing about sci-fi and horror films and the people who made them. He's the best!

Also, to Gary and Susan Svehla for their courage and commitment of time, money and many hours of hard work to lay out the book, send it to the printer and present it to you, the reader, to whom we *all* dedicate this volume. Thank you.

—Robert Clarke

TABLE OF CONTENTS

INTRODUCTION

At no point during my many years as an actor did I foresee myself writing a book about my experiences on stage, in films, on radio and television. But I also did not foresee the enduring popularity of so many of the movies in which I appeared. The funny part about it is, some of the movies which are among my best-remembered are exactly the ones I'd like to *forget*!

After working as a contract player at RKO (1944-7), on the stage (Broadway and summer stock in the late 1940s) and in two of Ida Lupino's well-respected "message pictures," I began to accept offers to star in B movies. Not that that's something to be necessarily ashamed of: The two Lupino movies I made, *Outrage* and *Hard, Fast and Beautiful*, certainly fall into the category of "small pictures," and *The Man from Planet X*, the first-ever "man-from-space" movie, is a cult picture today despite its lack of means. (We cranked *that* one out in just six days!) I'm also not ashamed of what we did on *Three Musketeers, Tales of Robin Hood* and *Sword of Venus* (made during my "swashbuckler phase"), pictures like *The Fabulous Senorita* and *Street Bandits*, and of course the two films I produced and starred in, *The Hideous Sun Demon* (which I also co-wrote and co-directed) and *Beyond the Time Barrier*. But there were also a number of films which I looked upon, then and now, as steps backwards in my career.

I've found out in recent years, though, that there's still a sizable audience for the B-type films of the 1950s and '60s, even some of the least of them; in fact, the low-budget pictures seem to have as much (or more) appeal as some of that era's bigger productions. My friend Wade Williams once paid me the compliment of saying that, while I never made "stardom," many of my films will be remembered longer than other films made by people who are more famous. At first that was hard to accept, but I've since recognized that there may be more than just a grain of truth to that. To this day I am receiving fan mail, requests for autographs (some of it from overseas) and requests for interviews. In recent years I've been profiled in a number of movie magazines, among them *Famous Monsters of Filmland*, *Fangoria*, *Filmfax* and *Psychotronic*.

But what really drove home the realization that there was a devoted following for the B-films was the response to my appearance at conventions. I think the first one I experienced was a *Starlog* convention, held at the Marriott Hotel out near the L.A. airport. At that con, I saw that not much attention was being paid to Mark Hamill ("Luke Skywalker" in the *Star Wars* movies), a "current" star, but there was *great* interest in Kirk Alyn, who played Superman in the old Sam Katzman serials. Years later I appeared as a guest at a movie memorabilia convention for the first time; it was held at the Beverly Garland Hotel in North Hollywood, and I attended at the suggestion of my friend and fan Eric Caidin, owner of the Hollywood Book and Poster shop on Hollywood Boulevard. I didn't know what to expect, but when it was announced over the public address system that I had arrived, suddenly there was a line out to the door of people waiting for autographs, asking questions and telling me how much they had enjoyed movies like *Planet X*, *Sun Demon* and *Beyond the Time Barrier*. Needless to say, it was quite a surprise, realizing that the interest in those pictures had not only been sustained, but was blossoming. Since that time I've appeared at a num-

After receiving the FANEX Guest of Honor Award, here I am posing with actor George Stover and producer Sam Sherman.

ber of such events locally, and I've also been a guest of honor at the Chiller Theater convention in Hohokus, New Jersey, at FANEX (Gary and Sue Svehla's yearly Baltimore-based con) and at the 1995 *Famous Monsters* con in L.A., where I was interviewed on stage (together with actors John Agar, Ann Robinson, William Schallert and Michael Fox) by director Joe Dante.

Modern-day directors like Fred Olen Ray and Joe Dante (pictured) like to have some of us old "monster fighters" around.

I had no inkling that any of this was in the cards 20 years ago, when I attended a Screen Actors Guild seminar about pensions. They read a finding from some study made about actors and employment, and the gist of it was that, come the age of 50, activity for the journeyman actor really begins to fade. The statistical information we were being read, unfortunately, applied in my case quite closely. In the mid-'70s I

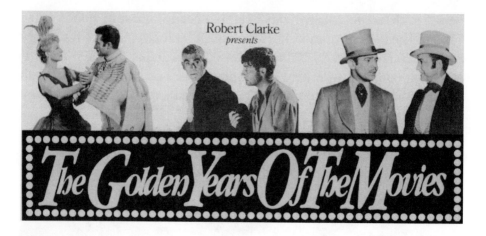

Robert Clarke
presents

The Golden Years Of The Movies

worked back and forth between the King Family's concert tours and TV specials (I married Alyce King of the singing King Sisters in 1956) and the inspirational TV series *Westbrook Hospital*. But once Alyce and her sisters and bandleader Alvino Rey decided to hang up their dancing shoes, and *Westbrook Hospital* ceased production, the number of calls I was getting from my agent gave me an indication that I was no longer going to be as busy as I previously had been. It was at that point that I determined to use some of my background in film and TV for what are commonly called "platform appearances," as a public speaker. I became a member of the National Speakers Association and I came up with a title for my presentations, "The Golden Years of the Movies." In my "Golden Years" lectures I told stories and anecdotes that I had gathered during my years in the world of entertainment, and it was a suitable transition from being actively involved in films and/or television and/or King Family activities and this new period of reduced acting work. The public speaking produced some very good results, but it wasn't what I most wanted to do—act.

Acting was my "lifelong dream," I suppose, right from the days when as a kid I used to pay a dime to attend the Saturday movie matinees in downtown Oklahoma City. I don't remember seeing *many* silent films, but Tom Mix, the great cowboy star of the silent screen, was my first Western hero (along with his horse Tony). Seeing Tom Mix and the senior Douglas Fairbanks and other actors like them gave me (and millions of other kids) an opportunity to live vicariously, to place themselves in the shoes of the hero. To me, it seemed like being an actor was a wonderful way to have a lot of different experiences as different per-

4

sons, different personalities, that one would not have otherwise. (Being a youngster, I didn't realize that an actor's "acting life" in front of the camera or on stage was one thing, but life off-screen, off-stage was quite different.)

My dad and mom were very good about taking us to the movies in those days; we'd get in the car and go to a movie as a family perhaps once a week, Dad, Mom, my brother Bill, sister Genevieve and I. The very first talkie we ever saw was *In Old Arizona* with Warner Baxter as the Cisco Kid. I still remember Dad saying as we were getting ready to leave the house that night, "We're going to take you kids to a movie, and you're going to hear the people on the screen actually *talk*!" (Of course we kids were just amazed by the picture; it was a never-to-be-forgotten experience.) I went to the movies more than once a week, however: We still had streetcars in Oklahoma City then, so my friend Cy Crum and I would buy round-trip tokens for 15 cents, ride downtown and get into the movies for a dime. (Cy and I are still friends 65 years later!) There was a main street in downtown Oklahoma City on which there were perhaps four theaters running first-run pictures; some of the movies that made big impressions on me when I was a kid (or, later, as a teenager) were *The Public Enemy* with James Cagney, *The Great Ziegfeld* with William Powell and *China Seas* and *It Happened One Night* with Clark Gable. Later we got some neighborhood theaters that would run second-run features, including one (the Victoria Theater) which was near our house. I would see movies downtown first-run, and then (weeks later) walk to the Victoria Theater and see them again! I'm sure my folks thought I was a little touched.

It was then, I guess, that the notion of wanting to be an actor was first instilled in me, but I had terrible stage fright. Years later, while I was trying to "make a name" for myself in Hollywood, my junior high school speech teacher Maybelle Conger wrote a little article about me in the school paper. "Bob was so bashful that he would hardly answer the roll call," Miss Conger wrote. "During the year the students always had a campaign assembly in which the various candidates appeared and were introduced and extolled by their campaign managers. Naturally it was very important to get a popular student for your campaign manager if you wanted to win your office. Bob was always popular with the student body so several of the boys asked him to be their campaign manager. He chose one of his best friends to campaign for, and when the fatal day came for the assembly, Bob was backstage, pale as a ghost and with his knees sounding like a trap drum solo. When his time came, he walked out on the stage and opened his mouth. Nothing came out. Not even a sigh. He was literally frozen to the spot. He tried to speak and nothing happened. Everyone in the audience was suffering with him, but finally he turned and walked off with his head bowed. I honestly believe that particular incident had more to do with Bob's determination to be an actor than anything before or since."

Actually, Miss Conger had the facts a little wrong, although it made a better story her way. What really happened was that *I* was running for the presidency of the graduating class, and as the candidate I had asked my friend Roy Mack Franks to be my campaign manager. At the assembly he stood up in front of the student body and introduced me, I came out and started the speech. I got off to a good start, but I was about two or three lines into it when I forgot the rest. I had the notes right in my hip pocket, but I was so petrified I just *stood* there, afraid that people would laugh if I pulled out the speech and read it. So I just snuck off the stage. (By the way, I won the election, I think because people felt *sorry* for me!)

When the all-school play *It Never Rains* came around, I was the first one to try out. It broke Miss Conger's heart to have to give me a walk-on part instead of a lead, but she was afraid I might get stage fright again on the big night. Even the responsibility of that small part made me nervous, and I kept moving back and forth across the line of doubt and determination as to whether I could do it or not. Miss Conger had most of her students as friends as well as pupils and I was no exception. I'd go to her home in the evenings, and we would discuss my speech problem. I confided in her that my ambition was to go into the theater, but she told me she thought I didn't stand a chance and that I'd better put any theatrical thoughts out of my head!

Even though Miss Conger felt I didn't have what it takes, she would work with me on breath control and volume. She would also sing the praises of *her* former teacher, Miss Gertrude E. Johnson of the University of Wisconsin, and tell me that if I was determined to "follow my dream" (acting), I should go to school there.

At Classen High School (which Dale Robertson attended a few years after I did), the only play I acted in was a production of Shakespeare's *As You Like It*; I was the shepherd boy and Van Heflin's sister Mary Frances played my girlfriend. I would read for leading parts in many of the different plays that the high school put on, but there were two or three fellow students who would *always* get those roles; I would rarely get anything. (I guess I didn't much impress the high school speech teacher.) To tell the truth, my high school days were full of fun and games; we had social clubs and sports activities, and I was more into those pursuits than hitting the books. After my final year of high school I felt that I was still in need of some "book-learning," and with the threat of World War II looming, going to a military school seemed to make a lot of sense. It was at that point (1939) that I went to Kemper Military School, a small junior college in Missouri. (Kemper's most famous cadet was the great Will Rogers, who attended in the late 1890s.) They didn't have any kind of theatrical activity at Kemper apart from public speaking and debating teams, and I wasn't into that at that time.

I took one year at Kemper and then in my second year I went to the University of Oklahoma in Norman. At O.U. I was going somewhere all the time: In addition to taking classes, I had a "meal job" in the Kappa Alpha fraternity house (working in the kitchen or out in the dining rooms, waiting on tables), and in the evenings I would take part in the university radio station plays. I don't know if anybody was listening or not, but *we* thought we were being heard and we'd reenact Sherlock Holmes stories and do dramatic adaptations of the works of authors like Gui de Maupassant. I felt I was lucky to be "cutting my teeth" a bit on some of that activity. The producer of these student plays was named Homer Heck and he encouraged me. I still remember one wintry night when he and I were leaving the radio station and I asked him if he thought I could succeed in the acting profession. Fifty-five years later I still remember his response: Quite wisely he said, "I don't think it's important whether *I* think you can or not. The question is, do *you* think you can?" He was tossing the ball right back to me, but that *was* the right answer to my question.

Then, summer of 1940, I took a course with a visiting professor from the University of Wisconsin, Gertrude E. Johnson—the very teacher Miss Conger had recommended back in my junior high school days. Miss Johnson was a woman in her 60s; she had taught Fredric March at the University of Wisconsin in 1918. She told me, "If you're serious about trying to get into theater or radio, you should get *out* of the southwestern geographical area, because you have a definite southwestern

7

twang." She suggested I go to the University of Wisconsin for my final two college years, and I took her advice. The tuition for an out-of-state student was reasonable, and I had the notion that if I followed this wonderful teacher I could come somewhere near emulating March.

I went up to the University of Wisconsin in the fall of 1940 and I got my first break in a university stage production. I played the lead in *Stage Door* at the Wisconsin Union Theater (part of the speech department) and I was thrilled to get that opportunity. It was my first time acting with some confidence, and I was beginning to feel that *this might actually work.* I was hedging my bets, however: In my academic courses, I was majoring in economics and minoring in speech. (And I was right to this extent: Later on, when I went into the insurance business when the movie business got tough for me, having that University of Wisconsin diploma helped me get a job as an insurance underwriter. For me, it turned out to be the right thing to do. So many kids want to be actors, that's all they can see, and when they don't succeed at it—*most* of them don't—they get left in the lurch.)

I was in two or three more plays at the University of Wisconsin during my two years there, with some good response from the school paper and others. Miss Johnson also got me a job interview with one of the producers at the university-owned radio station WHA. I wanted to do the same sort of work there that I'd done at O.U., but when the producer heard my southwestern accent, he said, "We've got *just* the job for you—sound effects man!" My accent was still so thick, he didn't want to let me on the air as an actor! (Actors like Dennis Weaver and Dale Robertson never lost their accent; in fact, they made capital of it. That wasn't the case with me.) After association with people, living there in Wisconsin for a year, I managed to lose a bit of that Oklahoma drawl and I finally got a $15-a-week job as a disc jockey at a local commercial radio station, WIBU in Madison. We used to borrow 78 RPM records from one of the local record shops for each day's program; I'd pick up a dozen or more on my way from the campus to the station, and then return them on the way home and thank the lady for the use of them! On the air I played records of the Big Bands, including songs that were being made famous by Alvino Rey and the King Sisters—whom I never dreamed of even *meeting*! I was there at WIBU four or five months, then I went to work as a newscaster for the nearby NBC affiliate.

My parents (Dad especially) had a very supportive attitude about my acting aspirations. Dad had had ambitions to be an actor when *he* was a young man, but he didn't have an opportunity to follow his dream. Dad was quite one with the jokes and the funny stories and he was very good at dialects, and I've told my son Cam (now an in-demand voiceover actor) that perhaps his talent for dialects and mimicry came down to him through the family tree—an "inheritance" from his grandfather! Mom was a bit more apprehensive about it; to her it seemed like a wild shot in the dark. (Which it was *then* and which it still is even *today* for so many hundreds, maybe *thousands* of kids who have ambition to be on television or in movies.) Never at any point did Dad or Mom try to set their foot down and say, "No, you can't do it"—they were helpful and hopeful through every step of the process.

I had not been able to follow my military training at the University of Wisconsin because I was asthmatic; I'd had two years of training (one at Kemper, one year R.O.T.C. training at O.U.), but I wasn't able to take the advanced course because I couldn't pass the physical. After graduating from U.W. (class of '42) I went to Chicago and became friendly with some employees of the Chicago Signal Corps Inspection Zone (part of the U.S. Army Signal Corps). My limited experience as a radio announcer enabled me to get in as an attached civilian employee, and for a year I spent time working for the Signal Corps in Chicago. When the draft call came, I went back to Oklahoma City, but because of the asthma, I was once again turned down. It was at that point that I decided to come to California—to finally make a grab for the brass ring, to pursue my ambition to get into the movies. I didn't want to follow the well-known advice that the best way to get into movies was to go to New York and start as a stage actor; I knew that actors could be discovered right in the shadows of the studios, at places like the Pasadena Playhouse. I hoped that would be my good fortune.

I arranged to hitch a ride to California with my friend Fox Wood, who was on his way to military training in Palmdale. I paid part of the gas and the two of us headed west. It took two and a half days to travel the 1500 miles; Fox left me off in Palm Springs and I took a bus into Los Angeles, where I stayed at a downtown hotel for three or four dollars a night. I had a few bucks in my pocket, a letter of introduction to a small-time agent named Gus Corder and unbridled enthusiasm about the career I was about to embark on in Hollywood. Somehow I just thought that big things were going to happen.

In my first screen role I appeared with Tom Conway (pictured) in RKO's *The Falcon in Hollywood*.

A BEGINNING ACTOR

So many of the great Hollywood stars were "discovered" in funny or colorful ways, and some of the stories of how they broke into the business are as well-known as the stars are famous. As for *my* entry into the movie business, I had to do it "the old-fashioned way," making the rounds of the different studios, holding "real" jobs on the side (for example, at Douglas Aircraft in Santa Monica), contending with disappointments and setbacks, and just generally "paying my dues" as a beginning actor. In fact, if there are any lessons to be learned from the way I broke in, they might be more accurately described as "how-*not*-to"!

My first screen test would take place at Twentieth Century-Fox in August or September of 1943, shortly after I had arrived in California. The scene that the dramatic coach gave me involved a young man (I was then 23 years old) who was dying of cancer—*very* heavy stuff. At that time I probably weighed about 128 pounds soaking wet, and they could tell I might not photograph well. "Kid, go over to wardrobe," I was told. "Maybe they can give you something to build you up a little bit."

Not many people know that a number of stars wear special vests, or "body pads," to give them a more robust appearance than they actually have. Don Ameche used to wear a body pad because one of his shoulders had an unattractive slope to it. He wore this lightweight, padded vest under his shirt and it gave him a better-looking physique. They got out Ameche's body pad and handed it to me, saying, "This'll give you a little more beef on your bones, a little more of a he-man look." George Sanders was making pictures at Fox at this same time, too, and the type of characters that Sanders played often wore smoking jackets. As they were putting Don Ameche's body pad on me, it occurred to them that I should also wear one of Sanders' smoking jackets. They couldn't adjust the length of the sleeves, because they were raglan, so the sleeves came down over my knuckles. "This'll make you look real *debonair*," the wardrobe guy announced. I had my doubts.

A young actress named Donnive Lee was to appear with me in the test, and we had worked on the scene with the dramatic coach for four or five weeks, until every bit of spontaneity we might have brought to it was gone. The scene was shot on the test stage at Fox and photographed by one of the studio's top cameramen.

My agent Gus Corder had gone to high school in Oklahoma with my father; it was Gus who got me that Fox screen test. Five or six weeks after the test, Gus got word back from Fox. This comment about my test went from Darryl F. Zanuck, the head of production at Fox, to the Fox casting director, to Gus, and then to me: Zanuck's advice was, "Don't show that test to *any*body." I was shocked and disappointed, but when we later watched the screen test, I could understand why it got that reaction: My head looked about the size of a pinball! I looked so odd in this big coat, the sleeves running down to my knuckles, and with the body pad creating the impression that my head was too small for my body. I was probably the strangest-looking would-be leading man who ever screen-tested—I looked more like some sci-fi/horror spook! With admirable understatement, Gus said, "Look, kid, we'll just forget that."

So we did. Several months went by and nothing much happened. During that time I was working in a cafeteria on LaBrea near Wilshire, doing a job that I had gotten used to in college—busboy. I lived in an apartment in Beverly Hills and I had a roommate (also from Oklahoma) who ran a Union Oil Company gas station. It was a furnished apartment with a bedroom—which the *other* guy got. I slept on a foldout bed in the living room. The rent control was still on, and we were lucky enough to find and rent that place for 50 bucks a month. That apartment building still stands, and adjacent to it is the Academy of Motion Picture Arts and Sciences.

During those months, things came to a sudden halt: Gus Corder seldom (or never) called. I knew that he was depressed over that terrible test at Fox, and I began to wonder whether it had shaken his confidence in me.

Through a lucky happenstance, I saw a little ad in a little Beverly Hills "throwaway" paper that the Geller Workshop Theater[1] was auditioning actors, and I decided it was time to take matters into my own hands. I went to the theater, which was located at the corner of Fairfax and Wilshire, and said that I'd like to read for whatever play they were getting ready to produce. Next up at the Geller Workshop was a play by

Rachel Crothers called *When Ladies Meet* which had been done on Broadway in the early 1930s. They were doing readings for parts, so I went up to the second floor and read for a director-type fellow, a nice, "older" gent. (At least, that's how I thought of him at that time; he was probably 40!) The "director" had a thin little mustache, a theatrical manner and a very enthusiastic response to my audition: He said, "You read *very* well. Go down and tell 'em I think you'd do very well as the lead." I thought to myself, "Boy, that's great"—I knew it was simply a matter of time before *somebody* realized that I had what it takes, and now it had finally happened.

My self-esteem once again intact, I marched down to the administration office and said, "Mr. Johnstone White said to inquire about the possibility of me doing the lead." They were just as enthusiastic in the administration office as Mr. White had been upstairs: They said, "Oh, fine. Here's an application, and here's the way we work: *You* pay *us* $60." Well, that came as quite a surprise—somehow I'd gotten the funny idea that *they* were going to pay *me*! No, this was how the theater supported itself—through actors paying to be showcased. It was a pay-as-you-go operation where *actors* paid *them* (the people who ran the theater) for the chance to be seen.

Feeling I had nothing to lose—except the 60 bucks!—I anted up the money for the opportunity to act in *When Ladies Meet* for two nights. It was money well-spent: During those two performances, one of the guys working backstage kept coming to me and giving me the cards of various agents who were in the audience. I was delighted by this acknowledgment of my competence as an actor, and by the end of the second night I had a fistful of cards from agents who saw and liked my performance.

As a result, I soon had the opportunity to go with a bigger agency, one which arranged for me to be screen-tested at Columbia. One of my most vivid memories of that visit to Columbia was my meeting with Max Arnow, the studio's casting director. I was introduced to Mr. Arnow, and one of the first things Arnow asked was, "Kid, do you have any stills?" I had my pictures in my hand and I promptly stood up and started walking toward his desk. But before I got there, Arnow said in a contemptuous tone of voice, "I never look at 'em!" And there I stood, caught between my chair and his desk—most embarrassed—with no idea what to do. Was I supposed to take the stills to him anyway, or go back to my chair and sit down? What I *wanted* to do was fall in the nearest hole.

(In a way that small experience encapsulated how I felt about Hollywood at the time. Being from Oklahoma and Wisconsin, coming to Hollywood, was like coming into a fantasy land. Seeing where the pictures were really made. Visiting the sound stages. Meeting the people who made the pictures. I think part of the reason that I made such a lousy test at Fox was that I was literally scared to death.)

My Columbia screen test took place on a Saturday. They were not only testing actors that day, they were also giving some of their dialogue directors a chance to direct test scenes. (One of the dialogue directors was Budd Boetticher, who later directed me in *Three Musketeers* for Hal Roach.) There were four actors being tested that Saturday: Gerald Mohr, Ron Randell, Loren Tindall (a fellow Oklahoman) and myself. I was sent to makeup at 10:30 in the morning and I was due to go before the camera at about one o'clock. I was going to be the fourth and last one tested.

The dialogue directors who were handling the tests had decided that they were going to try to show their abilities as directors—in a way, they were "auditioning," too! As a consequence, they immediately began to fall behind schedule. *Way* behind schedule. One o'clock came and went, and then two o'clock, and I was still waiting. Three o'clock... four o'clock... I was *still* sitting around, getting more and more nervous, and my makeup began running. At 5:15, Max Arnow came down to the set and he said the words I did not want to hear: "What's holding things up? You gotta be out of here in a half-hour!" At that point, it was my turn. Arnow peered at his watch with a look of exasperation and he said to my director, "You've got less than a half-hour. Whatever blocking the dramatic coach has done—forget it. Sit the guy down"—I don't think he knew my name! "Sit him down here in the corner of this couch, and just shoot it." I sat down on the couch and immediately sank way down into the cushions. I was about to get my chance.

The scene was out of Gable and Colbert's *It Happened One Night* and the gal who was testing with me was Ann Savage, who later co-starred in *Detour* with Tom Neal. Arnow said, "Ann, you just stand behind him." Somebody called *action* and the camera began to roll in on tracks, and all I could think about was the fact that I was getting this *one* take—*no* more—to say dialogue to a person (Ann) who was standing *behind* me. And as the scene began, and as I struggled to see her out of the corner of my eye, the camera got closer and I began to hear the sound of its motor. The sound of the motor distracted me and disrupted my concentration.

Needless to say, this test was another bomb—perhaps the *second* worst test in history. I could see my Columbia contract going right out the window—which it did. I was the only one tested that day who was not signed.

My new agency, the Frank Vincent Office, seemed to lose interest in me after the disastrous Columbia test, just the same way Gus Corder did after my flop at Fox. My next chance came via a talent scout named Don Dillaway, a fellow who had been a pretty well-known young actor back in the 1920s; his was one of the cards that had come backstage to me during the two-night run of *When Ladies Meet*. Don seemed to think that I should give it a go at the studio where he worked, which was RKO. I called the Frank Vincent Office and I told them that I was being asked to try-out at RKO, and their response to that was, "Well, go on, go over there!" Normally your agency has someone take you out to the studio, but they didn't even do *that* for me this time—they had apparently lost faith in me, because they just gave me their blessings to go by myself!

I took a bus over to RKO and I read for the dramatic coach, a wonderful woman named Lillian Albertson. Miss Albertson—as I always addressed her—had been an actress back in the 'teens, before I was born. Miss Albertson had me read a scene from a John Garfield picture called *The Fallen Sparrow* and she must have thought I had potential, because she wrote a nice report about me and sent it to Ben Piazza, the head of casting. Ben Piazza's most famous "find" was Spangler Arlington Brough—an actor you'd probably know better by his screen name, Robert Taylor. The funny part of that was the fact that, in my high school days, I used to get kidded about the fact that I looked a bit like Robert Taylor. Some of the kids used to call me "Robert Taylor Clarke," trying to embarrass me, but I thought Robert Taylor was a handsome guy and I took it as a compliment! Ben Piazza, the man who "discovered" Robert Taylor, now had in his hands the fate of "Robert Taylor Clarke."

Mr. Piazza told the Frank Vincent Office that they liked me, and (luckily) the Vincent Office had a lot of clout with RKO; some of their top clients, including Cary Grant and Rosalind Russell, were working in RKO pictures. To my great relief, the Vincent Office was able to push through a stock contract for me with*out* my having to test for RKO. If I had tested for RKO, it's hard to say what would have happened—my Fox and Columbia tests were so nerve-wracking, an RKO test might have had the same result. I can admit that because I'm not alone in that respect—I've heard a lot of people say that they just can't stand to do a test. So much is hanging on it, so much is dependent on whether you do well or not, that the natural inclination is toward extreme nervousness. So I was lucky—*very* lucky to get into RKO without a test.

I went under contract to RKO in July of 1944 (Robert Mitchum had been there just a month). Of course I couldn't *wait* to get into a picture, and I hustled one of the producers there, Maurice Geraghty, for a part. Shortly afterwards, my folks came out to California for a visit and I met them when they got off the train down at the Union Station. As we were walking up the ramp to leave the station, the first question Dad asked was, "Well, tell me, are you in a movie yet?" and I said, "Yeah, I'm in *The Falcon in Hollywood*."

He practically jumped for joy.

1 The Geller Workshop had originally been Max Reinhardt's theater, and people like Jack Carson, Alan Ladd and Maria Manton, the daughter of Marlene Dietrich, had "apprenticed" there.

Back home in Oklahoma City for Christmas 1944. Left to right: my dad, William Arthur Clarke; my sister, Genevieve, who joined me in California a few months later; my mother, Genevieve Irby Clarke; my brother, William A. Clarke Jr., "on leave" from the Navy; and me, "on leave" from RKO.

THE OKLAHOMAN IN HOLLYWOOD

I really was too young for my role in *The Falcon in Hollywood*, but I sold myself so hard to the producer Maurice Geraghty that he cast me anyway. *Falcon in Hollywood* was part of the RKO series of *Falcon* mysteries that had started out with George Sanders playing the renowned playboy/sleuth; when Sanders went on to bigger and better things at 20th Century-Fox, his brother Tom Conway stepped in to play the role Sanders had vacated. This entry was set at the Sunset Pictures studios in Tinseltown (actually the RKO lot), with Conway investigating the series of accidents and murders that is plaguing the production of a picture called "Magic Melody." I had a supporting role as the film-within-a-film's assistant director Perc Saunders (and, no, I wasn't the one who-done-it).

The director Gordon Douglas seemed to have some slight reservations about having me play the a.d., presumably because he thought I was too young, but that's funny in retrospect because (I later learned) Gordon had started *directing* when he wasn't much older than I was in *Falcon in Hollywood*, and I was only playing an *assistant*! Gordon was in his mid- to late-20s when he cut his teeth directing "Our Gang" shorts for Hal Roach back in the '30s. He worked for RKO for years, then at Columbia, then Warners and 20th Century-Fox, directing a lot of top stars in some pretty good pictures. Gordon was from New York City and a bit of a tough guy; Gordon was the type to call it like it was.

There was one scene in *Falcon in Hollywood* that I shared with several people, and I made some kind of a reaction that Gordon liked. But when he said, "Let's do a single on Bobby Clarke," and the camera started moving in for the closeup, I could not for the life of me remember what the hell I did! Gordon said, "Go ahead, do it again, do exactly what you did before," and I didn't know what to do. I did something that I hoped would satisfy him, but he said, "Kid, that's not quite it. Let's try it again. Take two." Lights, camera, action, and I did something *else*, hoping it was what I did the first time. It wasn't. So they tried it a third time, and that was the third strike; Gordon said, "Okay, it was a good try. Thanks anyway, kid." ("It was a good try" translates, of course, into "You *blew* it!")

Needless to say, all of this was new and exciting to me. When I got on the RKO lot and was permitted onto sound stages, I was stepping into a whole new world. The dawn came up like thunder at RKO—from early morning on, you'd see electricians and camera people hurrying around, prop men working, actors rehearsing, *everybody* expending a tremendous amount of energy, even for the less prominent pictures. And in those days, you worked six days a week. You would get a call for six o'clock in the morning, come in to makeup, get on the set by eight or eight-thirty, have an hour for lunch at midday, and then go on 'til six in the evening. Think what life must have been like for the guys in the *crew*, who went immediately from one picture to another. (It's still that way in this business to a large degree—the hours are just interminable. That's especially true for the guys who work in TV: They get up at four-thirty or five in the morning and get home at eight at night.) But for people who are "artistic," who see their work as a culmination of their dreams, it can be fulfilling and gratifying.

I started out at RKO making $100 a week. I finally saved up enough to buy a car about three months or so after I got my contract, but until that time I was riding the bus from Wilshire and Doheny and then changing busses to get into Hollywood. Finally I bought a used Ford from a friend from Oklahoma for 250 bucks. It was a little 1935 Ford coupe, an old clunker, but it got me there and home every day. That was the first car I ever owned.

Speaking of "firsts," I think the first big star I met at RKO was Ginger Rogers. There was a little park-like area not far from the main entrance of RKO, where people sat and had lunch, and she was either entering or exiting the lot. I approached her and told her what a fan of hers I was, and how much I liked those wonderful musicals she had made with Fred Astaire. I asked her a question I'm sure she had been asked many times: What was it like working with Astaire? She responded in three words: "Lot of work!"—and then proceeded to tell me how rehearsals would go on and on. And *on*! Astaire was a perfectionist, and it showed in his artistry—he left nothing to chance. I once heard that in her dancing slippers or her rehearsal shoes, there were bloodstains—she had worked so hard that the skin had been rubbed raw. When she described the tremendous amount of work, it made quite an impression on me, because I was still kind of under the illusion that making motion pictures could be a lot of fun. Having been a fan, way back in Oklahoma, it *looked* like fun—and it *can* be fun, and gratifying. I had no idea how pictures were made, or the kind of work that was involved, or the type of hardships that practically all actors must face at one point or another in their careers.

The one time I actually worked with Ginger Rogers was in an episode of Cecil B. DeMille's *Lux Radio Theater*, the most prestigious dramatic radio show on the air in the 1940s. Basically, what *Lux Radio Theater* did was dramatize in one hour a current, popular motion picture. The episode I shared with Ginger Rogers was an adaptation of *Lady in the Dark*, which she had done with Ray Milland for Paramount. It was the story of a career woman who, as the title implies, was "in the dark"— she had psychiatric problems and had to undergo psychoanalysis. In dream sequences, she had a teenage boyfriend, and that was the part which I played. Of course, I was thrilled. (I was under contract to RKO then, of course, but I could freelance radio as long as it didn't interfere with any of my picture commitments.) The program took an entire week to rehearse, and then we were "on the air." In those days they would do one live show broadcast to the East Coast and then, three hours later, a live show for the West Coast.

•   •   •   •   •   •

Speaking of radio series, during my first year at RKO I auditioned to replace one of the regular actors on a program called *Those We Love* with Donald Woods and Nan Grey. It was a Sunday afternoon series, and I think I made all of $35 per episode, but I was thrilled to be on it. But I guess I should have kept my mouth shut about it: I remember writing a letter about my involvement with that show and distributing it to the directors and producers at RKO. Ben Piazza, the casting director, had a fit; he said, "What if you have to go on location for a picture, and you have this radio commitment? I don't think this is a good idea at all!" Ben got very upset. But I had thought that writing that letter was a good idea; it would give people some inkling that I was doing something besides sitting around RKO's casting office, waiting to be called.

I *was* called—frequently—but many of the parts they gave me were so minuscule. I was not alone in that regard: RKO, and all the other studios, liked to keep their contract players busy, and it didn't matter to them if you played a good-sized supporting part in one picture, a co-starring part in the next—and then a five-second walk-on in something else. Other actors who played tiny parts in some of the RKO pictures that I was in were Bill Williams, Lawrence Tierney, Myrna Dell, Nan Leslie, Walter Reed, Raymond Burr and Lex Barker. It was good training, of course, but you never knew whether your next picture was going to be two weeks' work, one week's work, one day's work—or one *hour's* work.

Occasionally—not often, but occasionally—a small part can be a challenging one, for the simple reason that you're sometimes expected to convey a story point quickly. In *The Enchanted Cottage*, I had to get something across quickly and with*out* dialogue. Dorothy McGuire starred as a homely woman and I had an unbilled bit as a soldier who sees her from a distance, sitting alone at a ballroom dance. I started to walk up to her, presumably to ask her to dance with me, but then I saw how unattractive she was and I stopped dead in my tracks and bent over and retied my shoe. It was an interesting bit, one that had to be done just right in order for it to mean anything.

Dorothy McGuire's co-star in that film was Robert Young, for whom I had a lot of respect. To my mind, the sign of a *true* star is when you're an actor in the league of Robert Young or James Stewart and yet, when the actor you're sharing the scene with gets a closeup, you stand off-camera and give that other person off-stage dialogue. Not all actors will do that. People like Bob Young and James Stewart not only did that, they delivered their dialogue in those situations with the same emphasis and the same intensity and the same sincerity as when they were in *front* of the camera. That's being a professional. George C. Scott once said in an interview that Stewart would even put on the *wardrobe* and stand off-camera and deliver it just the same as if the camera was on him! To me, that's a very gracious thing—and, again, something that not every actor does.

Kevin McCarthy told me several years ago that Fredric March, when he starred in the film classic *Death of a Salesman*, had it in his contract that he could quit every day at 5:30. There were many big, dramatic scenes in *Death of a Salesman*, and one of the biggest was the scene where March is confronted by his son (McCarthy). They got

March's closeup and then it was time to get McCarthy's, but March noticed that it was 5:30 and he left the set and went home, leaving McCarthy to deliver his lines to the off-camera script clerk. (And when a script clerk reads dialogue, it's like they were reading it out of the dictionary— just awful. No animation, no nothing.) And Fredric March was the actor that I was trying to emulate by going to the University of Wisconsin! Kevin McCarthy told me, "I never forgave him for that," and I said, "I can't blame you."

•　　•　　•　　•　　•　　•

My one opportunity to work with the greatest Western star of all time was in a picture called *Back to Bataan*. Bill Williams and I, both of us RKO contract players, were assigned to go out to the RKO Ranch with a company and play medics in a war scene. Our job was to lift John Wayne out of a slit trench (two or three feet deep) and carry him at least 20 feet, out of camera range, while bombs and smoke and a lot of other activity was going on around us. Bill Williams had been an adagio dancer during his early days and he was a well-built guy, so I said to him, "Okay, Bill, you take the heavy end—the shoulders—and I'll grab him around the knees." Wayne wouldn't be able to help us at all, because in the scene he was supposed to be unconscious.

When Wayne came to work that morning, I remember that he drove his own car, which surprised me. In those days, you weren't allowed to drive your car on location, (a) because the teamsters wanted to have the job of driving everybody, and (b) because the studio's liability insurance would not protect the actor in case of any kind of automobile accident. (Bill and I had gone out there to the RKO Ranch by bus.)

Back to Bataan was a big-budget picture and the work pace that day was more leisurely than it was on some of the smaller pictures I had been doing. The director was Edward Dmytryk, and Eddie told us, "Bill, Bob, you don't have any dialogue here"—he tried to make us feel very important!—"but you've gotta do it right." We said, yes, sir, we sure would.

Wayne had come in and he stopped at the makeup table. His hair was beginning to go on him, so he took his cap off, borrowed an eyebrow pencil from the makeup guy and just scribbled on the top of his head—filled in with color what wasn't there. And there was a *lot* that wasn't there! *That* was his makeup. He took this grease pencil, glanced in the mirror (he didn't seem to care too much!), lowered his head so he could see the top of his head, and just colored an area at the top of his head. I thought that was kind of amusing.

Wayne was a big, big man, at least 6'3", and Bill and I started worrying again. I said, "Well, Bill, you're used to doing the lifts with the gals," and he said, "Yeah, I know, but this guy is *huge!*" We went in at Eddie Dmytryk's signal, after some of the explosions, and fought our way through the possible danger of grenades or mines. Bill got a-hold of John Wayne's chest and I picked up around his knees, and we lifted him together fine. But as I started to step up out of the slit trench, I stumbled and fell—right on top of Wayne! Of course, that loused up the scene, and Dmytryk yelled, "Cut it! Cut it!" But Wayne was patient, and he said (with his inimitable delivery), "It's okay, fellas. I *know* you can do it." We got another chance, and luckily this time we *did* do it. But that first take, falling right on top of John Wayne and spoiling the scene, will forever stay in my memory. So will Wayne's graciousness, the way he not only *didn't* get upset, but actually tried to encourage us! I found John Wayne to be a very pleasant, easygoing guy.

The best story I *ever* heard along those lines is told by an actor named Russell Arms, who was at Warners at the same time I was at RKO, working in the same capacity that I was: We were both small contract guys. Russell had been in the Air Force and he knew how to fly, so Warners cast him in a little part in a picture called *Captains of the Clouds* where he had to taxi a biplane. The very famous Michael Curtiz was the director, and Curtiz had a quite-complicated shot in mind: There would be a squadron of planes coming overhead, and his camera would follow the squadron. As the squadron came down and toward the airport, the camera followed the squadron, and as they came *over*, the camera then lowered and focused in on a biplane that was taxi-ing. Russell's job was to taxi the plane 50 feet or so, right up to a certain point, switch it off, get out, get a map out of his pocket, spread it out on a lower wing of the plane and then play out a brief scene with James Cagney, the star of the picture.

Russell was very nervous, but he managed to coordinate his actions with the squadron flying over, and then he taxied over to the right spot and climbed out. And, even though there was a breeze that almost took the map out of his hands, he spread it out just the way he was supposed to. And at that point, Cagney walked up to him—and Russ forgot

A toast to lovely Frances Langford with whom I appeared in RKO's
Radio Stars on Parade.

his line! Russell just stood there, speechless, knowing that he had just ruined a very intricate shot. But before he could blurt out an apology, Cagney—bless his wonderful heart—turned to Michael Curtiz and said, "Oh, Mike, I'm sorry. It was my fault—*my* fault. Let's do it again." Cagney took the rap, and (of course) Russell Arms could have hugged him! (And the second time they did it, Russ got the line out and the scene played perfectly.) But that apparently was the type of man that Cagney was, the sort that would extend himself for a nervous young actor.

> •   •   •   •   •   •

The one "romantic lead" I had early in my career was with a singer named Frances Langford. The picture was RKO's *Radio Stars on Parade*, which starred Frances and Ralph Edwards (later of *Truth or Consequences*). I had three or four scenes with her, as a young soldier, and I was afraid that she might say to the director or producer that I looked too young. (I did look very young: I was 24 in 1944 when I got a contract at RKO, and I could easily have passed for 18.) But she didn't say a word about it.

I recall that I had my hair combed in a particular way—I had the same tousled look that actors like Bob Mitchum and Clark Gable and Wallace Beery did. It was a device of sorts, "the practiced-casual look," to have a bit of hair hanging down over your forehead. (Back in the days of Valentino, and even into the sound era, the "look" of the leading men was very sleek; William Powell and people like that never had a hair out of place. But then along came the likes of Gable and Beery, and every-thing changed.) Anyway, I had this lock of hair purposely out of place and the hairdresser, who was fussing over Frances Langford, said to her, "Do you want his hair like that?" She didn't ask *me*, she asked Frances. Of course, I was really bugged at the remark, but I didn't say anything, because I knew that would only enlarge the situation. To my delight, Frances ignored the question completely: We just went right on talking, as if this overly-trained, over-conscientious hairdresser hadn't said a word. Frances was very genuine, very warm-hearted, *I* knew that *she* knew what I was thinking, and she did the right thing. (Also in that picture, incidentally, was Sheldon Leonard, who later went on to become a top TV producer. Sheldon and I had supporting parts in a number of the same RKO pictures, and I was impressed at how much the guy looked like a gangster. Sheldon had a *great* face, and when he put on a felt hat, he really looked as though he had guns in all pockets!)

Another gracious lady was the great Irene Dunne. She had just done (or was about to do) *I Remember Mama*, and a couple of the guys in the RKO publicity department invited me to a cocktail party honoring her. I went in to the cocktail lounge with one of the publicity department fellows, and who's standing at the door but Irene Dunne. The publicist was kind enough to present me—"Miss Dunne, this is Robert Clarke," he said, and I practically genuflected to her. Miss Dunne said to me, "Oh, how nice to meet you. Are *you* in the publicity department?" I said, no, I was under contract to RKO. With that, she *really* took an interest in me: She said, "Well, well, then you're one of *us*!", she crooked her arm into mine and we walked together into the cocktail lounge! She was gracious and charming, and I practically floated in. I was still at the age where seeing a star, *any* star, was an event in my life. But even now I still think back on that day, meeting Irene Dunne, and I still do consider that an event in my life.

By the way, I spent several hours on the set of *I Remember Mama* (I wasn't in it) watching George Stevens direct Miss Dunne and some others of the cast. Stevens was so meticulous and so careful, and it just seemed to go on and on and *on*. I marveled at the patience of the actors, the director, the camera people and everyone else who was working there. Every little detail was so important. Of course this was a great lesson, to be able to watch one of the masters of the directorial world (Stevens) doing a magnificent job. There was much decorum and quietness on the set when he was working, and I enjoyed it tremendously.

In '48 I appeared with Pat O'Brien in RKO's *Fighting Father Dunne*.

One very considerate director I worked with was Ted Tetzlaff, a former cameraman who directed a number of pictures at RKO around the time that I was there. I had a small part in a picture of his called *Fighting Father Dunne*, playing a priest, but to tell the truth I do *not* remember being in it. What I do recall is that they tested young people

"Gabby" Hayes (second from left), the comic relief in so many B Westerns, had the opposite effect on me in *Return of the Bad Men* with Anne Jeffreys and Randolph Scott.

like Darryl Hickman and several other juveniles for one of the leading parts in it, and they needed a Fighting Father Dunne to play opposite these young men in the tests. Of course Pat O'Brien (who played Father Dunne in the movie) wasn't available for tests, so I was sent down to the stage to do the dialogue (off-camera) in the tests with these young actors. I tried very hard, I was very conscientious about giving the guys in front of the camera all I could give them in the way of good readings and something for them to play to. For two or three days we did these tests and Ted Tetzlaff (who was directing) clearly appreciated the job I was doing. Ted went so far as to send a memo to the casting office complimenting me on the work I did. It didn't do any great things for me, but Ted went out of his way to thank me in the best way possible, which was by telling Dick Stockton and Eddie Rhine and of course Ben

26

Piazza, the head of casting, what he thought of my work. It was a small gesture but it meant a lot to me, a young actor, and I remember it to this day.

•　　•　　•　　•　　•　　•

A Western I did around this same time was called *Return of the Bad Men* with Randolph Scott, Robert Ryan and a "who's who" cast of desperadoes—Billy the Kid, the Dalton Gang, the Younger Brothers, etc. My part in this one was very small, just one scene, and in it I was taught how to fire a rifle by old "Gabby" Hayes (who was *not* as old as he wanted to appear, with that beard and all). He was teaching me how to fire a rifle, and my line was, "You squeeze the trigger just a wee bit." Hayes kept reading me the line and coaching me as to how *he* thought I should read it. He wanted me to put a real emphasis on the "wee," "You squeeze the trigger just a *weeeeeee* bit"—in other words, the way *he'd* deliver the line if it were his. We shot the scene four or five times—Hayes kept telling the director, "Let's do it again!", "Let's do it again!", and I can't *begin* to tell you how sick I got of being coached by "Gabby" Hayes. He was a funny guy on screen—he was the comic relief in some of the John Wayne and Roy Rogers Westerns—but, working with him, he sure had the opposite effect on me! That's another "small gesture" I still remember to this day, just a very different kind.

•　　•　　•　　•　　•　　•

I had a good part in a crime picture called *San Quentin*, but director Gordon Douglas didn't want me in that one, either. The picture was produced by Martin Mooney, who actually knew a little about prison life: Martin had been a crime reporter for a paper called the *New York Journal-American*, and he once served a prison term for refusing to reveal some of his news sources. It was while Martin was incarcerated in the Queens County Jail that he started writing for the movies, and pretty soon Warner Brothers brought him out to Hollywood to write *Bullets or Ballots* with Edward G. Robinson, Barton MacLane and Humphrey Bogart. MacLane was also in *San Quentin*, playing a mad dog killer whose escape from the famous prison has jeopardized its rehabilitation program; Larry Tierney plays the upstanding ex-con who seeks to recapture him.

I had a good-sized role in the opening reels, playing a young convict with a chip on his shoulder who ties in with MacLane, and is shot and killed while helping MacLane escape. Gordon Douglas fought

Lawrence Tierney, myself, Harry Shannon, and Barton MacLane appeared in *San Quentin*.

against having me play that part; he said, "Clarke is too handsome, too 'pretty.'" I understood why he was reluctant to put me in the picture; that *was* a problem I had during the early years of my career. The 1940s was the era of stars like Bogart and Larry Tierney and Robert Mitchum and others who had a more rugged physique. (In more recent years, of course, handsome guys like Paul Newman and Robert Redford have made it big because of their extremely fine acting.) Gordon Douglas tried to make me feel good by saying, "Kid, you're just too nice-looking, too handsome," but that wasn't much of a consolation—I wanted to play a tough guy! Fortunately for me, the head of RKO's B picture unit, Sid Rogell, overrode Gordon Douglas's objections: Rogell said, "We've seen Bob's work in the Westerns with James Warren. He plays the same type of characters there, a young kid who's gone wrong. We don't need a Dead End-type of kid in this part, it's better if the guy *does* look like he's on the clean-cut side."

Larry Tierney was a real character. At lunch he would go over to Lucie's, a restaurant across the street from RKO, and have three martinis—or four—or five—and get pretty bombed. One day, when everybody came back from lunch and Tierney wasn't among them, the assistant director had to go look for him. The a.d. found Tierney at Lucie's, but Tierney said that he wasn't going back to work unless the producer asked him personally. Martin Mooney went across to the restaurant and asked Tierney to come back, but now Tierney said, "I won't come back unless you bring one of those messenger bikes over. I'll ride it back." So they got Tierney a bike, he got on and he turned to Mooney and said, "Get on the handlebars and I'll ride you back with me." And, by God, they crossed Melrose Avenue—a very busy street!—on this bike, Tierney peddling it and Mooney sitting on the handlebars!

One scene in *San Quentin* found me in the back seat of a car between Tierney and Barton MacLane. I didn't have any dialogue in the scene. After we rehearsed it, Tierney said to me, "Look, Clarke, when I say so-and-so, *you* get into the scene a little bit." I said, "It's not in the script," and Tierney said, "Oh, to hell with the script! You should say a few words, it'll make you look a lot better." I did it, and appreciated the interest that Tierney had taken in me. And after my part of the picture was done, I found it heartwarming that Gordon Douglas came up to me and said, "You know what? I was wrong. You did a terrific job, Bob."

•   •   •   •   •   •

I had a good, long run at RKO and picked up a lot of valuable experience there which put me in good stead for the freelancing career that followed. Of course I wish they had given me more good parts than they did, but I can't complain, because the experiences I had, the stars I met and the training I got were vital. And I was paid to *act*—something which (if I'd had the money) I'd have paid *them* to let me do! My first year I got $100 a week, my second and third year, $200 a week—I agreed to go without a raise the third year because I knew how lucky I was, being paid to be trained. Working at RKO was a wonderful three years and a very important part of my life as an actor.

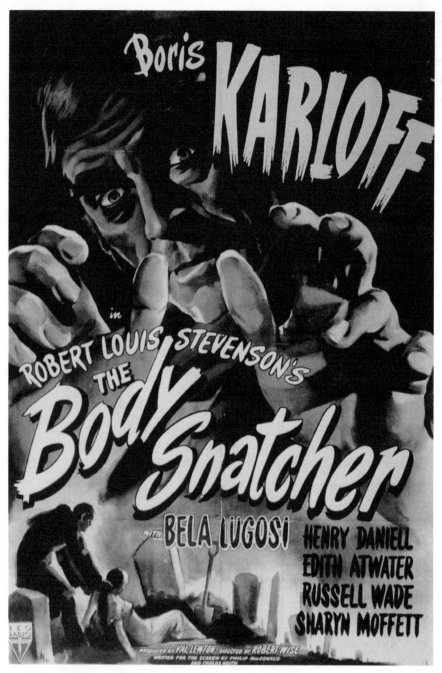

Boris Karloff gave one of his all-time best film performances in Val Lewton's *The Body Snatcher.* [Poster courtesy Ronald V. Borst/Hollywood Movie Posters]

VAL LEWTON

During my first years in the business, while working as a contract player at RKO, I encountered a number of talented directors, some of them well-established, others up-and-coming: Gordon Douglas, John Cromwell, Edward Dmytryk, Anthony Mann. But I only worked with one producer whose name now stands out in the movie reference books: Val Lewton.

I didn't know much about Mr. Lewton's background when I was acting in his pictures in 1944 and '45, but I was able to learn much about him years later, when his renown as one of the great producers of horror films made him the subject of articles and books. He was born in Yalta, Russia, not long after the turn of the century, and he came to the U.S. when he was seven, accompanied by his mother. (Lewton's aunt—his mother's sister—was the great Russian stage and screen star Alla Nazimova.) Lewton attended Columbia University and became a prolific writer, authoring a number of books (fiction and non-fiction), a book of poetry and even a book of pornography. He broke into the business as an editorial assistant to David O. Selznick and worked for Selznick for eight years before he became a producer of B movies at RKO.

I certainly had no idea when I was assigned a small part in Mr. Lewton's *The Body Snatcher* that, years later, this would become one of the RKO films for which I'd be best remembered. (Of course, at *that* point in time I had no reason to suspect that anybody would remember me in the 1990s at *all!*) The reason that I'm so often asked about *The Body Snatcher* is that it gave me my first chance to observe Boris Karloff, and my one and *only* opportunity to work with Bela Lugosi. Of course, it was odd to find these two "horror stars" in a Val Lewton movie: Lewton went in for a subtler type of fright film, filled with shadows and eerie atmosphere and the sort of unseen, *suggested* terrors that allowed the audiences to use their *imaginations*. The "horrors" that an individual with an active imagination can "custom-design" for himself are of course

My only opportunity to watch my "horror hero" Bela Lugosi was in RKO's *The Body Snatcher* with Russell Wade (left).

far more frightening than anything that Lewton, or any *other* filmmaker, could put up on a screen. That's what made Lewton's films unique, particularly in the 1940s, and that's why it was somewhat unusual to find two "overt" horror stars like Karloff and Lugosi acting in one of his movies; I have to assume that that might have been a decision made by the front office or by the executive producer, Jack J. Gross.

Karloff, however, was a kindly, well-educated gentleman, and from what I've heard and what I've read, he and Lewton got along famously. Both Karloff and Lewton were thoughtful individuals with great capacities for kindness; in fact, the two of them went on to make two more pictures together, *Isle of the Dead* and *Bedlam*.

The Body Snatcher was derived from a story by Robert Louis

Stevenson, which was based in turn on the real-life 19th-century graverobbers Burke and Hare. Karloff had the lead as John Gray, a cabman in 1832 Edinburgh. Gray is a grave robber selling cadavers to Dr. MacFarlane (Henry Daniell), the head of a medical school, who supervises his students in dissecting them. Gray has a strange "hold" over MacFarlane which baffles MacFarlane's young assistant Fettes (Russell Wade); Gray even compels the unwilling MacFarlane to perform a delicate operation on a crippled girl. Eventually it's revealed that MacFarlane was saved from prison years before by Gray, who went to jail for MacFarlane and has been holding it over him ever since. MacFarlane kills Gray in a fight, but Gray has his revenge in the macabre finale.

Meeting Karloff and watching him work in *The Body Snatcher* and *Bedlam* was an education. He was a considerate fellow who took a genuine interest in the young actors working opposite him. His dressing room door was always open to visitors and he would talk to you at any time, one-on-one. One of the stories I remember Karloff telling (we were in his dressing room, between takes on the set of *Bedlam*) concerned the time that he went back East to do *Arsenic and Old Lace* on Broadway. At that point, he hadn't been on the stage in so many years that he found that he was suffering from stage fright. For the first week or so of rehearsals, they allowed him to sit in the audience, and he was very nervous. He told me, "The night of dress rehearsal, I walked the streets of New York, trying to get up the nerve to go on. Then on opening night, someone *pushed* me on the stage and I don't remember a thing—except that I had diarrhea for three weeks!"

Bela Lugosi was quite different from Karloff, at least at that point in their lives and careers. When I was a youngster, Lugosi was *my* "horror hero," and for many years I defended Lugosi as being better—or I should say more *horrifying*—than Karloff. I can still remember going to see *Dracula* with my friend Billy Jay at the Midwest Theater in Oklahoma City in 1931. I had read the novel by Bram Stoker and, boy, was I excited about seeing it! After one frightening scene, Billy said he had to go out to the men's room, and from that point on he kept going out and coming back, going out and coming back. Finally I went out into the lobby and Billy was standing out there, too scared to come back into the theater! So when I finally saw Lugosi in person, on the set of *The Body Snatcher*, I was saddened—*very* much saddened—by what nature, what growing *older* had done to him. Bela was having terrible problems with his back, and he was on drugs because of it. (In *The Body Snatcher*, he played a servant who learns that Karloff has committed a murder, and makes a clumsy attempt to blackmail him.) During the time that I was involved on the film, Lugosi was so darn sick that he hardly came out of his dressing room unless the assistant director came and told him they had need for him in the scene. They had a daybed in there, and the guy was flat on his back on that couch nearly all the time. He talked very little to anyone, and obviously he wasn't well at all. It was very difficult for him to perform. It took away from the thrill of seeing Lugosi in person, the fact that he was incapacitated to such a degree. (I was in two other Lugosi films at RKO around that same time, *Zombies on Broadway* and *Genius at Work*, but I didn't act with Lugosi—or even *see* him—on those.)

Along with Bill Williams and Carl Kent, two other RKO contractees, I played a medical student of Henry Daniell's. Daniell was a smooth, accomplished and very professional English actor who had provided villainy in some of the great Hollywood films of all time, including *Camille* with Greta Garbo and *The Sea Hawk* with Errol Flynn. But I found Daniell to be a bit condescending in his attitude. In one scene, Daniell was performing the operation on the little girl as his students looked on. I had one line in that scene—"Bravo!"—and when I missed my cue, Daniell went right by my line in his dialogue. But Robert Wise, the director, stopped the camera and said, "Wait a minute—Bobby Clarke has a line there. Now, let's go back and start again, and let Bob get his line in." Unlike Karloff, Daniell was apparently not the type to have empathy for young actors; "aloof," I guess, would be the best word to describe him. It was his scene, and we were just window-dressing. Unlike Karloff, who would never try to upstage you, who would never try to get the best of you in a scene, Daniell probably couldn't have cared less whether we were there or not.

That experience with Daniell not only demonstrates the type of individual that he was, it's also indicative of the type of individual Robert Wise was: Bob treated us very, very equally. He took more pains with the stars than he did with the supporting players—naturally—but he never berated anybody, and he seemed to be the type of director who would go out of his way to afford an actor a chance to "give it his best." Not every director was that way; in fact, some were just the opposite. Lewis Allen was a good English director, make no mistake about that, but he had a lot to learn in the area of dealing with his actors. The same year I did *The Body Snatcher*, I had a *very* small part in a picture that Allen directed, *Those Endearing Young Charms* with Robert Young and Laraine Day. In one scene Young was in the waiting area of an airport, talking on the phone, and Paul Brinkman and I were also in the scene, dressed as Air Force officers.[1] Paul and I had no lines; as contract actors, we were being used, literally, to do extra work. (There was no fighting the casting office.)

Lewis Allen was shooting a master shot, sitting back under the camera as Bob Young was talking on the phone. Then, all of a sudden, he started hollering at me and Brinkman! "You two guys in the uniforms!" he yelled—he didn't even use our names. "Come on, *show* me something, *do* something. You're not doing *any*thing." Paul and I were supposed to be listening, and—well, what *can* you do when you're listening, when you have no dialogue? All you can do is *act as if you're listening*. Paul and I tried it again and, son of a gun, Allen lit into us again! Now, a kindly, *smart* director would have come up to us, without telling the whole crew, and tried to convey to us what it was we were doing—or *not* doing—that made him unhappy. Robert Wise was considerate enough to give us the directions in a *sotto* voice. So was Mark Robson, who directed *Bedlam*. But not Lewis Allen. He called us two or three times, yelling that we were just standing there like we were nothing, and it was embarrassing as hell for Paul and me to take his abuse, time and again.

To my mind, Robert Wise was a much better director, the sort of fellow who was not only considerate but also careful about details, leaving nothing to chance. To a director like Wise, everything was important. I watched Wise work with Mr. Karloff, and Wise spoke to him in a low, confidential tone. In my experience, he never showed any disrespect, not even for the least of the actors. He was not like Cecil B. DeMille, who often chided his actors openly.

I never worked for DeMille, but I've heard good and bad things about him from people who did appear in his pictures. He was kind, for example, to Lillian Albertson, the dramatic coach at RKO, whom he had known for many, many years. When Miss Albertson played the part of Jimmy Stewart's mother in *The Greatest Show on Earth*, DeMille was nice enough to call her in a day early, for which she got an extra day's pay. He knew that he didn't need her that day—and *she* knew that *he*

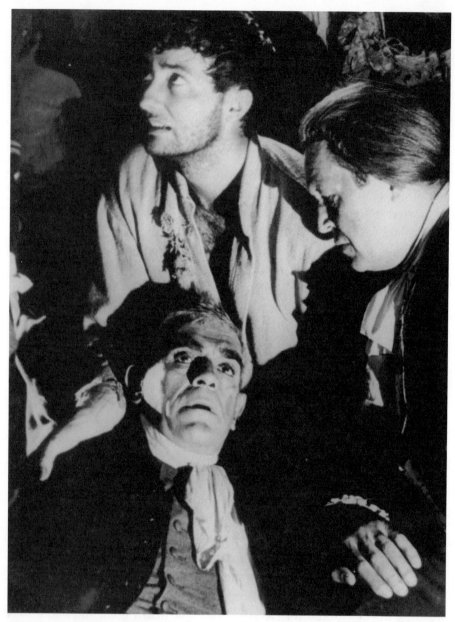

Jason Robards Sr. (right) played one of my fellow "loonies" in
Bedlam. **[Photo courtesy John Antosiewicz Collection]**

knew he didn't need her. It was just a nice way of getting her an extra
$500. But then from another actor, I heard a very different story. This
fellow was in *North West Mounted Police* with Gary Cooper and

Dan the Dog helps overpower Master Sims (Karloff) in the climax of
Bedlam. **Looking on are Anna Lee, Ian Wolfe and Ellen Corby.**
[Photo courtesy John Antosiewicz Collection]

Madeleine Carroll, and he was working on a sound stage where they
were doing some process shots. Scenes of Indians were being projected
on a screen, and the principals who were there on the sound stage were
firing at the Indians on the screen. This actor had never done this sort of
thing before, and when he began firing, he was apparently firing at the
wrong angle. DeMille laced into him right in front of all the people who
were there, and embarrassed him terribly. DeMille later came over to
him and said, "Son, I'm sorry, but you see, I can't do this to my *stars*"—
DeMille could not treat his stars the way he was treating this poor guy.
Which I think is awful, taking things out on the "little people," the people
who need help.

In contrast to DeMille and Lewis Allen, Robert Wise was extremely considerate of those whom he thought would need help. (It's hard for a young actor to stand up in front of that camera unless they're *very* outgoing, and he can use all the encouragement he can get!) As for *Body Snatcher* itself, it was a first-rate horror drama because Wise and Mr. Lewton made certain that it had all the necessary components: A compelling story, authentic atmosphere, interesting characters and good performances. Many of the movie's fans feel that it was one of Boris Karloff's best performances, an opinion which I would enthusiastically second.

I had a much more substantial part in my second picture for Val Lewton, *Bedlam*. (By the way, I did not call him Val, I called him Mr. Lewton. I remember Mark Robson called him *Vol*.) This was another "historical" type of horror film, depicting the terrible abuses committed against inmates at the notorious 18th-century London asylum. Boris Karloff played the evil head of the institution and Anna Lee played a high-spirited young woman who becomes such a thorn in Karloff's side that he uses his influence to have her committed to Bedlam.

I had a nice supporting role as "Dan the Dog," a harmless lunatic who is obsessed with dogs, and sometimes acts like a dog (and who Karloff presumably beats like one!). This was a good, unusual part and I wanted to do my best, and I went so far as to visit a mental hospital in the southeast part of Los Angeles. I hoped to pick up the *feeling*, the *attitude* of how they (the mental patients) really *were*, what they really *looked* like, and to get from a visit to that facility the feeling of what being inside as a patient was like. My father and I drove to the place and the head of the hospital gave me a guided tour. I didn't have direct contact with any of the inmates, but the superintendent was very informative, and he made an interesting comment which I still recall quite vividly: "Most of those who are here, the *large* majority, are here because of problems related to religion or sex." According to the superintendent, those two problems loomed highest on the list of reasons for mental disorders (at least among the people that were there as patients at his facility). They were *ab*normal because of their outlooks and approaches to matters sexual or religious.

The asylum scenes for *Bedlam* were shot on an RKO sound stage where we worked for over a month. In the story, Anna Lee befriends three of the more placid "loonies"—Ian Wolfe, a lawyer with a persecution complex, Jason Robards, a writer placed in Bedlam by his family to

Dan the Dog was an unusual part and I wanted to do my best, and I went so far as to visit a mental hospital. [Photo courtesy John Antosiewicz Collection]

keep him from drink, and my character, Dan the Dog. In one scene, Anna, Wolfe, Robards and I were seated at a table playing a card game called paroli, and (being demented) instead of betting money I was betting dogs—whippets and bassets and bulldogs. Mark Robson, the director, made practically every little move for me—"When you place a card here, you do *this*, and then *that*," and so forth. It's been 50 years since that day, but I've never forgotten how careful and meticulous he was. Robson, like Bob Wise, and like Mr. Lewton, was a caring person, and he treated actors with respect, which is wonderful. (Directors today don't have the time to do that.) Robson laid it all out for me, and I was much better in that scene than I would have been without his direction.[2]

Karloff portrays the evil head of Bedlam, a man who abuses the harmless lunatics inside the asylum, such as my character Dan the Dog.

Bedlam, like *The Body Snatcher,* was intelligent and moody and impeccably acted, and both films rank high on the list of horror classics.

One day my dad and mom visited the set. A scene involving Karloff and Jason Robards was being shot, and my mom watched them photograph half a dozen (or more) takes. At that point there was a little break and I came over to chat with them, and she said, "Oh, what hard work! I hope you never have to give me any of the money that you make from working this hard!" And it's true, film work *is* very hard, more than the average person thinks.

The other funny thing I recall about *Bedlam* is that the actors in those asylum scenes, many of them extras, looked (to me) more insane than some of those I saw in the actual mental hospital! The casting was beautifully executed, probably through Lewton, Mark Robson and the RKO casting office, which was headed up by Dick Stockton. In my four or five weeks on the picture, I got the feeling that those extras were more demented and dangerous than the people I saw in the hospital!

There was an unfortunate upshot to my *Bedlam* experience, however. When the picture was finished, a screening was scheduled one evening at the studio, in one of the larger screening rooms. I was there along with Mr. Lewton and Mark Robson (I don't think Mr. Karloff was there). Sitting next to me was Lillian Albertson, a strong supporter of mine. The movie began with the RKO logo, and then the credits came on. I saw the names of Jason Robards... Ian Wolfe... Glen Vernon... Leyland Hodgson...

I read all these names, and then I re-read and *re*-re-read them. My name wasn't there.

"Miss Albertson," I whispered, "my name's not there."

"Oh, I think it was, Bob, I think it was." Then the picture began...

I had put quite a bit of effort into that role, like going to the mental hospital to gain insights that would help me in delineating the character. I thought that my performance seemed to be pretty true to the form of a person that was mentally ill, and it shook me up to see that my name may have been omitted.

The very next day I went up to Mr. Lewton's office. He was either out of the office or he was not available, because I did not get to see him, but I did speak with his secretary and I told her, "Would you please tell him that I don't think my name's on the credits?" She said she

My name was accidentally omitted from the screen credits of *Bed-lam.* Years later I "rectified" matters, amending my copy of the poster.

would. And Mr. Lewton, the kindly man that he was, did phone me: He said, "I understand you think your name's not on the credits."

"I know it's not, because I saw the picture," I said in a firm (but very careful and diplomatic) way. Lewton seemed nonplused. "I'm quite sure I would have seen it," I reiterated. "Would you mind having someone check the credits?"

"Oh, we'll be glad to," he said. "I *want* you to have credit, because you did a fine job, very, very fine, and we appreciate it."

It was shortly thereafter that I got a letter from him—apologizing. He said that there *had* been a mistake, and my name *was* inadvertently left off the credits; in the letter, he promised, "We will do whatever we can to try to make amends for this error." Then I got a call from his secretary, who said, "Mr. Lewton deeply regrets what happened. But to change the credits and add your name would mean that we'd have to re-do the whole first reel. The expense involved is, unfortunately, too much to make that correction." I was very saddened to hear that, but there was nothing more I could do. It was a regrettable situation, and Mr. Lewton was certainly a gentleman about it.

The last time I saw Boris Karloff was a year or two later, right after we had finished a picture called *Dick Tracy Meets Gruesome*. Karloff and I shared no scene in that one: He was Gruesome, a master criminal, Ralph Byrd played Dick Tracy and I had an unbilled role as a police lab man. But I was on the set the day that principal photography wrapped and they threw a "party." (I put "party" in quotes because it was hardly that. We were on a very bare stage at RKO, and somebody brought out a couple of bottles of bourbon. I thought it was rather crude.) And here was Mr. Karloff with 8x10s, handing them out to anybody who wanted one. That last encounter with him reinforced in my mind yet *again* what a good-hearted individual he was. He wrote on the picture he gave me, TO BOB CLARKE—BE AS LUCKY AS I AM, which to me demonstrated how very modest he was. He was more talented as an actor than a lot of people have given him credit for; so often, people think of him only as the Frankenstein Monster. But he had *tremendous* acting ability, and not just in monster roles like that one. Now, I don't mean to slight in any way the job he did in *Frankenstein*: To take a role like that, with no dialogue, and do what he did with it, was miraculous. But Mr. Karloff was capable of so much more, as he proved time and again throughout his long career.

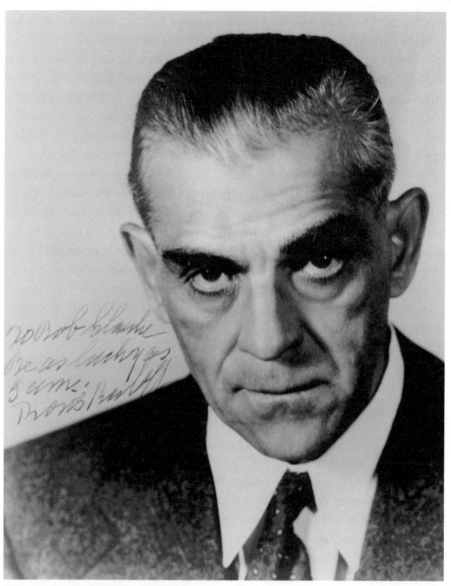

TO BOB CLARKE—BE AS LUCKY AS I AM. BORIS KARLOFF

My final encounter with Val Lewton came a few years later, after he had left RKO and gone to work at MGM. He had gotten a one-picture deal over there and I was being interviewed for some part in the A-film he was going to be producing. (I felt as if I was in over my head even to be considered for this part, because actors like Mark Stevens and others, all of them bigger names than mine, were in the running.) But it was nice to see Mr. Lewton again; he remembered me and called me by my first name, and it made me feel welcome. I also recall some comments that he made, and thinking they were kind of funny: Lewton said, "We were just sitting here talking about DeMille's latest picture. DeMille has made money on every picture he's ever made." Lewton said it with a little bit of a wistful, wish-*I*-could-do-that type of feeling. He went on to talk about the type of pictures DeMille had done, and I could tell that he looked rather condescendingly at DeMille's films because *he* thought DeMille was "playing down to the masses." Lewton simply couldn't understand the success that DeMille had had, and was *continuing* to have.

I may not have had prominent parts in *The Body Snatcher* and *Bedlam*, but for me they are two of the most memorable movies I made at RKO. It was an eye-opening experience to work with conscientious men like Robert Wise and Mark Robson, and of course Val Lewton. Mr. Lewton had very high ideals, and his artistic endeavors were far above those of most horror film producers. As for Boris Karloff, I never worked with any man for whom I had more admiration. With this sort of talent behind them, *The Body Snatcher* and *Bedlam* emerged as very fine pictures, and they are still widely recognized as two of the best horror films of the 1940s. It gives me a good deal of pleasure—and pride—to be able to tell people that I was in them.

1 Paul was another contract player at RKO; he would later marry Jeanne Crain. Paul was a nice-looking guy with a mustache, and we all thought he might become another Errol Flynn. But he didn't. He became a husband of Jeanne Crain!
2 Karloff seemed to get on as well with Mark Robson as he did with Robert Wise. Karloff was *very* flexible in dealing with his directors, and I never saw him question or object to anything that the director called for.

UNDER WESTERN SKIES

I've always had a fondness for Westerns, partly because I enjoyed them as a kid in Oklahoma, and also partly because it was the RKO B Westerns that provided me with some of my first decent-sized screen roles. Some of my earliest memories of growing up in Oklahoma City are of playing cowboys and Indians with the other kids in the neighborhood. Our role models were such known names as Tom Mix, Buck Jones and Hoot Gibson. (William S. Hart was before our time.) I recall my dad taking me to a Saturday matinee in which Hoot Gibson rescued the leading lady from a runaway horse by lassoing her and quickly tossing his lariat over the limb of a tree, then pulling her up as the horse sped on past. The next anxious moments saw Hoot and the girl seesawing from the ground up to the top of the tree and back down until finally they both ended up on the ground. I couldn't wait to get home and try the trick with my little brother. But the rope broke, and he came tumbling down on top of me.

I also vividly recall having our own motion picture show in the backyard on summer evenings, when my friend Cy Crum brought his Keystone projector (hand-cranked) to show a Tom Mix ten-minute short. We charged a nickel admission and two cents for a drink. In those days, kids under twelve got into the Saturday matinees for a dime, and that meant two features, maybe a serial chapter, a comedy short and a newsreel. The Westerns made such an impression on us kids that, as I described above, we'd go home and try to do what the cowboys did!

Throughout my career I've appeared opposite several of *the* most famous cowboy stars: Tim Holt at RKO, Guy (*Will Bill Hickok*) Madison, Clayton (*The Lone Ranger*) Moore and others on TV, John Wayne (although not in a Western) and more. I've also worked with some very unusual and *unlikely* "cowboy heroes," like bandleader Harry James. But the first several Westerns in which I worked starred what you'd have to call a "forgotten" Western actor, James Warren.

In the late 1930s and early '40s, before I came on the scene at RKO, their top B Western star was Tim Holt, son of the actor Jack Holt. Tim made his first film appearances in some of his famous father's silents, and by 1940 he had risen from bits and supporting parts to being the star of his own low-budget Western series at RKO. (Tim also occasionally "broke out" of the Western mold and played supporting parts in top features like Orson Welles' *The Magnificent Ambersons* and John Huston's *The Treasure of the Sierra Madre*, which was unusual for a cowboy star of that type.) In 1943, at the height of World War II, Tim was inducted into the military. His father was also in the service at the same time, and in fact rose to the rank of major.

In Tim's absence, RKO initiated a series of B Westerns based on novels by Zane Grey. The first two, *Nevada* and *West of the Pecos*, starred Robert Mitchum, who was at the beginning of what would turn out to be a very long and distinguished film career. The producer of these Westerns was a fellow named Herman Schlom, and the story went around that Herman suggested to Bob Mitchum that he change his name to Mitch*ell*. Mitchum asked, "Well, why?", and Herman said, "'Mitchum'—it doesn't look so good on the screen." To which Mitchum replied, "Well, *your* name's on the screen, and your name is *Schlom*!"

Needless to say, Mitchum wouldn't change his name, much to his credit. Prior to working at RKO, he had acted in some Hopalong Cassidy Westerns with Bill Boyd, and even in those early days when Mitchum was busy in these low-budget cowboy pictures, the people working with him could tell that he was headed onward and upward. I remember that one of the actors that played heavies in some of these pictures, Harry Woods, once said, "We thought, seeing Mitchum in the Hopalongs, that he was certainly destined for bigger things." Mitchum's performance in MGM's *Thirty Seconds Over Tokyo* with Spencer Tracy impressed a producer named Sid Rogell, and Sid signed Bob Mitchum to a long-term RKO contract. With Tim Holt in the service, RKO put Mitchum into some of these little Zane Grey Westerns, and the next thing anybody knew, his career was off and running.

After Bob Mitchum's two Zane Greys, the reins were handed over to James Warren, who starred in three, *Wanderer of the Wasteland* (1945), *Sunset Pass* (1946) and *Code of the West* (1947). I also acted in all three of those, playing either the renegade son of some rancher, or the undisciplined brother of some pretty cowgirl. It wasn't art, but I enjoyed

As Jay Collinshaw in my first Western, *Wanderer of the Wasteland*.

doing them. The parts were substantial and they actually called for some acting; being placed in dramatic situations gave me an opportunity to *act*, which was what I wanted to do. The other roles that RKO handed me were often so limited, some of them so *small*, that the Westerns seemed to offer me many more opportunities.

Jim Warren was a very agreeable, easygoing kind of a fellow. He had been under contract at MGM before he came over to RKO, he was tall and slender—almost Gary Cooper-ish—and he had the look of a Western type. My first picture with him was *Wanderer of the Wasteland*, based on a Zane Grey novel that had previously been filmed by Paramount in 1935 with Dean Jagger, Buster Crabbe and Gail Patrick. Warren played a character who had been orphaned as a child when his dad was slain on the Mojave Desert. He was taken in by a middle-aged couple and grew up with *their* young son. Now adults, Jim and his lifelong friend Chito Rafferty (Richard Martin) find a clue to the killer's identity which leads them to the ranch of Robert Barrat. Warren admires Barrat and accepts the job of keeping Barrat's disreputable young nephew (myself) away from the gambling tables in the local saloon. Warren also falls in love with my sister (Audrey Long), but avoids her because he fears that her uncle may turn out to be his father's killer.

"Chito Rafferty," the slow-witted, girl-crazy Mexican/Irish sidekick, was played by Richard Martin, a prince of a guy and one of my best friends. Dick was the type who would do you a favor and, if you tried to thank him, tell you, "Well, that's what friends are for." I remember seeing Dick my first day on the RKO lot, and I recall thinking that he was about as handsome a guy as you could find. Dick was standing in the doorway of the casting office and I said hello and introduced myself, and we had a brief conversation. I was so impressed with the looks of the guy that I felt sure that he was headed for stardom. And he *was*, in a manner of speaking; "Chito" became Tim Holt's sidekick in Westerns once Tim got out of the service, and Dick stayed with that series right up into the 1950s. (Dick had grown up in West Hollywood where he had a lot of friends who were Hispanic, and he found out he could do a very good Spanish or Mexican accent.) But Dick didn't reach the Robert Taylor or Tyrone Power pinnacle that I thought he might have achieved. He once said that he never really felt that he had the acting qualities or charisma that goes with being a superstar. He never quite felt comfortable playing "himself" and so he enjoyed playing Chito. (He could also tell very funny stories with that accent.) Of course, if that part was cast today, they would cast a Hispanic person, not an Anglo-American, because the Screen Actors Guild now is very pressed to give opportunities to those of different ethnic backgrounds. But Dick did get the chance to play Chito, and he found that he could work "behind" that accent and feel comfortable.

Another thing I recall distinctly about *Wanderer of the Wasteland* is how surprised I was at the first daily rushes. I saw them and I thought to myself, "Is that *me*?" I heard the voice and *it* sounded familiar, and then I looked at myself and thought, "Gee, I didn't know I looked like that!" (I don't know *what* I expected!) I was quite young then, 25 approximately, and I looked even younger than *that*, and I was kind of taken aback. I also found, seeing rushes the first few times, that I kept seeing in my mind's eye the setups of the cameras and the lights and the sound equipment and all—I couldn't get into the scene as a viewer. *That* soon passed, but my first reaction to rushes was one of not only seeing what was on the scene but of remembering what was all around.

The second James Warren Western was *Sunset Pass*. In this one, he was an express company agent who sets out with Chito (this time played by John Laurenz) to stop a series of Arizona train robberies. On a train they meet Nan Leslie, returning home to her family's ranch, and Jane Greer, an entertainer. Bandits hold up the train, and evidence points to my character (Nan's brother—of course) as one of the robbers. Through the influence of Warren and Nan, I decide to reform, but I refuse to expose other members of the gang because they are in a position to frame me for a murder. In the end, Jim saves me from a lynch mob before the desperados are killed and I'm cleared of the murder charge.

I'm sometimes asked if I was ever asked to do things that were beyond my capabilities in Westerns or in some of the other action-type pictures I was in. The truth is that they generally had stuntmen on hand to double the actors in any sort of dangerous situation, because an injured actor can throw an entire production behind schedule. I did like doing my own stunts whenever I was permitted, because I'd heard that some of the biggest stars, Douglas Fairbanks Sr., for instance, were renowned for doing that. (It wasn't until years later that I found out that even Fairbanks and other stars like him *did* have stuntmen for some of their hairier stunts, regardless of *what* they said!)

It was on one of the James Warren pictures that I was in my first Western chase scene. I had done some riding back in Oklahoma, where we used to be able to get a horse rental for 50 cents an hour when I was a kid, and so I wasn't unfamiliar with horses, but I was *not* what you'd call an experienced horseman. However, I wanted them to *think* I was. The scene called for me to ride my horse behind the camera car and fire my gun, supposedly at whoever it was I was chasing. (This was in the Alabama Hills, just outside of Lone Pine.) What I realized once we started was that I also had to keep my hat from blowing off. With your left hand handling the reins and the right hand firing the .45, that's not always so easy! (Once or twice, the hat *would* blow off and we'd have to go back and start again. I learned later that it was a good idea to put the hat on as tight as you could.) And then, of course, you were firing right over the horse's head, near his right ear, which the horse didn't like. There were three different sizes of blank cartridge (the full load, the half-load and a quarter-load), and the full load really was a loud bang.

The horse I was riding evidently had a problem with his front hooves, because as he ran, he kept clicking them together. So not only was he stumbling, but every time I'd fire the gun, it would scare him a little bit. The camera car was going 35 or 40 miles an hour and I had to keep up with it; the men in the car were waving me on, "Come closer—closer," and the driver was watching me in his rear view mirror. Well, this was a first for me, needless to say. With every shot of the gun, the horse would bow its neck and veer to the right, to get its ears away from the noise. By the side of the road was a drainage ditch, and every time I fired the gun, the horse got closer to the edge of it. To make a long story short, I got through the scene in one piece: I didn't get thrown, and we didn't go into the ditch, but I sure did have trouble staying aboard, and I don't mind admitting that I was glad when *that* particular ride was over. After the first one or two Westerns, it got to be easier, of course, and I became more adept in riding with a posse and that sort of thing. I also realized that most horses were well-trained for use in movies—sometimes better-trained than the actor!

The last of the James Warrens was *Code of the West*, in which I had less than usual to do. I was once again the brother of the leading lady (Debra Alden), and this time Jim and John Laurenz (as Chito) clean up a gang terrorizing the Arizona strip. It was on *Code of the West* that I had my first opportunity to observe Raymond Burr in action. He had just come out from New York, and this was one of his first experiences in front of a camera. Ray and I had a dialogue scene together, and after I'd done my dialogue with the camera on me, the camera switched around to Ray's closeup and I stood alongside the camera to give Ray *his* cues. Ray was so nervous, he began to perspire like you wouldn't believe. Of course, later he became very confident as an actor and so adept at the

Becoming an adept rider was one of the fringe benefits of working in RKO's B Westerns.

parts he played in movies and on TV (Perry Mason and Ironside and so on), and he developed into such a really good "type." But in that little part in *Code of the West*, he was extremely nervous, fighting to get the words out, and the perspiration just poured out of him. The makeup man was there with a sponge, trying to keep him dry, and we had two or three takes before he finally got it. It's amazing the way actors can change and grow, from modest beginnings and a "stage fright" attitude; once they get going, they suddenly sprout and blossom and they've got the world in the palm of their hand. That was certainly the case with Raymond Burr.

Tim Holt got his discharge in late 1945, but instead of returning to RKO, he first played one of the Earps in director John Ford's *My Darling Clementine* with Henry Fonda and Victor Mature. After that he came back to RKO, replacing James Warren as star of the Zane Grey series. (Jim now makes his home in Maui, Hawaii, where he works as a professional painter.) I was in four of Tim's B Westerns, two while I was under contract to RKO and then two more after I had begun freelancing. I know from reading about Tim and from meeting some of his fans that my first film with Tim, *Thunder Mountain* (1947), has the reputation of being one of his best. In the movie, Tim returns to his Grass Valley homestead after agricultural college to learn that an old family feud between Tim's clan and the Jorth family is still going strong. Steve Brodie and I played the Jorth brothers and Martha Hyer played our sister. The real villains keeping the "feud" alive are a pair of sidewinders (Harry Woods and Tom Keene) and a crooked sheriff (Harry Harvey) who have gotten advance word that an irrigation company intends to build a dam on the Holt land, making it the most valuable ranch in Arizona.

The gals who worked in these Tim Holt Westerns enjoyed them for some of the same reasons that I did, not the least of which was the fact that they were a "start" in the business. Jane Greer, who was also in *Sunset Pass*, was a pretty sophisticated gal (and a good actress, as she later proved), but I got the impression that she didn't care too much about being in the thing. She was a bit blasé about it, to put it frankly, but she was *funny*—she had a great sense of humor. It was a job, she was a contract player and she did what she had to do or RKO would put her on suspension and lay-off.

But Martha Hyer, who was in *Thunder Mountain*, was quite an ambitious actress even then, and she seemed to be more into putting her career ahead of everything else. And I mean *everything* else. She didn't have a car then, and I remember picking her up in my second-hand Ford to go to the bus the morning we were leaving for Lone Pine. (She had a rented room in a nice neighborhood not far from RKO.) As she got in my car she said, "Oh, my teeth are *killing* me." I asked, "What's the matter?" and she said, "I just had all my four front teeth capped *yester-*

day." She was in so much pain, but it meant so much to her to look her best that she'd gone through this *very* painful procedure. Nobody does that all at once, but *she* did, in order to be ready for the picture. I remember too that she was very aware of her weight and felt that she had a weight problem, and she was trying desperately to reduce. She later got it completely under control, after which she got into bigger pictures and better parts. Like Jane Greer and Barbara Hale and other contract actresses there at RKO, Martha later enjoyed quite a career.

Steve Brodie was also ambitious. Steve was a Kansan who'd gotten into the picture business after working in stock, and he certainly didn't seem to lack any self-esteem. I remember that in one of the Westerns (we were in several together) he was practicing the fast mount of his horse. He wanted to be able to run and hit that stirrup and get on the horse in one leap, rather than running up to the horse and stopping and stepping up. Some of the stunt guys were very good about helping him, and the director, whoever it was on that particular picture, told him that if he missed the stirrup, they'd let him do it again. Steve was trying to make things look professional and to make his own character look good, and always seemed to have things pretty much under control. He liked to laugh a lot, and he was always joking off-screen.

Tim Holt wasn't that way at all. I found Tim to be a very serious person as well as a very serious actor. He was a quick study who always came to the set prepared, always knew his lines, and could handle a gun or a horse as well as any other actor working in pictures. He never said or did anything to make you aware that *he* was the star, that his was the name in big capital letters above the title while yours was the one in smaller letters below. He also never felt that he had to be "on" between takes; Tim wasn't into entertaining the crew. Many actors feel that they've got to be as good between sequences, and they *use* and *lose* a lot of the energy that they could save for the camera. Tim behaved as though he was part of the production office: He knew that this was a business and he'd do everything he could to keep the pictures on schedule. The other thing I recall about Tim was that he really came across as though he could have been a real-life cowboy. I read not too long ago that, even when he was in military school, Tim expressed a desire to be a cowboy star, and years later he achieved it. His acting career could have gone in another, more dramatic direction, as one can see from his performances in movies like *The Magnificent Ambersons*, but he chose to stick

Disarmed by Tim Holt in *Under the Tonto Rim.*

with his Western motif.

Thunder Mountain was a good "comeback" picture for Tim as he returned to his old RKO stamping grounds. Lone Pine was no Monument Valley, but it was rugged country, highly photogenic, and it gave the movie some wonderful atmosphere and the same "look" as a much bigger budgeted Western. (The town street scenes were shot on the Western Street at the RKO Ranch in Encino, barely a mile from the Bank of Encino where I later worked for years.) *Thunder Mountain* also featured plenty of action and even a few laughs courtesy of Dick Martin, who returned (for good) in the role of Chito.

I had a much smaller part in *Under the Tonto Rim* (1947), my second picture with Tim. In this one, he was the owner of a stage line whose best friend, one of his drivers, is killed by a gang of outlaws who swoop down on the stagecoach to kidnap a girl (Nan Leslie). Tim devotes himself to tracking down the killers, who are known as the Tonto Rim Gang. "You know what the word 'tonto' means in Spanish?" Dick Martin (Chito) asks. "It means 'fool'!" (I wonder if Jay Silverheels ever found that out!) Tim infiltrates the gang and locates Nan, who is being held prisoner in a small house in the desert by a bad guy named Hooker (myself). One of the big action scenes in the picture is my fistfight with Tim. I was doubled in the fight by one of the best stunt men in the business, Dave Sharpe.

Under the Tonto Rim was another well-done Western that looked like a more ambitious picture than it actually was because the director (Lew Landers) and his cameraman got the most out of the Lone Pine locations. Again playing the villain was Tom Keene, who acted in these movies under the name "Richard Powers."[1] Keene had reached the point where things were not going as well as they had when he was younger. I also remember him telling me on one of the Zane Grey pictures we did together that I was playing the part that *he* had played in an earlier version!

Playing a small part as a sheriff's deputy was another RKO stock player, a handsome son of a gun named Lex Barker. I didn't get to know him too well at the time, but I remember seeing him again several years later in New York, after he'd gotten the part of Tarzan, and we chatted for a few minutes about old times. He said, "Boy, you think it's tough acting when you first start out as a Western actor, using guns and learning how to use 'em and all. Try acting without any *clothes*!" He told me that when he played Tarzan, he never knew where to put his hands—he had no pockets, he didn't have anything except that loincloth! Like a lot of actors, Lex knew that it helps your career to date the right kind of people, and so he not only dated but he *married* Lana Turner, and I lost track of him after that.

When we'd go up to Lone Pine, RKO would save money by putting two actors in the same hotel room. I roomed with Jason Robards Sr., who had been a star on the stage in New York years before. Until he told me about it, I was unaware of the career he'd had in the theater. He mentioned that one of the long-running plays he did in New York was called *Lightnin'* (which was later made into a movie with Will Rogers), and that after *Lightnin'*, he came to California to work in films. By the time Jason and I were doing these Westerns together, he was a man in his 50s, now a contract player (a character man) at RKO. I recall Jason's

Richard Martin (right) was a sweetheart of a guy and one of my best friends. A scene from *Riders of the Range*.

attitude about the movie business and how difficult he said it could be for some actors. He said, "Sometimes I go into the grocery store and I'll be standing there at the meat counter, and I'll look up into the mirror and say to myself, 'Who *is* that old face?'" Years later, Jason Robards Jr. said he could always have the greatest sympathy for his dad because of what Hollywood *did* to him. (You could say that Hollywood did it to him, or you could just call it "the accidents of a career." In Hollywood, the careers of most actors are filled with peaks and valleys, and it's very hard for the actors who don't make it in a big way. They have to have some kind of extra employment or extra income to sustain themselves.)

I've been asked if there was any sort of "family feeling" or sense of camaraderie making these Tim Holt Westerns, which often had the same casts, the same assistant directors, the same prop guys and so on.

In *Riders of the Range* I once again played the reckless kid brother, this time victimized by gambler Reed Hadley (left).

We did have a nice camaraderie when we'd be up at Lone Pine. We'd spend three, four, five days, perhaps a week, up there whenever we'd make a picture. One of the things I remember best about Lone Pine is how terribly, terribly hot it could get in the summer. But, as unbearable as it was in the heat of the day, at night it was cool and beautiful. In the evenings we would have dinner and sit around the lobby of the Dow Hotel, or sometimes take a walk, just for something to do. At night there wasn't much *to* do in Lone Pine: There was a local saloon or two, but I didn't join in the fun there—I wasn't much for the booze. (The story was that that's where Bob Mitchum used to do some of his best fighting. After a few drinks, he'd want to fight everybody. He was pretty rough, they say.) I think there was one movie theater in Lone Pine, and of course no television.

My right-thinking sister in *Riders of the Range* was played by Jacqueline White.

I came back to RKO as a freelancer for the other two Holt Westerns, *Riders of the Range* (1950) and *Pistol Harvest* (1951). RKO didn't exercise my option in the summer of 1947, so I left the studio and went to New York to work in summer stock. When I came back from New York, I went over to the RKO casting office to see Dick Stockton and Eddie Rhine. I told them about the work I'd done back East, including a Broadway play with Louis Calhern and Faye Emerson, and they asked me if I'd be interested in doing a Tim Holt Western. They told me that it was a very good part, running the length of the picture, and they said they'd up my pay a little (I got $500 a week instead of $400).

I went for it, but what Dick and Eddie didn't know was that (by offering me this Western) they were reinforcing the feelings of doubt I was having about my career. Here I was, coming back from New York

ROBBERY AND MURDER SET BORDER ABLAZE!

TIM HOLT

Pistol Harvest

with RICHARD MARTIN • JOAN DIXON • Directed by LESLEY SELANDER
WRITTEN BY NORMAN HOUSTON

After years of playing different characters in his Westerns, Tim Holt began playing "himself" in the 1950s.

and a Broadway play, and the first job I got was right back in a Tim Holt Western! "What have I *done*?" I asked myself. "Have I made the wrong choice of professions here?" To get back to California from New York, I had hitched a ride with a songwriter, an older guy who wanted somebody to share the cost of the gas. We had come through Oklahoma, where we stopped for a few hours and I visited two or three friends who had become quite successful in business. It seemed like they were making it real big, and now here I was back in Hollywood and, in effect, starting from scratch by agreeing to do this B Western.

By this point, Tim's Westerns were no longer based on Zane Grey's novels (not that they really ever were). In *Riders of the Range*, I was back to playing the troublesome brother, this time opposite Jacqueline White, and I am deep in debt to saloon owner Reed Hadley. To square the debt, I agree to help his henchmen rustle Jacqueline's cattle. The villain in this one was played by Tom Tyler, who (like Tom Keene) wore the white hat in Westerns for years and then, when he got older, started

61

With Tim Holt in our fourth and final Western, *Pistol Harvest*.

wearing the black one. The movie also featured the wonderful Robert Barrat, who was in several of these Holt pictures with me. Not only was he a very nice man, he was also a really good, stalwart character actor. He was born in New York City and had worked on Broadway before he went into the picture business. He told me interesting stories about some of the things that he experienced in his career; one story in particular I recall is how Barrat acted opposite Edward G. Robinson at Warners, and how dominant and selfish Barrat said Robinson was to work with. Barrat said Robinson "wanted it all," he wanted to be the center of everything, and he didn't want to give any of the spotlight to any of the other actors. Ida Lupino later expressed the same kind of attitude about Robinson, so apparently Robinson didn't have too many people that liked him—not actors, anyway!

In addition to his Westerns, Tim Holt also appeared in the occasional A picture—a rarity for B cowboy stars.

By the time of *Riders of the Range*, RKO was starting to cut corners a little bit on these B Westerns. (At this point you could see Westerns on TV for free, so I guess it didn't make much economic sense for the studios to put as much effort into their B Westerns as they once did.) The director of *Riders of the Range*, Lesley Selander, was very adept at what he did, one of the best illustrations I can give of a fast Western director. By the time we actors would finish shooting a scene, Les was already walking away; from 15 or 20 feet away, he'd hear it finish, look around and say, "Okay, cut!" And Les would already be halfway to the *next* place that we had to shoot! The crew would have to *run* to keep up with Les. That was what Les was famous for, he was off and running to the next setup before the crew had broken down the last

Robert Wilke, one of the great Western heavies, was my *Pistol Harvest* partner in outlawry.

one.

My final picture with Tim Holt was *Pistol Harvest*. Tim had played different characters (always with the same "amigo," Chito) in the earlier pictures, but now he was playing "Tim Holt" in his Westerns the way Roy Rogers played "himself" in his. He was a ranch foreman in *Pistol Harvest* and Robert Wilke and I played a couple of saddle tramps who are hired by a crooked banker (Mauritz Hugo) to ambush Tim and Chito. Bob Wilke was the lead heavy and I was the "kid outlaw" because we were physically two different types. Bob had that great, "mean" face that made him a good actor to have in Westerns. A year or so later he played one of the badmen in *High Noon* with Gary Cooper and that was the beginning of better days for Bob. After *High Noon* his price went way up and he played good supporting roles in lots of top Westerns.

By the early 1950s, the B Western was nearing the end of the trail, done in by TV. As I mentioned before, these movies weren't art but for people like me, Barbara Hale, Lex Barker, Steve Brodie, Jane Greer, Dick Martin and a lot of others, they provided a great opportunity to "get our feet wet" in the picture business. Again, the Westerns I saw as a kid were such favorites that when I was assigned to *Wanderer of the Wasteland* (my first Western), it was a big thrill, because it hearkened back to my boyhood. I was delighted to be cast in these Westerns: We were kids, having fun making movies. Our hopes and dreams were up in the stars, and for some of us, many of them never came true. But it sure was fun to *dream*.

1 Keene started out in the movies under his real name, George Duryea; switched over to Tom Keene and was a cowboy star for 13 years; then changed it to Richard Powers.

Suspected of rustling, I'm made a prisoner by Tim Holt in *Pistol Harvest*.

THE PLAY'S THE THING

Robert Clarke

Who joins the cast of "The Play's the Thing" tonight at the Booth Theater

THE PLAYBILL

REGISTERED IN U. S. PATENT OFFICE

FOR THE BOOTH THEATRE

NEW YORK, NEW YORK

After RKO failed to pick up my option in 1947, I began to give some thought to trying my luck as an actor on the stage in New York. Somehow word got around about what I was contemplating, and Jason Robards Sr. heard that I might be going East. Jason, as I mentioned before, was one of the RKO stock players, a character man; one of the most prominent parts I saw him play while I was there was Oliver Todd, the institutionalized author in *Bedlam*. (When I made up a list of all my films, I was surprised to find that Jason and I were in at least 16 RKO pictures together!) Jason had been a star on stage and in the early days of pictures, but now he was at the point in his career where he may no longer have been making over $200 a week. He said to me, "My son is just getting out of the Navy in New York, and I'm sending him to the American Academy of Dramatic Arts. I'd sure appreciate it if you would give him a call when you get back there. Maybe you fellows might find something in common. And maybe you can help him!" (That, in retrospect, was the funniest line!)

Once I got to New York, I did call Jason Jr., and we agreed to meet on the second floor of Horn and Hardart, a famous automat. I got there first and sat where I told him I'd sit, and in walked this tall, gaunt... *homely* fellow. He had just gotten out of the Navy, as his father had indicated, and he was therefore still quite skinny, and his eyes were kind of sunken in his head. He was terribly nice, and we had an enjoyable conversation, but I certainly had no idea how to "help him," as his dad had requested; I was still trying to find my way around New York myself. The next time I heard of Jason Jr., he was doing some things on television, which was a brand new medium, and then the *big* springboard for him was the play *Long Day's Journey into Night* with Fredric March and Florence Eldridge (Mrs. March). From there, he took off like a rocket. Of course, the funny thing was Jason Sr. saying to me, "Maybe *you* can help *him*!"

Flash forward: For about eight years, starting in the late '40s, Jason Robards Sr. was unable to work because of blindness, but then in 1957 he underwent a series of operations made possible by the Motion Picture Fund. Later that year, his sight restored, he picked up his career again, working in TV. A year or so after that, I was in New York for some reason (I cannot recall why), perhaps with Alyce or with all the King Sisters; at that time, Jason Robards Jr. was starring in a play called *The Disenchanted*. And, happily, I noticed as we passed that theater that the marquee read STARRING JASON ROBARDS JR., JASON ROBARDS SR.—Jason Sr. had gotten back into the Broadway limelight with the help, and through the thoughtfulness, of his son.[1] Jason Jr. had become a very famous actor, and very deservedly so—he was brilliant. And I didn't help him a bit!

As for myself, the first job I got after arriving in New York was a two-week job in Detroit, acting with Brian Donlevy in the play *What Price Glory?* at the Music Hall Theatre. Brian had had a supporting part in the original Broadway production in 1924, but now he was the star (playing Captain Flagg), with Regis Toomey as Sgt. Quirt and me as Lt. Moore. Brian flew to Detroit to begin rehearsals, and I recall that we young actors in the cast were all curious as to what he would be like. We shared with each other what we already knew about him—including the fact that he wore a hairpiece. Brian arrived, rehearsals began, and in one scene, the girl playing the little French barmaid was supposed to sit on Brian's lap by the bar and get cozy with him. As she did so, Brian said to her, for all of us to hear, "Be careful, honey—don't spoil me doily!" We all got a kick out of that, and realized he was a genuine guy.

Detroit had one of those terrible blizzards, and sometimes there were as few as 15 or 20 people in that old barn of a theater. But Brian never stinted in his performance; he was always "up" energy-wise, and went at it full tilt. He never tried to be the big star, upstaging any of us. And he treated us very well, inviting us up to his hotel suite for a cast party, which he provided. He seemed to me a masculine, gutsy guy, and he was certainly generous to us. (And I remember that when he was around, the drinks flowed quite freely, as he was going through a terrible divorce at that time.)

After *What Price Glory?*, I came back to New York and did some modeling, acted on a few radio shows, and also looked for stage work (and didn't work much). My agency, the Max Richards Agency, was looking for some guys to go up to West Point and work as extras in a picture called *Beyond Glory*. (For years I've been mistakenly telling people the name of the picture was *The West Point Story*, but that was a later James Cagney movie which I'm *not* in. This one was called *Beyond Glory*, and it starred Alan Ladd and Donna Reed.) Having been at RKO as a contract player, I thought it would be kind of demeaning to do extra work, but I needed a job very badly. "Oh, hell," I thought to myself, "there'll be a lot of soldiers there and I'll just get lost in the crowd and won't be seen as an extra."

Now here I am, up at West Point, working on the picture, and who do I see but a guy named Russell Wade, one of my fellow contract players at RKO. (Russ was the juvenile lead in *The Body Snatcher*.) I saw him and he didn't see me, and I kept avoiding him all day; any time I'd see him, I'd turn the other way. But then at one point, we both came around a corner from opposite directions and we ran almost smack-dab into each other! I got away with telling him that I was playing a small part, but how I would have liked to have been able to avoid him altogether, because I didn't want him to know I had come down to this. But the punchline to this story is that I wasn't the only one playing a minuscule role in this thing: Years later I found out that Audie Murphy had a little part, courtesy of his actress-girlfriend Wanda Hendrix; so did Noel Neill, who later played Lois Lane on TV's *Superman*; and so did Kenneth Tobey, who was a struggling New York actor the same way I was. Knowing that they were in it too makes me feel a little better about taking that tiny part in *Beyond Glory*.

At one point during my New York "adventure" I decided to come back to California for a few weeks, and the one movie job I landed back here during that time was a two-line bit in a B-picture called *Ladies of the Chorus*. My agent then was Don Montgomery, the brother of actor Robert Montgomery, and it was Don who got me that one-day job over at Columbia. The stars were Adele Jergens and Rand Brooks, and the only reason the picture is still remembered today is because it's the earliest film in which Marilyn Monroe had a good-sized part. She was just an unknown then, but seeing her on the set, poured into a slinky red gown, it wasn't hard to tell that she was a good candidate for stardom. (Years ago I ran into Rand Brooks again, and I commented on the fact that it was obvious to me that Monroe was going to be a big star. Rand said, "I wasn't so sure—she had such big knees." I laughed, "Well, I never got down that far!")

I went back to New York after my California trip and I made the rounds trying to get a job in summer stock, which (luckily) I did—I landed one at a Newport, Rhode Island, theater. Working in summer stock is another interesting type of experience: You'd rehearse a show during the day and do a different show at night. In preparing to do a play called *John Loves Mary*, the cast had to rehearse without the actor who was going to be playing the comedy lead. That actor (I don't recall his name) didn't come in until a Sunday afternoon, because he was traveling around the circuit of summer theaters. (He was playing *John Loves Mary* for ten weeks during the season, at different theaters.) We rehearsed it with him all Sunday and part of Monday, and the show opened Monday night. But it was difficult to rehearse without a very important part of the cast.

The same sort of thing happened again when we did a play called *Fatal Weakness* with Glenda Farrell. When we got the "sides" for that play, I saw that I had 18 or 20 pages just acting with her alone. We got the sides from New York on a Friday and we started learning them, Glenda came in late Sunday, and we didn't even get a run-through with her until Monday. I got to do *one* rehearsal with her before we began doing the show in front of an audience. I managed to get through the scene the first night, the second night was easier and the third was a snap, but believe me when I say that initially I was quite nervous about doing this long scene which I had never properly rehearsed with her at all.

When summer stock closed and we went back to New York, my agent said that a job had opened up: an understudy for the juvenile in a Broadway revival called *The Play's the Thing* with Louis Calhern and Faye Emerson. It was a classic comedy by the Hungarian playwright Ferenc Molnár, originally seen on Broadway back in the mid-'20s, and it was set in a castle on the Italian Riviera. The characters were a playwright (Louis Calhern), his theatrical associate (Ernest Cossart), a young composer (Richard Hylton), a young prima donna (Faye Emerson) and an old actor (Arthur Margetson). Hylton is heartbroken after he overhears some spicy bedroom conversation between Margetson and Emerson, his fiancée. Calhern saves the romance by quickly writing a dramatic sketch in which the heated dialogue turns out to be quite innocent and ordinary. When Emerson and Margetson rehearse it, Hylton is greatly relieved.

The Booth Theatre

Central Theatres Leasing & Construction Co.

THE · PLAYBILL · A · WEEKLY · PUBLICATION · OF · PLAYBILL · INCORPORATED

Week beginning Monday, October 25, 1948 • Matinees Wednesday and Saturday

GILBERT MILLER
in association with
JAMES RUSSO and MICHAEL ELLIS
presents

LOUIS CALHERN

in

FERENC MOLNAR'S

THE PLAY'S THE THING

Adapted from the Hungarian by P. G. Wodehouse

with

FAYE EMERSON   **ARTHUR MARGETSON**
ERNEST COSSART   CLAUD ALLISTER
Francis Compton   Robert Clarke

Directed by Mr. Miller

Lighting by Ralph Alswang   Gowns by Castillo
Scenery designed by Oliver Messel
Costumes supervised by Kathryn B. Miller

CAST

(In order of appearance)

ALBERT ADAM .... ROBERT CLARKE
SANDOR TURAI .... LOUIS CALHERN
MANSKY .... ERNEST COSSART

It was Richard Hylton's understudy who had quit, and whose job I was competing for. I went over and auditioned along with a lot of other young fellows, and I thought I did a terrible job. There was a bright light in my eyes that made it impossible for me to see who was talking to me from the auditorium, and my voice sounded like it was in a cave. I thought I was awful, that I didn't even make sense, but lo and behold I got the job as Hylton's understudy.

I'd had about two or three weeks of rehearsals, doing the play with the other understudies, when all of a sudden *Hylton* gave his notice. I got *one* rehearsal with the real cast, on a Friday afternoon, before the producer Jimmy Russo asked, "Kid, do you think you can go in tomorrow afternoon?" I was afraid to say *no* because I was afraid I'd lose the chance, so I lied through my teeth and said, "Yeah, I'm all right." (To tell the truth, if I hadn't had the nerve-wracking experiences that I did in summer stock, I doubt that I would have had the courage or the confidence to go into *The Play's the Thing* with so little rehearsal.) Well, throughout the whole first act of the Saturday afternoon matinee, my whole body shook. The cast was very, very helpful, making every effort to work me in easily, and by that evening, I was a little more at ease. And that's how I got the part, my one shot at doing anything in New York. That was at a time when Brando was in *A Streetcar Named Desire* and Lee Cobb was doing *Death of a Salesman*, and it was a big thrill for me to be a (very) small part of the Broadway scene during those exciting days. There I was for three months, October-November-December, 1948, at the Booth Theater.

Faye Emerson, who played my fiancée, had acted in a number of Hollywood films before she made her Broadway debut in *The Play's the Thing*. Faye was not only a lovely gal but a bit of a fighter. She and Louis Calhern didn't get along because Calhern didn't want her playing that part, he wanted his wife, Marianne Stewart. (By a very strange little coincidence, I had worked with Marianne when she was a very young actress at the Geller Workshop Theater. After that, she went to New York and acted with Calhern in a play called *Jacobowsky and the Colonel*, fell in love with him and married him.) Eventually, when *The Play's the Thing* went on the road, Faye declined to go and Marianne took over the part. (We only lasted two weeks in Philadelphia—they had a terrible winter storm set in, and the box office was just terrible.) But I have very wonderful memories of doing four months on Broadway with one of the finest actors ever to grace the stage, Louis Calhern.

1 I heard Jason Jr. interviewed on TV quite a few years ago, and a question was put to him about working in films in Hollywood. His answer went something like this: "I saw what it did to my father. I have been fortunate that that hasn't happened to me." It was a sad note, but on the other hand, his dad did get a late-in-life "re-visit" of better days by being in a play on Broadway with his son, and that must have been a most gratifying experience.

As Edmond Dantes Jr. in *Sword of Venus*.

SWASHBUCKLING STAR

Like many movie fans of my generation, I grew up with the classic Hollywood swashbucklers and looked up to their stars. In the silent days, the undisputed king of sword-and-cloak movies was Douglas Fairbanks, the zesty, acrobatic, devil-may-care star of *The Mark of Zorro*, *Robin Hood*, *The Three Musketeers* and other pre-talkie blockbusters. Fairbanks not only starred in these films, he was in the ideal position where he also produced and often co-wrote, insuring that each of them was the perfect showcase for his talents. Once movies "broke the sound barrier," the baton was passed to handsome Errol Flynn, the Tasmanian-born actor whose "big break" came when he was chosen as the last-minute replacement for Robert Donat in Warner Brothers' 1935 pirate epic *Captain Blood*. The movie was a hit with audiences, and so was Flynn, who went on to play in a long series of costume adventures at Warners; Jack L. Warner wrote in his autobiography, "To the Walter Mittys of the world, Flynn was all the heroes in one magnificent, sexy, animal package." Tyrone Power, Cornel Wilde and Fairbanks' own son Douglas Jr. were other gallant actors who fit the swashbuckling mold a decade later. It was my privilege to join this illustrious circle of actors—on a more modest level—during the early years of television.

Hal Roach Jr., the son of the legendary comedy producer, had broken into the business collaborating with his dad, then later branched off into the infant medium of TV. In 1949, Roach Jr. let it be known that he was going to produce a film for television, *Three Musketeers*, in partnership with producer Bob Lippert. (I think their arrangement was that Lippert would put up some cash. How much I don't know, but certainly not much, because the budget on the thing couldn't have been more than $25,000!) Roach had access to the sets that were used in the Ingrid Bergman film *Joan of Arc*. In those days, it was common practice for a producer to keep an eye peeled for expensive standing sets and work them into his next production; this saved him the cost of set construction

Following in the imposing footsteps of Douglas Fairbanks Sr., I took on the role of D'Artagnan in TV's *Three Musketeers*.

while giving his film a pricey look which he could not otherwise achieve. I can't say for certain that this was the case with Roach and *Three Musketeers*, but it was standard operating procedure then. In fact, those same *Joan of Arc* sets were later seen again in two other films I starred in, *Tales of Robin Hood* and *The Man from Planet X*, in addition to who knows how many other film and TV productions.

For the role of D'Artagnan in *Three Musketeers*, the scuttlebutt was that they wanted Scott Brady. Brady was a good actor, as was his older brother Lawrence Tierney, but he was a husky fellow and very "New York-y." Both Scott and Larry looked and sounded like they came from Brooklyn (which they *did*), and I was having a tough time picturing Scott Brady in that part. I was a fan of Fairbanks Sr. and Jr. and Errol Flynn and, quite frankly, I thought, wouldn't it be fun to play D'Artagnan! Hoping that Scott Brady had not yet been signed, I sent Roach a tele-

Four against six—all in a day's work for the Three Musketeers and D'Artagnan.

gram saying that I thought I could do a very good job of it. And, to my delight, I landed the part. Of course, I later asked Roach if my telegram had had anything to do with persuading him to cast me in the picture, and he said, yes, he certainly took note of it. (In truth, I've always suspected that Scott Brady simply refused to work for the kind of money that the rest of us did!)

It was my good fortune on *Three Musketeers* to work with the marvelous Jack P. Pierce, who had created the Frankenstein Monster, the Mummy, the Wolf Man and other classic monster makeups during his many years at Universal. By this time, of course, he had left Universal and he was freelancing, working on movies and in TV. I wanted to sport a mustache in *Three Musketeers*, but they hadn't cast me in time for me to grow one. (And I was young enough then that I probably couldn't

The actors in *Three Musketeers* worked for $55 a day because the Screen Actors Guild had not yet set a minimum wage.

have grown much of one anyway!) Instead of just taking a mustache that had already been made on a piece of lace and sticking it on me, Jack Pierce took the painstaking route that demonstrated the type of craftsman he was. He applied spirit gum to my upper lip and then took several dozen long pieces of raw makeup hair and cut them. He laid each little bit of hair onto the spirit gum, piece by piece, in a straight line, and then trimmed it. We went through this procedure every morning, and the mustache that Jack so carefully created felt flexible, stayed on all day and gave me no problem. (In *The Man from Planet X* I wore a false mustache which was *not* that type and at times it was so stiff that my upper lip wouldn't move easily.) Jack P. Pierce was a true artist who was incapable of doing a second-rate job—a trait which sometimes worked to his detriment (his time-consuming attention to detail had cost him his job at Universal). It was a pleasure to work with Jack Pierce on several different occasions throughout my career. (More on Jack later.)

Equipped with Jack's mustache, my period costume and a scabbard full of youthful bravado, I embarked on the first of what would turn out to be a series of low-budget swashbucklers. The story, which followed (as best it could!) the original Alexandre Dumas novel, was set in 1625 France. King Louis XIII (Don Beddoe) sits on the throne, but the power has been wrested from him by his scheming prime minister Richelieu (Paul Cavanagh), who plans to instigate a war with England. Into this political powderkeg struts D'Artagnan, a young man from Gascony adventurously seeking the headquarters of the King's Musketeers. "Monsieur de Treville," D'Artagnan tells the Captain of the Musketeers (James Craven), "ever since I could lift my father's sword— from the moment I could sit astride his horse—I dreamed of one thing only. Of becoming a Musketeer."

D'Artagnan is accepted as a cadet, and through a comical series of incidents antagonizes Athos (John Hubbard), Porthos (Mel Archer) and Aramis (Keith Richards), the best swordsmen in the King's Musketeers. D'Artagnan is set to duel Athos at noon, Porthos at one and Aramis at two. But just as D'Artagnan is about to cross swords with Athos, six soldiers appear and threaten to place them all under arrest for duelling.

Porthos: There are only six of them to our three—two for each of us!
D'Artagnan: It appears to *me* that we are *four*!

D'Artagnan joins the fray, driving the soldiers off. The *four* musketeers are now inseparable and their motto ("All for one and one for all!") is born. To thwart Richelieu's plans to incite a French-English war, D'Artagnan goes to England, collects the 12 diamonds given to the Duke of Buckingham (Charles Lang) by Queen Anne (Marjorie Lord), and returns them to the Queen in Paris. Had he failed, the Queen would have appeared at a ball without the gems, which would have been a declaration of war and revolution. D'Artagnan and the Musketeers are triumphant and Richelieu is foiled.

We shot the picture in four days under the direction of Budd Boetticher, who I had known when he was a dialogue director at Columbia. Before that, Budd was a professional matador in Mexico; he broke into movies working as technical advisor on Tyrone Power's *Blood and Sand*. (Budd taught Power the necessary cape work.) Budd later made a name for himself via his bullfighting pictures (his *Bullfighter and*

One of the perks of playing a dashing, romantic lead.

the Lady was semi-autobiographical) and a well-regarded batch of
Randolph Scott Westerns. (Hollywood insiders also remember his 22-
day marriage to Debra Paget!) Budd was the type of director you liked
to be around. On *Three Musketeers* he was gung ho and enthusiastic,
very much *for* the project, and (like Edgar G. Ulmer) he tried to get a
variety of shots, to try different camera moves, to use a dolly when he
could, and not just make static shots with the camera. Even though *Three*

Three Musketeers played on TV in Los Angeles on New Year's Day, 1950. A few years later it was released to theaters under the new title *Blades of the Musketeers*.

Musketeers was a low-cost TV production, Budd wanted to make it look the very best he could; he didn't treat it as something to be sloughed off or run through as fast as possible. He was a fun-type guy who loved to make pictures and who gave the actor the first nod insofar as priority. He afforded every chance to those of us out there in front of the camera to give as professional a performance as possible.

I prepared myself for the D'Artagnan role the best I could: On the side, I took some fencing lessons (which I really couldn't afford). Fortunately, we also had a fellow on the set who was a very good fencer; I worked with him as well, and tried to absorb as much as possible. At appropriate times I was doubled by a fencer, to make it look even *more* authentic. Permit a bit of immodesty: I thought I came off fairly well, all things considered. One thing that's very important in any business or any art (and I don't mean to imply that *Three Musketeers* was art, necessarily) is your attitude toward the job. My attitude on *Three Musketeers* was one of being delighted to have gotten the chance. Part of what carried me through was my feeling that this was something I could handle and could do as well or better than any actor that *they* could get at that time. I am *not* putting myself in the class of an Errol Flynn, but for this small production, I was able to come up to what was expected.

The costumes were fairly decent and so were many of the actors, particularly Paul Cavanagh, who played Richelieu. I admired Cavanagh because he was in one of my favorite pictures, *The Hard Way* with Ida Lupino, Dennis Morgan, Jack Carson and Joan Leslie. Cavanagh was an excellent actor, and I got the feeling, knowing some of his acting credentials, that *he* knew that something like *Three Musketeers* was beneath him. The actors in it worked for 55 bucks a day because there was no minimum wage set by the Screen Actors Guild in those days. I never talked to Cavanagh to any great extent because there was something about him that didn't seem to invite "chitchat." I don't mean that Cavanagh *wasn't* a kindly man; in fact, he probably was. But I got the impression that he just didn't seem to be too interested in anyone else, that he was there to do the job—which to him was belittling, probably. He didn't let it be known through his acting, he did not stint in any way in his efforts. He was letter-perfect in his lines, a consummate actor, and just by being in it, he lent some dignity to the proceedings.

Don Beddoe, who played the King, was very effective, and the ladies (Marjorie Lord and Kristine Miller) were also good. Marjorie, of course, went on to play Danny Thomas's wife on TV's *Make Room for Daddy*. Mel Archer, the portly actor who played Porthos, looked the part (he was built like a bull) but he had a voice like a *canary*. They later "looped" him—they had another actor replace his dialogue via dubbing—but they went to the *other* extreme. The voice that you heard instead of Archer's was a big, low voice, sounding like it was coming out of a barrel, and it was so terrible that it became very distracting. John Hubbard (Athos) was a very smooth, professional actor, and also a pleasant guy. He was a "light leading man" type who had been under contract to Roach Sr. years before, and had starred for Roach in a movie with Carole Landis called *Turnabout*. *Turnabout* was very much like a recent Blake Edwards movie called *Switch*, it was about a husband (Hubbard) and his wife (Landis) who end up in each other's body. It was meant to help John's career but it actually didn't do *anything* for his career (except, perhaps, hurt it), because it gave the effect of his being effeminate. I remember that when we were doing *Three Musketeers* John pointed to a sizable dressing room there on the lot and said, "That was built for *me!*"—and there he was, back on that very lot, doing this little TV thing for just $55 a day. Like many actors who find it necessary to make a transition to other jobs during the course of their careers, John later became a maitre'd at a well-known restaurant out here called the Tail o' the Cock, and then following that he worked as a dialogue director.

Three Musketeers was made in 1949 and it played on TV in Los Angeles on New Year's Day, 1950; it was, to my knowledge, the first feature film shot for television. A few years later it was released to theaters—all 51 1/2 minutes of it!—under the new title *Blades of the Musketeers*. There were no residuals when it went to the theaters and no residuals when it played who-knows-how-many-times on television. But I was excited about getting to do it, and if I'd had the money, I'd have paid Hal Roach Jr. $55 a day to let me do it!

Roach Jr. later proposed a second feature in the same vein, *Adventures of Robin Hood*. Roach had me under contract—a quote-contract-unquote, a *verbal* contract—and told me that I should stay available for *Robin Hood*. (Normally a producer would "take an option" on an actor, pay him to keep his schedule open; what Roach did as he lined up *Robin Hood* was say to me, "Just stay available!") We shot the film under the title *Adventures of Robin Hood* but before it went into theatrical release the name was changed to *Tales of Robin Hood*. (Roach was apparently afraid of infringing on Warner Brothers' *The Adventures of Robin Hood* with Errol Flynn.)

Stage star Mary Hatcher was my Maid Marian in *Tales of Robin Hood*.

Robin Hood was meant to kick off a television series, although this "pilot" never got off the ground. I, however, had my own alternative

Taking aim at a TV career, I hoped that _Tales of Robin Hood_ would launch a small screen series.

plan. My agent's brother was a man named James Schwartz, and in advance of production on _Robin Hood_ I decided that we should try to launch a _Robin Hood_ radio series, in case the TV series didn't go. James lined up Fine and Friedkin, well-known radio scriptwriters, to bang out a script and we went to the McGregor Sound Studios and recorded our pilot episode. I played Robin and Alan Reed, the voice of TV's Fred Flintstone in later years, was Little John. Our logic was, let's get our radio *Robin Hood* on the air before the TV *Robin Hood* is shot, and that way we'll lock up the radio dramatization no matter *what* happens to the TV.

For the feature I had time to grow my own mustache, saving Jack Pierce a lot of time and bother every morning. But I did have to wear a "fall"—a wig for the back of the head—so that my hair would be long in the back, in the style in 12th century England. That, I thought, was a very glaring error, for the simple reason that the hair in the back is long but my sideburns and the hair around my ears was cut like a modern-day haircut. The hairdressers (who were under time constraints, as we all were) were quite creative in the way they devised that fall for me, but it hurt to wear the thing. They put it on with hairpins and rubber bands at seven o'clock in the morning and I couldn't take it off until we were finished shooting that night. I perspired through it all, doing all the swordfights and running around which the story entailed.

Like *Three Musketeers*, *Robin Hood* adhered closely to the source material (the Robin Hood legends). The Earl of Chester (John Vosper), master of Locksley Castle, is one of the few Saxon nobles who refuses to bow to the arrogance of the Norman conquerors. Sir Gui de Clairmont (Paul Cavanagh), the Norman overlord of Nottinghamshire, dispatches his representative Sir Alan (Keith Richards) to collect taxes from the Earl. When the Earl resists, Sir Alan shoots him in the back with an arrow. The dying Earl entrusts his young son Robin (David Stollery) to the care of faithful retainer Will Stutely (Whit Bissell).

Robin grows to manhood in Sherwood Forest while Sir Gui's rule becomes more ruthless and oppressive. Robin Hood (Robert Clarke) and his band of outlaws become the champions of the people, routing Sir Gui's soldiers and returning tax money to the people. (Somehow Robin managed to grow to adulthood while nobody else in the story got a day older!) Robin Hood adds Little John (Wade Crosby) and Friar Tuck (Ben Welden) to his marauding band of Merry Men while Sir Gui lays elaborate plans to effect Robin's capture. Lovely Maid Marian (Mary Hatcher), Sir Gui's ward, is detained in the forest by Robin Hood and his men; Robin and Marian are attracted to one another, but Marian wrongly

I had time to grow my own mustache for *Robin Hood*, but this time I got stuck with a wig which was painful to wear.

believes that he is a scoundrel. Robin, disguised as a Crusader, enters an archery contest, staged by Sir Gui and Sir Alan in order to flush him out. Sir Alan and his men chase Robin, and Sir Alan is accidentally killed by his own soldiers. Other skirmishes, escapes and rescues follow before Robin gets Sir Gui at sword's point and persuades the Norman to return his estates. Marian sees Robin for the hero that he is, and Friar Tuck calls for the Merry Men to prepare for a wedding.

Like *Three Musketeers*, *Robin Hood* was filled with the type of action designed to appeal to youngsters. My grandson saw the picture not too many years ago, and when it was over he said, "There sure was a lot of *laughing* in that picture!" Which there was—I led the *merriest* band of Merry Men in Robin Hood's long screen history, I think! We felt it was in the nature of the swashbuckler to be *having fun* and we were trying to reach a young audience. This was an underlying attitude of the swashbuckler genre right from the very beginning. Douglas Fairbanks was the type of hero that would hit his opponent on the butt with a sword, run away and hide, and swat at the bad guy again as he'd run past.

(Later, Fairbanks Jr. did that same sort of thing at RKO in a picture called *Sinbad the Sailor*.) We attempted to approach *Three Musketeers* and *Robin Hood* in much the same way, where the bad guys were made to look like buffoons, as if they couldn't *think* their way out of any situation. They were the goats. There would be serious moments, and of course a bit of romance, but overall it was just a fun chase, with hardly anybody having to endure anything worse than a fall on his ass. *Robin Hood* was adventurous and fun, and not as dark and deadly as the more recent production (with Kevin Costner).

I delivered the archaic dialogue the best I could, put up with that uncomfortable hairpiece and crossed my fingers that the actors who were coming at *me* with swords were as well-prepared as I tried to be. Actually, that was not much of a concern, since they cast as the soldiers men who were not only actors but stuntmen. Harvey Parry, who was our stunt coordinator on *Robin Hood*, was the granddaddy of stuntmen for many, many years. Harvey had started out as a Keystone Cop, worked with Fairbanks Sr., stood in for Harold Lloyd climbing the building in *Safety Last* and doubled for Jimmy Cagney throughout most of Cagney's career. He did stunt and double work for Humphrey Bogart, Elvis Presley, Ronald Reagan and even Shirley Temple(!). He was also a sweetheart of a guy. I don't think that Harvey ever doubled me in *Robin Hood* (they had a guy that looked a lot more like me than Harvey did), but I considered it a real honor in picturemaking to have him coordinate the stunts. Harvey worked right up until just before his death; in 1984, one year before he passed away, he received the first Stuntman's Life Achievement Award.

In one of the scenes I had to fight Wade Crosby (Little John) with a staff on a log bridge over a stream. Wade was a fun guy and he did a good job. He was the right type physically and he had a good sense of humor about it all. I remember they really wanted to cast Alan Hale Jr. in that part, probably because his dad had played Little John in the Errol Flynn version, but Alan Jr. wouldn't work for the 55 bucks a day. (Later I worked with Alan Jr. in *Captain John Smith and Pocahontas*.)

The director of *Tales of Robin Hood*, James Tinling, was a very cooperative type, but not the same caliber as Budd Boetticher. Budd had a lot of creativity, and Jim Tinling was a journeyman-type director. I had to jump into one scene unexpectedly (from off-camera), land on a table and point a sword at Paul Cavanagh, who was sitting at the table. I could

Starring
ROBERT CLARKE · MARY HATCHER · PAUL CAVANAGH
WADE CROSBY · WHIT BISSELL · BEN WELDEN · MARGIA DEAN
An R. & I. Production · Produced by HAL ROACH, Jr.
Directed by JAMES TINLING · Original Story and Screenplay
by LEROY H. ZEHREN · Released by LIPPERT PICTURES, Inc.

Villain Keith Richards is about to get his just deserts.

tell that Tinling was giving no special consideration to the scene, so I asked him, "Could I make an entrance here? I could leap up over the top of the camera, make a kind of a half-turn in the air, and land on the table in a position of pointing my sword right at the camera." "Sure, sure," he said, "let's set it up"—and we did. He was very amenable and we got a good shot as I made my entrance, but Tinling wasn't the sort of director who'd have come up with something of that sort on his own; he was more concerned about the tight schedule than with my entrances! Once more we shot on the *Joan of Arc* sets and the cast held up very well for the four days of shooting. Looking back now, it's almost amazing what we were able to do. There was a lot of action in *Tales of Robin Hood*, and it's hard to get that amount of action on film in just four days. And, once again, it was fun to do in the sense that I was getting the opportunity to do it first on television.

As I mentioned, *Robin Hood* failed to blossom into a TV series. Later on in the '50s, there *was* a *Robin Hood* television series, made in England, and it was better (I think) than ours would have been because Robin Hood was an English character and they were there on the actual locales. (Richard Greene played Robin in the English series.) Our radio series also didn't sell, but the one episode did get played on KNX CBS radio out here, and I think we got back part of the money I invested.

Tales of Robin Hood was also co-produced by Bob Lippert, who released it to theaters. I'm fuzzy now whether it played on TV first or not. Lippert was the kind of guy that would call a project one thing and it'd come out something else. That habit got him in trouble with exhibitors, who naturally expected to have exclusivity when they ran pictures— only to find out in the case of some of Lippert's they were already airing on TV! Lippert became notorious for that; later on, in order to get some production going again, he made a deal with 20th Century-Fox where he would produce second features (which *wouldn't* have his name on them) and Fox would release them in theaters, on the lower halves of double-bills with A-type Fox pictures. As for Hal Roach Jr., while he didn't have much luck in the swashbuckler vein, he did eventually succeed in getting a number of other TV series going, including *Racket Squad, Duffy's Tavern* and *My Little Margie*; he was one of the founders of the Academy of Television Arts and Sciences, and later one of its presidents. He died much too young in 1972.

My swashbuckling days were not yet over. By this time (1952) I had made a pair of science fiction pictures for the screenwriting/producing team of Aubrey Wisberg and Jack Pollexfen, *The Man from Planet X* and *Captive Women*. Wisberg and Pollexfen knew that I was hooked on wanting to do swashbucklers, and as part of the slate of pictures they were making for RKO, they added their own modest version of Alexandre Dumas' *The Count of Monte Cristo*. Actually, *Sword of Venus* was a sort of sequel to *Count of Monte Cristo*, set a generation later, in 1832 France. I played the Count's son Edmond Dantes Jr., a playboy whose escapades get him into scrapes, causing his invalid father heartache. When it is impressed upon Dantes that his father's life depends upon his actions, he promises to leave the temptations of Paris for the family castle. However, a scheming trio, Claire (Catherine McLeod), Baron Danglars (Dan O'Herlihy) and Valmont (William Schallert), have sworn to wipe out the House of Monte Cristo and obtain their fortune. Claire makes the acquaintance of Dantes and lures him into her bedroom where, as planned, "the jealous husband" challenges him. Dantes is made to believe that he killed the man, and Danglars kills one of his men to provide the corpse. Dantes' framing is complete when he is sent to prison. However, he

My "swashbuckler" career continued with *Sword of Venus,* **in which I played the son of the Count of Monte Cristo.**

escapes and, making his way to Paris, learns that his father has died and that his fortune is about to change hands. Arriving at the castle, Dantes is able to put an end to the scheme. Danglars is slain and Claire, who has come to love Dantes, goes off with him.

The director on *Sword of Venus* was Harold Daniels. Hal was a nice-enough guy but he didn't do too much more than pick the angles and then give the cameraman (and everyone else involved) a free hand. The cameraman would suggest a certain lens and Hal would say, "Yeah, I'll buy that"; and as far as directing actors, he didn't seem to be into that very much. We were pretty much on our own. Perhaps there just wasn't

The greatest swashbuckler stars always seemed to be having fun, a trait I tried to emulate.

time—although Budd Boetticher found time for it on the four-day *Three Musketeers*, and *Sword of Venus* took perhaps ten days. Hal was a good craftsman, though. My salary on *Sword of Venus* was $350 a week and we were in and out of there (RKO Pathé) in a week and a half.

My leading lady Catherine McLeod had been under contract to Republic and was very pleasant to work with. There was an accident on the set of *Sword of Venus* the very first day: We were about to shoot a scene where Catherine was required to cry. One way of doing this with actors who can't bring on the tears involves menthol crystals, which have a strong odor. The makeup man took a Kleenex tissue, laid it out flat, put the crystals on it and then enclosed them in the Kleenex by bringing the corners of the tissue up and around them. Then he blew gently through the Kleenex into Catherine's face, so that her eyes would tear up. But the Kleenex tore and one or two menthol crystals lodged in one of Catherine's eyes. She was unable to work all day: She couldn't see because her eyes kept watering, and she was in great pain. (Catherine was quite nice about it all, and didn't get terribly upset.) On a picture with that tight a schedule, it took a monumental effort to get around such an obstacle, but we managed and by the next day Catherine was okay.

Les Guthrie, the production manager, was the type who tried to make sure that accidents didn't happen. Toward the end of the movie there's a scene where Dantes leaps off a balcony, and I said that I wanted to make the jump myself. But Les wouldn't let me. He pointed to my stunt double Bill Ward and said, "That guy, from 20 feet away, looks as much like you as *you* do. If he sprains an ankle or breaks a leg, we can go on and finish the picture. But if *you* do it and *you* have an accident, you're gonna hang us up. So you stay right here and you watch." Well, there was no arguing with that.

Sword of Venus was the best of my swashbucklers from a standpoint of production; it was better-produced, more "finished," and had a slicker look. But it broke the cardinal rule: Instead of having a sense of fun, it was (*I* felt) quite heavy-handed and dramatic. A few years later, in 1954, I was in Central America doing a movie called *The Black Pirates* with Anthony Dexter, and the distributors down there heard that Tony and I were in their country. They tried to capitalize upon the fact that we were there by running in a theater Tony's movie *Valentino* and my *Sword of Venus*. (It was kind of interesting, seeing the film again, this time with Spanish subtitles, in San Salvador!) And neither in English nor Spanish was I ever able to figure out what the title meant.

By 1953 *The Hollywood Reporter* was calling me a "specialist in TV swashbucklers," but by then I was at the end of the line as far as that type of picture was concerned. I played another historical character in an episode of TV's *Favorite Story*, a syndicated dramatic anthology series hosted by Adolphe Menjou. In it I played Francois Villon, the roguish poet immortalized in film by Ronald Colman in *If I Were King* many years before. The casting director on *Favorite Story* was Ralph Winters, who had been at RKO, and I was able to show him some stills from *Three Musketeers* and *Robin Hood* and I think that helped me get the part. This experience would just be a footnote to this chapter, but I remember it well because I was so pleased to arrive at the studio (Califor-

By 1953 *The Hollywood Reporter* was calling me a "specialist in TV swashbucklers."

nia Studios) and find that the episode was going to be directed by old Lewis Allen. Allen, you'll recall, was the director who gave Paul Brinkman and me such a hard time on *Those Endearing Young Charms*, continually harassing us for "doing nothing" in a scene where Paul and I were supposed to stand off to one side and simply watch Robert Young speak on the telephone. Allen didn't seem to remember me, and I didn't bring up the incident, but it was fun having the good feeling of, "Here I am doing the principal role in this half-hour TV segment. I am now the principal, the lead." *I* had moved up, and Lewis Allen had moved down— *wa-a-a-y* down. Mr. Allen had come a long way from directing at Paramount and RKO to directing a two-day TV shoot for a fledgling outfit like Ziv.

I don't kid myself that this is any great achievement or any tremendous claim to fame, but I must be the only actor who has had the opportunity to play D'Artagnan, Robin Hood and the Count of Monte Cristo. I can't think of any other actor who did all of those characters— and certainly not as inexpensively as we did 'em! We worked our tails off on these little features and, despite all their shortcomings, I've always looked back upon that phase of my career (pardon the pun) as a feather in my cap.

THE PRICE OF FAME IN THE BIG-TIME SPORTS RACKET!

THE FILMAKERS *present*

HARD, FAST *and* BEAUTIFUL!

Distributed by
R K O
RADIO
PICTURES

AN IDA LUPINO PRODUCTION STARRING
CLAIRE TREVOR · SALLY FORREST
Directed by IDA LUPINO   Produced by COLLIER YOUNG   Screenplay by MARTHA WILKERSON

IDA LUPINO

Some of my best film opportunities came my way shortly after my return from New York: In the early 1950s, I played my first starring and co-starring roles in movies which ranged from the swashbucklers to the dramatic *A Modern Marriage* with Margaret Field (Sally Field's mom) to *The Man from Planet X*, the first "invasion from space" science fiction film. But it was the two pictures I made for Ida Lupino's independent production unit, *Outrage* and *Hard, Fast and Beautiful*, which gave my career its biggest boost.

My association with Ida began as a result of an appearance I made on an episode of a radio series. In those days, advertising agencies put together "packages" of shows for radio; for instance, *Lux Radio Theater* was done by the J. Walter Thompson ad agency. An ad agency called SSC&B (Sullivan, Stauffer, Colwell and Bayless) had a radio series which showcased up-and-coming Hollywood "hopefuls"—actors and actresses who had given some indication that they might become stars, or at least better-known actors.

The title of the series now escapes me, but one of its gimmicks was that the aspiring actors and actresses would be introduced by a well-established star. My "presenter" was Brian Donlevy. In 1947, after I left RKO and went back East, the first role I landed was a feature part in the Detroit stage revival of the old World War I play *What Price Glory?* That experience may have had some bearing on the fact that it was Donlevy who was selected to present me. With Donlevy as my "introductory star," I was highlighted in one episode of this half-hour radio show as an actor who might later be fortunate enough to become someone of some renown in the business.

Writing scripts for the program was Martha Wilkerson, a lovely lady who was married to an NBC executive back in New York. At that time, I was dating an ad agency secretary, a beautiful redhead named Virginia Reed, and Virginia was great friends with Martha. Martha

Director Ida Lupino (wo-manning camera) was marvelous with actors, putting their needs ahead of her other concerns.

seemed to be impressed with my ability and she said, "I'm working with Ida Lupino's production company. If there's any part in her next picture that you'd be right for, maybe I can get you in for an interview." (Ida had recently begun to branch out from acting into writing, producing and directing.) I thanked Martha but, to be honest, I then kind of dismissed it from my mind.

But Martha, true to her word, did make the recommendation. One rainy afternoon I was lucky enough to be home when the telephone rang; it was Martha, and she said, "Ida is auditioning actors for the second lead in her new picture. If you can get over here as soon as possible..." Needless to say, I rushed over to RKO in the rain and did a quick read-through with Don Weis, the dialogue director. I was then ushered in to meet Miss Lupino.

I had never before met Ida Lupino, although of course I was quite aware of the success that she had had in Hollywood. Ida made her first films in her native England before she came to the United States in the mid-1930s on a Paramount contract. In the 1940s, she was signed by Warner Brothers and subsequently made some of her best and most famous pictures there: *They Drive By Night, High Sierra, The Sea Wolf, The Hard Way* (a particular favorite of mine) and many others, often in *femme fatale* roles. Ida had the respect of the industry (the New York Film Critics named her Best Actress of 1943 for *The Hard Way*), but for whatever reason she once said that she considered her acting career a failure. In fact, she once referred to herself as a "poor man's Bette Davis"!

In 1948 Ida had married a Columbia executive named Collier Young, and the following year, she and Collier formed an independent production company, The Filmakers. Their plan, I had read in the Sunday section of *The Los Angeles Times*, was to produce budget pictures with socially important themes—stories that would have human values and social significance. Their first was *Not Wanted* (1949), produced and co-written by Ida, and starring her "discovery" Sally Forrest. *Not Wanted*, true to the course that Filmakers had charted for itself, concerned an unwed mother (Sally) seeking understanding. When the director of *Not Wanted*, Elmer Clifton, fell ill, Ida stepped in and did some uncredited directing. Ida made her "official" directing debut with *Never Fear* (1950) with Forrest, Keefe Brasselle and another of Ida's discoveries, Hugh O'Brian. Again, the story (Sally Forrest battles polio) was sensitively told, its screenplay dealing with the psychological and emotional plight of polio victims. These were inexpensive pictures, but the critics treated them with respect because they were also earnest statements on society. (Ida once said that she "liked to do pictures with poor bewildered people, because that's what we are.")

The film I was auditioning for was *Outrage* and the plot concerned the traumatizing effect of a rape upon a young girl (Mala Powers). Entering the office and meeting Miss Lupino (I *always* called her Miss Lupino), I noticed immediately that Ida was quite theatrical as a person, very dramatic in the way she did things. Everything was *ter-ri-bly im-port-ant, dah-ling*, very Tallulah Bankhead-ish or Bette Davis-ish. (Bankhead and Davis were probably even *more* so, but Ida certainly fell into that category of a dramatic personality.) I mentioned to her that

Traumatized by rape, Mala Powers recoils from her fiance's touch.

I'd recently been in the Broadway production *The Play's the Thing* with Louis Calhern and Faye Emerson (that seemed to impressed her) and I told her about a picture called *A Modern Marriage* which I had just finished making at Monogram. I then read my part opposite Don Weis (who was reading the *girl's* part!), and when we finished, Ida said, "*Oh!* That's wonderful. That's *marvelous*, dah-ling. That's fine for me. You're *it*." I almost fell through the floor. When Ida said, "You're *it*, dah-ling," I knew that this was one of the luckiest days of my life.

I felt I was a competent actor and that, if given a chance and the right kind of atmosphere and the proper role, I might be able to finally "make my mark" in Hollywood. I was the second male lead in *Outrage*—not a tremendously large part, but I would have some good scenes, and one *very* dramatic, emotional scene. *Outrage* would also enjoy the same sort of status as Ida's previous "meaningful message" pictures. It wasn't going to have a big budget—none of Ida's films did—but there was going to be a certain amount of prestige attached to it and to working with Ida (Hollywood's only postwar woman director).

Coincidentally, the Monogram picture I had just finished, *A Modern Marriage*, had an adult theme similar to that of *Outrage*. In it I played a newlywed whose bride (Margaret Field) runs out on him on their wedding night and attempts to commit suicide. Rescued by quick action, she is placed in a rest home where a psychiatrist (Reed Hadley) attempts to get at the root of her mental condition. It turns out that Margaret is afraid of the commitment of marriage, particularly the sexual part of it, and her problem stems from her relationship with her possessive mother (Nana Bryant).

A Modern Marriage had the small budget and short schedule (six days) for which Monogram was famous, but it also tried to convey a message about the problems of young love. It was the first film of a director named Paul Landres, who arranged for the three of us (Paul, Margaret and me) to do some pre-production rehearsing of our scenes. That helped a great deal. Paul wanted to make *his* mark with *A Modern Marriage*, just as Margaret and I did. Paul's desire to do a better-than-average job was communicated to the crew as well: About two hours into the first day, Margaret and I noticed that (for example) the cameraman William Sickner was beginning to take more care in lighting the scenes. He had realized rather quickly that here was something a *little* higher quality because Paul Landres, Margaret and I didn't just come in cold and grab the script and start firing away with the dialogue. *A Modern Marriage* was tastefully done, and the rewards for Paul and Margaret and me came later in the form of several complimentary reviews.

On February 20, 1950, production began on *Outrage*. Mala Powers played an office worker in a Midwestern town and I played her boyfriend, whose $10-a-week raise puts him in a position to propose. (The scene is set in a busy park, and my conversation with Mala is constantly being interrupted—by a shoeshine boy, by the staring of a smiling old lady, etc.) The next step is to announce our plans to her mom (Lilian Hamilton) and dad (Raymond Bond), a straight-laced, old-fashioned schoolteacher. As I nervously wait to break the news, I absent-mindedly begin to pull the stuffing out of a tear on the arm of the couch, until Mala alerts me to what I'm doing and rushes over to sit on the arm of the couch, concealing the damage.

Leaving work the next night, Mala is followed through the dark, empty streets of the warehouse district by a man (Albert Mellen) who finally catches her and "criminally attacks" her. (The word "rape" wasn't—and probably *couldn't* be—used, which shows how far we've come since then.) Mala walks home in a daze, and becomes hysterical when she is later questioned by the police. The incident has filled her with feelings of guilt and anguish and changed her attitude toward me. Ida got this across by showing Mala looking out her bedroom window as my convertible pulls up to the curb in front of her house; Mala walks over to her bedroom door, closes it and locks it.

When Mala arrives at police headquarters to look over a lineup of suspects, I'm already there. I sit next to her and I take her hand, but she quietly pulls it away—another small touch which spoke volumes. (Ida also wrote the screenplay in collaboration with her husband Collier Young and Malvin Wald, the third partner in Filmakers.) These scenes were well-written and also well-directed; as a director, Ida was excellent. Ida was so wonderful in the way that she put the actors' needs ahead of everything else. She was concerned about the performances, *that* (to her) was of the uppermost importance, and she would make little suggestions to the actors about pieces of "business" that might improve a scene. You knew that she cared, and that she wanted *you* to do the very best you could. To her, the first consideration was to make her actors and actresses feel at ease, to help *them*. Don't be worried whether it's the right aperture of the camera, the cameraman will take care of that; don't worry about the key light, the lighting director will handle it. She being a director *and* a high-caliber actress, she took care of the actor. Ida Lupino was the first and only woman director I've worked with; I don't consider her as fine a director as Robert Wise or Mark Robson, but she was certainly *very* considerate of actors. I *would* place her up alongside Wise and Robson as being kind, concerned, thoughtful individuals.

My best scene in the picture followed. I drive Mala home after her ordeal at the police station, and in the car in front of her house is

I thought *Outrage* was a good picture, partly because of the realistic performances.

where we have our first conversation about the attack. I tell her that my feelings for her haven't changed, but Mala has decided to close me out of her life and she bolts from the car, near tears. I chase her and catch up to her on the porch. Mala's experience has affected her reason, and she hysterically accuses me of never being able to forget what happened to her.

This was an important, volatile scene—*my* big scene in the picture—and I asked Ida to help me on it. I will never forget how marvel-ous she was about it. I said, "Tell me how to do this scene," and she *did*: She instructed me line by line. "'Nothing matters except us,' and then pause. 'You know that, don't you?'—*beat*." She acted out my dialogue for me, recommending how to play it, when to raise my voice, when to wait a beat—it was almost like she was directing a musician or a dancer, fine-tuning their performance.

It must also be said, however, that Ida did have a certain austerity about her, and the young actors in the pictures she directed (myself and Mala Powers and Sally Forrest) always referred to her as "Miss Lupino." She certainly never *said*, "Call me Miss Lupino," but we did, because we never quite felt we were on any sort of equal footing with her. Mala and Sally and I—*and* Hugh O'Brian and Keefe Brasselle, too, I'd imag-ine—we *all* put Ida up on a pedestal, and I think rightfully. She was the type of actress who couldn't read a line wrong if she *tried* to, she just had that innate sense of dramatic correctness, the inborn ability to be a fine actress—which she truly was.

Outrage went on from there, as Mala's emotional state worsens amidst all the whispering and knowing looks which follow in her small town. She suffers a mental lapse and leaves home in search of anonym-ity. She settles under a new name in California, where she is taken under the wing of a clergyman (Tod Andrews) and given a bookkeeping job on a fruit farm. But when Jerry Paris, another worker, tries to kiss her, she relives the attack and, imagining Jerry to be the rapist, hits him with a wrench. Mala is then jailed and her true name and background are dis-covered. Her attacker has been apprehended in the interim, and she is returned home to her family and her fiance. The implication is that her recovery will be complete.

I thought *Outrage* was a good picture, partly because of the real-istic performances with which we—*and* Ida—had taken such great pains. Tod Andrews was a good actor who had done a play in New York about the same time that I had, and Jerry Paris later became a very good direc-tor in television. In some of the supporting roles Ida used people out of radio, including Hal March, who later became quite well-known as the host of TV's *The $64,000 Question*. (Ida's sister Rita Lupino even played a small part; according to the news reports, Rita was at Ida's bedside when Ida passed away in August, 1995.) The film was publicized as "The Picture That Ida Lupino Said Had To Be Made And Must Be Seen," and many of the reviews were very positive; *The Motion Picture Exhibitor* called it "an honest, affecting, adult drama set forth with much integrity and simplicity," which was precisely the intent. (Again, not much was spent on the picture; for instance, during some outdoor shooting, there were planes buzzing overhead. Rather than delay shooting by waiting for them to pass, an expedient line of dialogue was added to the scene, referring to the "busy little airport nearby.") But the movie's admirable honesty of purpose shone brighter than its few flaws, and it got the reviews it deserved.

At the same time that we were shooting *Outrage*, Patricia Neal was also on the RKO lot. She saw some of the rushes of *Outrage* and afterwards, when she and I met on the lot, she complimented me on the work I had done. Of course, I was very pleased. I also got a note from Jerry Wald, the head of production at RKO (and the brother of Malvin Wald), saying how much they liked the rushes. Coming on top of Patricia Neal's compliment, it added a lot to my confidence as an actor.

Martha Wilkerson, who recommended me for the part in *Outrage*, was assigned to write the screenplay of Ida's next picture, *Hard, Fast and Beautiful*, one of the first (and one of the *few*) movies about the sport of tennis. Once again, Martha thought of me: She said, "There's a part that I'm writing in *Hard, Fast and Beautiful*, a young guy who works at the country club where some of the activity takes place. It'd be ideal for you. If the opportunity arises, I'll mention it to Ida." Martha did put in a word for me with Ida, who was pleased with what I'd done on *Outrage*; and, since the role I wanted in *Hard, Fast and Beautiful* was that of a character who plays tennis in one scene, I mentioned to Ida that I had been on a tennis squad at Kemper Military School in my early college days. Ida promised me the part, and during the next four or five months I kept my fingers crossed that she would remember her commitment. When *Hard, Fast and Beautiful* got underway in mid-July, 1950, I was there, playing the second male lead in a cast headed by Claire Trevor and Sally Forrest.

Unlike *Outrage* and other Filmakers productions which pointed to social blights, *Hard, Fast and Beautiful* was a more conventional story highlighting corruption in the amateur tennis industry—and mom-ism. Sally Forrest played a high school tennis champ who is being "pushed" by her ambitious mother, played by Claire Trevor. (The production title of the movie was *Mother of a Champion*, which was also the title of the

105

Getting guidance from Lupino on the set of *Hard, Fast and Beautiful*.

novel on which Martha Wilkerson's screenplay was based.) "By gosh, my daughter's gonna have everything!" Claire tells her long-suffering husband (Kenneth Patterson). "Everything I *missed*!" When Sally takes a liking to my character, a cleancut young fellow who works at the local country club, Claire begins nudging Sally up the ladder of success, encouraging her to play tennis with the blue-bloods there. This leads to Sally competing in junior title matches and then a series of tournaments. Tennis promoter Carleton G. Young, as unscrupulous and ambitious as Claire is, proceeds to court Claire and make large under-the-table payoffs of expense money to her.

Sally is blind to the way that Claire and Young are manipulating her but *I'm* not, and my disapproving attitude eventually leads to the breakup of our romance. During a European tennis tour, Sally finally

My days on the Kemper Military School's tennis squad may have helped me win the lead in *Hard, Fast and Beautiful* with Sally Forrest.

begins to see Claire for the ruthless, greedy woman that she is, and as a form of "self-defense," begins to behave the same way. But when her father becomes ill, Sally rushes to his side and comes back down to earth. She competes at Forest Hills and wins the title of world champion, then

At poolside with another Lupino "discovery," pretty Sally Forrest.

announces that she's retiring from the sport to become my wife. Spurned by all, Claire is left behind at the stadium. When night falls, she's still there, surrounded by blowing newspapers and thousands of empty seats as the closing credits appear.

True to the title of the novel, the film was really about Sally's mom, the "mother of a champion," played by Claire Trevor as a selfish, unloving woman who uses her daughter to get the things that she (Claire) wants. Claire was very pleasant and she always took a professional attitude toward things—she was one of my favorite actresses—but I found in working with her that she was not overly friendly. She was a little cool toward the rest of us, and I never felt that I was being "accepted" on *her* level, whatever that was. I also recall that Collier Young and Malvin Wald were concerned that there might be friction between Ida and Claire. (There wasn't, to *my* knowledge.) Claire Trevor *was* the star of *Hard,*

The proud "mother of a champion," Claire Trevor is about to be spurned by Sally Forrest in *Hard, Fast and Beautiful.*

Fast and Beautiful, but her part wasn't very sympathetic; and there was some conversation to the effect that she had not been so gung ho about doing the picture, that she had kind of been persuaded. (By whom, I don't know.) She was a little distant and she didn't let her hair down like (say) Frances Langford did on *Radio Stars on Parade*. Claire did a very good job, of course, and I remember that she and Sally got along fine.

Since *Hard, Fast and Beautiful* didn't deal with a touchy theme, the critics were able to take off the gloves and point more frankly to its defects. It was Filmakers' most expensive picture to date, but there were still a lot of corners cut. For the finale at the Forest Hills stadium, they made a facsimile at the RKO Ranch. It was a very modest recreation, and a lot of the shots had to be carefully planned by Ida and the camera

Broadway in Manhattan was closed off when Sally Forrest, Bobby Riggs and I took part in a *Hard, Fast and Beautiful* publicity stunt.

man Archie Stout so as not to have to show too much grandstand (there *wasn't* much!). In showing the radio commentator Arthur Little Jr. for example, the camera angle was from the base of the court up; Little was sitting in a chair above the court and the camera shot up past him into the sky. They also cut in a number of shots of the actual stadium, filled with crowds, to give a feeling of the size of the place, but these clips tended to make the scenes *we* shot at the RKO Ranch look even more small-scale and restricted. (During that climactic tennis match, by the way, the character name of Sally's opponent was Virginia Reed. Martha Wilkerson had named the character after her friend.) By working quickly and efficiently, we finished the picture a full four days ahead of schedule.

Once again, I had a good part as Sally's beau. Unlike *Outrage*, where I vanished from the movie once Mala Powers ran away from home, I was in *Hard, Fast and Beautiful* from start to finish; I had some nice, romantic scenes with Sally, including another "proposal" scene, and then

True to the title of the novel, the film was really about Sally's mom, the "mother of a champion." [Photo courtesy Eric Caidin/Hollywood Book & Poster]

some dramatic, confrontational ones with her later in the picture. *Variety* said in its review, "Robert Clarke has his best role to date and makes the most of it with a good performance."

Howard Hughes, who owned RKO, became quite enamored of *Hard, Fast and Beautiful* and he set up quite a publicity campaign. To advertise the picture, a junket went up to San Francisco: Me, George Murphy, Bill Bendix and other actors that had multiple picture deals at RKO. Then later, when the picture opened in New York, Hughes had Sally and her mother and me entrained on the Super Chief. That was a great trip. We stayed at the Plaza Hotel, where the food was just great; one evening, I remember, I really overdid it, and I got the old "green-apple stomach ache" from overindulging in the cuisine! Sally and I also played a mock tennis match in Times Square against Bobby Riggs. The street was blocked off and a tennis net was set up and there we were, playing tennis in the middle of Broadway, between 46th and 47th Street. Bobby Riggs being a professional tennis player, we didn't actually *play*; this was strictly for the cameras. We just hit the ball back and forth a few

Less of a "message picture" than Ida Lupino's other films, *Hard, Fast and Beautiful* received a harsher critical reaction. [Photo courtesy Eric Caidin/Hollywood Book & Poster]

times, Sally and me on one side of the net and Riggs on the other, as the photographers clicked away. The photos made all the papers. Another evening, we went out to a Yankee game and made a personal appearance out on the field, Riggs, Sally and I. Hughes had told the publicity department at RKO to give *Hard, Fast and Beautiful* first-class treatment, which they did.

Acting in these Ida Lupino movies did more for some of us than for others. Hugh O'Brian went on to have a long and lucrative career, first in movies and then later on TV where he had his own series *Wyatt Earp*. Sally Forrest parlayed it into a contract at MGM. Mala Powers, who starred with me in *Outrage*, was a very good actress and a beautiful girl who was supported by the constant presence of her mother. She co-starred with Jose Ferrer in *Cyrano de Bergerac* that same year (1950) and she did a fine job as Roxane.

As for myself, I had hoped that appearing in these pictures would get me into either a TV series or at least into the type of pictures that were a step or two up from the exploitation things. (As it turned out, of course, it's the "exploitation things" that have endured while films like *Outrage* and *Hard, Fast and Beautiful* have sort of faded from people's memories!) But participating with Ida Lupino on those two pictures gave me a boost, a kind of a "leg-up" in the business which lasted awhile, and which did lead to other starring roles. I look back on them now as two of the best breaks I had in my career.

Rushed into production to make capital of *The Thing*'s publicity, *The Man from Planet X* beat that Howard Hawks film into release.

THE PLANET X FILES

In recent years, science fiction has grown to become one of Hollywood's most high-profile and profitable genres; among the biggest moneymaking hits of all time are movies like *Alien*, *Star Wars*, *The Terminator* and *Jurassic Park*. But science fiction wasn't always the popular film genre it is now: Until 1950, science fiction movies tended to be relatively few and far between. Before that time, with just a few exceptions, most of the sci-fi that Hollywood *did* have to offer could be found in Saturday matinee serials like *Flash Gordon* or *Buck Rogers*.

That all began to change in the 1950s, when reports of flying saucer sightings were commonplace, and when outer space exploration moved from the comics page to the front page. George Pal's *Destination Moon* (1950), depicting a manned space flight to the Moon, was one of the first—but not *the* first—science fiction adventures to capitalize upon the public's new appetite for sci-fi entertainment. The first movie out, actually, was an *imitation* of *Destination Moon*: As George Pal put months of work into his film, producer Robert Lippert saw its box office potential and cranked out a similar movie, *Rocketship X-M* with Lloyd Bridges. Probably no more than eight weeks passed between Lippert's initial announcements and the film's first reviews, and Lippert had on his hands a movie pre-sold by all of the intense advance publicity that George Pal's film had generated. The people who saw articles and news items about *Destination Moon* in the major magazines and newspapers blithely bought tickets to *Rocketship X-M*, probably assuming that this was the movie they had read about.

My first science fiction film, *The Man from Planet X*, was "born" under similar circumstances. Late in 1950, Howard Hawks began work on his own sci-fi film, *The Thing from Another World*. Hawks was one of Hollywood's biggest-name producer/directors; his career went back to the silent days and his list of credits included such hall-of-fame titles as *Scarface*, *Bringing Up Baby*, *His Girl Friday*, *Sergeant York*, *To Have*

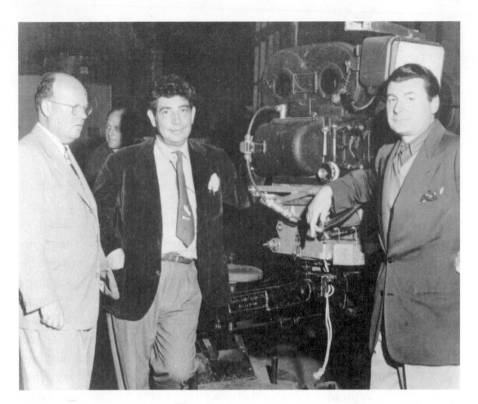

Jack Pollexfen, Edgar Ulmer and Aubrey Wisberg on the *Planet X* set.

and Have Not and *The Big Sleep*. *The Thing* was to be produced by Hawks and directed by his protege, editor Christian Nyby. (Today it's well-known that Hawks actually directed it himself, allowing Nyby to assist and to take the credit.) Hawks filled the cast with "new faces" rather than established stars, and production began in October, 1950. The success of *Destination Moon* and *Rocketship X-M* demonstrated that there was money to be made in the field of science fiction; the combination of sci-fi and the Hawks name probably spelled box office gold to a lot of people.

Two Hollywood writers, Jack Pollexfen and Aubrey Wisberg, decided to hop aboard the bandwagon. They wrote the script of *The Man from Planet X* with the intention of selling it but then, realizing that it could be made on a very low budget, they decided to produce it themselves. They formed their own independent production company, Mid Century Films, and set up headquarters on the Hal Roach lot. At this

"The odds are a hundred to one I too will be finished before another sun rises ..."

time, I was attending a course in screenwriting at U.S.C. The teacher was Malvin Wald, the third partner (with Ida Lupino and Collier Young) in Filmakers. Malvin told me that Pollexfen and Wisberg were auditioning actors for the leads in *The Man from Planet X* and he suggested that Margaret Field and I meet with them and try out for the roles.

Approximately one hundred actors and actresses were interviewed by Pollexfen and Wisberg before they selected us to star in the picture. Jack Pollexfen was a newspaper reporter, a playwright and a screenwriter before he and Aubrey Wisberg decided to take the production plunge. Jack was rather shy and diffident, but quite obviously an erudite man, someone you could picture plowing through volumes of research material in order to get correct details into his script. Aubrey, who was British, was much more vocal and more outgoing, and he seemed to be the "spokesman" of the two.

In charge was Edgar G. Ulmer, the great Austrian director whose modern reputation as a "miracle worker" of the B movie world is well-deserved. Edgar's history was the history of the movies: He began as a set designer and assistant director in Vienna and Berlin, working on stage productions and in films. He came to the United States in the 1920s and worked on Broadway and in Hollywood as a set designer before he returned again to Germany, where he collaborated with the great movie pioneer F. W. Murnau. Ulmer worked as an assistant on Murnau's Hollywood films as well, became an art director in 1930 and then a director three years later. One of his first films, Universal's *The Black Cat* (1934) with Boris Karloff and Bela Lugosi, has the reputation of being his greatest.

The script girl on *The Black Cat* was married to a member of the Laemmle family that owned and ran Universal. The story was that Edgar and the script girl, Shirley, became involved romantically, and that angered certain higher-ups at Universal. That was the point at which Edgar stopped getting work at the major studios; from then on, he worked exclusively for "Poverty Row"-type companies, both here and abroad. But according to Ulmer, this was how he *liked* to work; he once declared, "I did not want to be ground up in the Hollywood hash machine." At his side throughout the rest of his years was Shirley, whom Edgar married in 1935, and who shared his private and professional lives: She worked with him on most if not all of his future pictures. (Brian Aherne, who was in Ulmer's last film *The Cavern*, accurately described Shirley as "Ulmer's loyal, overworked wife, who acted as assistant producer, script girl, wardrobe mistress, secretary, cashier, and everything else necessary.")

Margaret Field was the very dedicated actress who co-starred with me in the Monogram film *A Modern Marriage*. (Before that, she was under contract to Paramount, where she played small supporting parts in a number of very good pictures.) We were both full of starry-eyed hopes and dreams, and so exuberant over getting a chance to do *The Man from Planet X* together. I remember that it was arranged for Margaret and me to rehearse (pre-production) at Edgar Ulmer's house, and we were so impressed by what we found just inside the door: Here in the foyer of his home was the rather large and imposing glass painting of the "broch" (Scottish for "castle") that would be seen in the movie. Edgar had painted it himself, and Maggie and I were quite amazed; nei-

John Lawrence examines evidence of the approach of Planet X.

ther of us knew that he had been a fine art director. We also met Shirley, Edgar's devoted wife, who would work as the script clerk on *The Man from Planet X.*

    The Man from Planet X was shot on the Hal Roach lot, on the impressive medieval *Joan of Arc* castle sets where I had made *Three Musketeers.* (Here they were being seen as the interior of the Scottish tower.) I had the feeling that we were racing to get the movie "in the can" in order to capitalize on *The Thing*; when we began *Planet X*, Howard Hawks and the cast of *The Thing* were up in Cut Bank, Montana, waiting for snow to fall so that they could shoot some location scenes. My hunch was confirmed when someone, I can't remember who (*not* Pollexfen or Wisberg), actually told me, "This will be a small budget picture, but what they're trying to do is capture some of the impetus, some of the momentum, the pre-publicity stuff that's gone out about *The Thing*."

My friend Robert Skotak (the special effects genius who has won Oscars for *Aliens* and *Terminator 2*) is a big fan of *The Man from Planet X*; he once wrote a very perceptive article about *Planet X* where he pointed out that it was an ideal link between the old Hollywood horror movies and the new science fiction genre. "The castle setting, the ever-foggy moors, the superstitions of the local villagers... all create a gothic atmosphere... Many elements in the film work in a gothic horror as well as science fiction manner." In the film, I play an American newspaper reporter, John Lawrence. The opening scene sets the mood immediately: The camera moves in on a tower-like structure situated on a foggy moor. Inside, Lawrence paces in a room equipped with a telescope. He moves back and forth across the room, but his face is always unseen. His thoughts are heard on the soundtrack:

"I don't know if she's still alive or not. They've had her now for the past 24 hours. I'm equally uncertain as to the fate of her father, Prof. Elliot. Both are probably dead. The odds are a hundred to one I too will be finished before another sun rises..."

The story is told in flashbacks. A mysterious planet is hurtling through outer space and will pass close to Earth. The elderly Prof. Elliot (Raymond Bond) plots its orbit and determines that the best vantage point is Burray, an island off the coast of Scotland. Elliot invites his friend Lawrence to visit him on Burray and witness the rogue planet's passing.

Prof. Elliot and Mears (William Schallert), a disreputable doctor who has imposed on Elliot's hospitality, have set up an observation post in the moldy fog-bound broch (tower) on the island's moors. While awaiting the approach of Planet X[1], Lawrence finds romance with the Professor's pretty daughter Enid (Margaret Field). Walking on the foggy moors one night, Lawrence and Enid discover a small projectile which they bring back to the broch. Prof. Elliot speculates that it's some type

Enid and Lawrence stumble upon the alien advance probe.

of alien advance probe; Mears analyzes its metallic structure and greedily contemplates the wealth that could be his were he to discover the formula.

Enid drives Lawrence to the inn in the nearby village, but on the return trip gets a flat tire. While covering the remaining distance to the broch on foot, she discerns an eerie glow on the dark moors and finds a small spacecraft—a diving bell-sized ball girdled by steel belts, buzzing and pulsating with a weird greenish light. A hideous figure in spacesuit and bubble helmet appears at the porthole, sending Enid racing back to the broch in terror.

Furtively tailed by Mears, Prof. Elliot and Enid creep back to the landing sight for a close look. A hypnotic ray emanates from the ship and Prof. Elliot, caught in the beam, goes into a strange trance. Like a docile sleepwalker he is led by Enid back to the broch, where he soon regains his senses.

Notice the top of the sky backdrop behind X's spaceship.

Prof. Elliot and Lawrence sneak out to the spaceship the next night and encounter the alien, "X," who holds them at bay with a strange weapon. When X appears to be suffocating inside his helmet, Lawrence turns a regulator valve on the shoulder of his spacesuit to re-establish the flow of air. (You'd think that if the X-Men were smart enough to travel through space, they'd be smart enough to put the air supply knob somewhere where they could reach it!) Unable to communicate with X, Lawrence and Prof. Elliot flee back to the broch, but they are followed by the seemingly benign alien.

In a dungeon below the broch, Lawrence, Prof. Elliot and Mears attempt to make themselves understandable to X. Left alone with X, the power-hungry Mears loses his patience and attacks him. X, now feeling threatened by the humans, escapes, taking Enid with him. Prof. Elliot, Mears and a number of villagers join the ranks of the missing as X uses his hypnotic ray to turn them into his slaves, digging trenches and

The first close encounter of the third kind.

fortifying his spaceship against attack.

While Scotland Yard men and the military converge on the moors to destroy the alien craft, Lawrence infiltrates the landing area to save X's human slaves. He grills the entranced Mears, who explains that X is the advance scout for an invasion force from the fast-approaching Planet X, a dying world turning to ice. If the people of Planet X do not escape to Earth before their planet swings back along its route through space, they will be doomed.

Lawrence evacuates Enid, Prof. Elliot, Mears and the other slaves. Mears revives and, fearing that he's about to lose his "meal ticket" (the alien), rushes back toward the ship just as the military opens fire. Both Mears and X are killed.

The Earth forces cringe in terror as Planet X swoops down out of space, creating high winds, then swings back up into the heavens. Lawrence and Enid wonder whether the arrival of men from Planet X would have been Earth's darkest hour or its greatest boon.

    •   •   •   •   •   •

The Man from Planet X was finished at the end of its sixth shooting day, at a cost of just $41,000. My participation accounted for a very small fraction of that amount: The actors in *Planet X* were paid scale (the Screen Actors Guild minimum was $175 a week then). We worked from 6:30 in the morning until eight or nine o'clock at night, every night, for those six days. Overtime payments boosted my paycheck to $210. While we were shooting, the cast and crew of *The Thing* returned in defeat from Montana: The snow they needed for their location scenes had failed to materialize, setting back the whole production.

In order to bring *Planet X* in for such a minuscule amount, every corner had to be cut. The little Scottish village seen in the film was no more than a painted backdrop. Much of the movie was set on the Scottish marshes between the broch and the village, but only one or two shots were actually done out of doors. The rest of those scenes were shot on a "foggy" marsh set at the studio. The heavy fog seen throughout the movie not only helped to create "atmosphere," it effectively camouflaged the tiny dimensions of our "exterior" sets. But it also created problems. We shot the picture in six days, and about the fifth day, some of the people began coughing because of all that simulated fog. Fortunately, I was able to get off the set every now and then; when the fog got to be too much, I could step outside and get some fresh air. As much as I was in the picture (I was the star), I wasn't "locked in" like the camera people, the crew, the electricians, etc.—not to mention Edgar Ulmer! The crew members' eyes became watery and bloodshot and their throats were all sore. That fog became a real hardship for the people who were there for 12 or 14 hours a day.

The grim castle sets from the Ingrid Bergman *Joan of Arc* also added to the somber atmosphere and helped a lot toward creating the impression that we were really in a dank Scottish tower. In one shot I walked through one of the corridors of the broch and, to give the scene a more eerie effect, they had one of the grips hose down the walkway with water so that there would be a sheen, so that the lights would reflect and it would shine. Touches like these, I believe, contributed toward making *Planet X* the cult film it is today. As Jack Pollexfen once said, Ulmer had a flair for creating mood; if silent films had lasted, he would have been one of the greats.

The Man from Planet X was John L. Russell's initial opportunity

Even the scenes set amidst the Scottish moors and rocks were shot on the Hal Roach sound stages.

as a first cameraman, and John worked very closely with Edgar Ulmer, doing everything possible to cooperate and to give Edgar what he wanted. In one scene, I was sitting at a table in the broch, writing in longhand about the Man from Planet X. My thoughts would be heard on the soundtrack via a voiceover recording, and the scene was meant to have an ominous quality. Here I was, just a young actor, certainly not the director, but I suggested to John Russell, "I'll be facing down toward the manuscript that I'm writing, John. Would it be possible for you to drop the camera low enough so that you don't get just the top of my head?" John said, "Oh, sure. Glad to!" So he lowered the camera about six or eight inches, and I thought that it was a most effective shot because the expression on my face could now be seen. I also remember that they wanted some tracking and dolly shots in the castle scenes, and they had to lay tracks for the camera. Because the floor was uneven, they

125

The *Joan of Arc* sets we used added to *Planet X*'s clammy atmosphere.

were constantly putting shims under the tracks to make for smooth camera moves. It was a lot of trouble, but the shots they got by doing this gave *Planet X* the feel of a bigger picture. John Russell worked very hard on the picture and I felt that he made a great contribution to the mood of *Planet X*. John was a nice man who later did fine work in television and on features like *Psycho* (for which he earned an Oscar nomination).

I had tremendous respect for Edgar Ulmer, and always will have. But Ulmer was a temperamental man, as temperamental as he was artistic, and there were times when he seemed somewhat condescending. He probably didn't mean to be, but he *was* difficult at times, with *every*one. Perhaps the one flare-up I had with Edgar was *my* fault to some extent. Some of the dialogue that Pollexfen and Wisberg wrote was tedious and

Lovely Margaret Field was my co-star in *A Modern Marriage,* *The Man From Planet X* **(pictured) and** *Captive Women* **before she married Western TV star Jock Mahoney.**

literary, and sometimes it was tough to get those words out. Edgar did some cutting, but it was still hard at times. Toward the end of the shooting schedule, I was in a scene with the actor who played Margaret's father, Raymond Bond. (Ray had played Mala Powers' father in *Outrage* several months before.) Ray and I were standing up on a rock ledge, looking out toward the area where the spaceship had landed, and there was a lot of exposition dialogue. I had a couple of fluffs in my dialogue. I don't remember exactly what Edgar said, but he made it plain that he was disgruntled over the fact that I'd blown a take. There wasn't any outburst on *my* part, I just said, "I'm up here doing the best that I can. I don't need criticism when I'm struggling to give the best that I can give." I was willing to accept the responsibility for having

Lawrence rescues Mears and Enid from the clutches of X.

forgotten the line, but I wasn't willing to let Edgar start to hammer on me. As I said, the dialogue was ornate and overwritten and we had a lot of it, and I wasn't the only one who blew a take here and there. Ulmer wanted *Man from Planet X* to be the best it could be, and he occasionally put pressure on me and made my job even tougher. But Ulmer had his own cross to bear: Because he made pictures so inexpensively, inexpensive pictures were all he ever got to do. He was a very talented man with some very innovative ideas, and I'll always admire him for his great ability.

Margaret Field and I played our parts to the best of our abilities, as did William Schallert, who contributed greatly as the villainous doctor who antagonizes the spaceman. Bill Schallert has certainly become the most well-known of us all, and is as fine an actor as I can name. I'm frequently asked to recall the name of the actor who played the gnome-

Sharing a cup of tea with the Burray constable (Roy Engel) between alien encounters.

like X, but all I can remember about him is that he was about the size of a jockey and that he complained—constantly!—about how little money he was making. (He also didn't get billing, which I thought was unfair; the producers probably thought that leaving X unbilled gave him a bit more "mystique.") Jack Pollexfen said in an interview that this fellow came out of vaudeville, where he did a slow-motion act that combined dance and acrobatics. The guy didn't like wearing the spacesuit, and the mask was hot and uncomfortable. He had a right to belly-ache, and he did—a *lot*. He was a nice-enough man and he did his job well, but as far as I can tell he went on to great oblivion!

Another person I remember fondly from *Man from Planet X* is the production manager, Les Guthrie. Les had been a first assistant at Warner Brothers, where his father was head of location scouting, and on *Planet X* Edgar gave Les his first chance to be a full production manager. All Les's life he felt very beholden to Edgar and had a great loyalty to him, because, to get that promotion, to get a chance to do a production manager's job instead of a first assistant's, was a big move and a great opportunity even on a small picture like *Man from Planet X*. (Unions were very much in control, even moreso than now.) Les was so very important on *Planet X*, keeping it on budget, keeping things under control. He was careful right down to the last penny; when Les told you that a picture would cost x-number of dollars, then that's what it cost.

Sherrill Corwin, the owner of a chain of California theaters and drive-ins, saw *The Man from Planet X* and paid Pollexfen and Wisberg $100,000 for a 75 percent interest in it. Corwin premiered it at the Paramount Theatre in San Francisco, and in just the first three days of its engagement there, it rang up a near-record gross of $10,000. (This was in March of 1951, and *The Thing still* wasn't finished!) More successful test engagements followed. The publicity received by *The Thing from Another World* helped *The Man from Planet X*; even the titles were alike, adding to the confusion of identity. Corwin went to New York and negotiated a distribution deal with United Artists, and with UA behind it, *The Man from Planet X* proceeded to do exceedingly well. (UA later took out a full-page back cover ad in *The Hollywood Reporter* announcing the holdover business that *Planet X* had done at the San Francisco Paramount and New York's Mayfair Theatre. At Philadelphia's Stanton Theatre, it opened to one of the biggest takes in UA history.) The movie went on to gross well over $1,000,000, which was a very substantial sum considering what the picture cost.[2]

I don't mean to imply that the success of *The Man from Planet X* had any negative effect on the grosses of *The Thing*. *The Thing* was and still is regarded as one of the finest pictures of that type, and acting-wise, I can't say enough good about it. *The Thing* was a big moneymaker as well, grossing *much* more than *The Man from Planet X*; but if one were to calculate what each picture *cost* versus what it took in, I'm sure that by *that* reckoning *Man from Planet X* was an even bigger success than *The Thing*.

Though small in budget, *Planet X* was the *first* picture about a creature coming to Earth from outer space, and one of the *few* pictures of that generation to depict an alien visitor as a sympathetic character. It paved the way for dozens of similar movies in the decade to come; some were better, many worse, but none matched *Planet X*'s unique atmo-

Sci-fi film scholars (and autograph hounds) have frequently asked me for the name of the actor who played X, but all I can recall about the man is his continual complaining.

sphere and quality. (It also went to television quite early. That did *me* no good, as there were no residuals paid to actors then, but it did the picture a *lot* of good, helping to establish its cult status.)

Over the years, *The Man from Planet X*'s reputation has continued to creep up the ladder. Pictures like *The Thing*, *The Day the Earth Stood Still* and *The War of the Worlds* certainly deserve their standing as science fiction classics, but remember that they had bigger budgets, the resources of major studios and great publicity behind them. With no "names" in the cast, a tiny budget and an even tinier shooting schedule, *The Man from Planet X* achieved the reputation of a stylish, artistic gothic science fiction classic. That's something that all of us—particularly Edgar Ulmer—could take a lot of pride in.

●　　●　　●　　●　　●　　●

Lightning so seldom strikes twice. No sooner had *The Man from Planet X* wrapped up than Jack Pollexfen and Aubrey Wisberg began announcing a second science fiction feature: *3000 A.D.* From the success of *Planet X*, they later got a three-picture deal with RKO, and the planned *3000 A.D.* became the first of those three features. But RKO also stuck them with an "associate producer," Albert Zugsmith. According to Pollexfen, the problem with *3000 A.D.* was that he and Wisberg were battling Zugsmith too much to pay attention to the production. That certainly could have been part of what went wrong.

I had my own (small) battle with Zugsmith just before we got started: I don't remember why, but he told me he wanted me to shave my mustache for the picture. I didn't think that was a good idea and I got stubborn. I told Zugsmith, "Why, you wouldn't ask Errol Flynn to shave *his* mustache." Zugsmith replied, "Yeah, but that's different." I said, "I don't know *why*," and that was the end of that; for whatever reason, Zugsmith didn't pursue it any further, and I got to keep my mustache!

The other problem was the director, Stuart Gilmore. Howard Hughes owned RKO at the time and Gilmore, a film editor, had cut some of Hughes' pictures. Hughes evidently had loyalty to the people who worked for him, if he liked them; he apparently took a liking to Gilmore, because he insisted that Pollexfen and Wisberg give Gilmore *3000 A.D.* to direct. (Gilmore had previously directed a Western, maybe two, but that was about it.) There was quite a bit of disorganization on the set, and it quickly became evident that Gilmore was in over his head.

When the film came out, *The Hollywood Reporter* called it "a pretentious, long-winded dissertation on the bleak future lying ahead for humanity," which pretty much hits the nail on the head. It combined science fiction with low-budget swashbuckling and Biblical references in a story set one thousand years in the future. A total atomic war enveloped the Earth, civilization is in ashes, and Man has been hurled back into his primitive past. In the ruins in and around New York City, three tribes battle for existence in the year 3000. I play Rob, the son of the chief of the Norms, a tribe that took refuge in the rocky caves and subways below Manhattan and has avoided mutation. The Norms worship the Devil. Across the river live the Mutates, a group of outcasts, persecuted because they are disfigured through gene mutations as a result of the A-blasts. The Mutates are Christians, although occasionally a raiding party of Mutates will slip into Manhattan and kidnap Norm women

Production problems and a disorganized director spelled disaster for *Captive Women*, the Pollexfen/Wisberg follow-up to *The Man from Planet X.*

for mating purposes; they hope that in future generations, their blight will be erased. The third tribe is the warlike, marauding Up-river people. (The whole movie took place at night, reinforcing the barbarous, "Dark Ages"-type atmosphere.)

Rob is engaged to Catherine (Gloria Saunders), daughter of the high priest, but Up-river men led by Gordon (Stuart Randall) infiltrate the celebration, kill Rob's father and take over the tribe. Rob and his friend Bram (Robert Bice) escape with their lives, and they are taken in by Mutate leader Riddon (Ron Randell) and his tribe.

The Mutates make a raid on the Up-river people, and make off with several of the Norm women they are holding captive. Riddon falls in love with one of them, Ruth (Margaret Field). Carver (William Schallert), a troublemaker banished from the Mutate settlement, tells Gordon about a secret underwater passage which will enable him to destroy the Mutates. Taking a page from the Bible, Rob, Bram, Riddon and other Mutates allow themselves to be chased by the Up-river men into the passageway and then, once they reach the far side, they pull out the ceiling supports. The river crashes in, filling the tunnel and drowning the Up-river men—just as Moses and the Israelites vanquished Pharaoh's army. Riddon and Ruth marry, with the minister commenting that since this was the first Mutate-Norm marriage of love, only good can come of it. The film fades out on the image of a cross, indicating that the human race will now be reborn.

It seemed to me that with *3000 A.D.*, Pollexfen and Wisberg had bitten off more than they could chew. On a modest picture like *Man from Planet X*, where an experienced director (Ulmer) was in charge, they did well, but here they went a little beyond their budgetary limits. *3000 A.D.* had a large cast, a number of different settings and a very involved story. The person *I* felt sorry for was Stuart Gilmore. It was a very fitful, frustrating time for the poor man, because he had so little experience as a director. He didn't have to contend with big crowd scenes—we didn't have the *money* for big crowd scenes!—but he did have to direct a lot of "small" crowd scenes, which is tough on a picture with a tight budget. There were dialogue scenes with four, five and six actors, and maneuvering all those actors, getting them in and out of the scenes, was tricky and difficult. Additionally, Gilmore had to direct lots of action, fight scenes, special effects people dropping rocks, etc. There was also quite a bit of re-writing going on while the movie was in pro-

With *Captive Women* villainess Gloria Saunders in a gag shot.

duction. Part of it was that Bill Schallert's part was expanded: He was coming across so well as the villain in the dailies that it was decided to make his part bigger. Stu Gilmore had no easy time on *3000 A.D.*, and the fact that he got a picture out of it was quite remarkable. After another Western or two, he returned to the editing room, and directed no more features.

My role was that of a sort of 29th-century Robin Hood: The costumes we wore were Robin Hood-ish and we fought with knives, staffs, bows and arrows. My character name was Rob (short for Robin?),

Margaret Field and I reteamed for *Captive Women*, a tale of life in New York centuries after The Bomb.

and my sidekick was actor Robert Bice, who later played Will Scarlet in my *Tales of Robin Hood*. There was one "lighter" moment during production involving Ron Randell, who played the leader of the Mutate tribe. We knew each other prior to making this movie; we both screen-tested at Columbia on the same day a number of years before. We were

After working together in *Captive Women* and *Tales of Robin Hood*, Robert Bice and I knew our way around a bow and arrow.

about to do a scene together, on one of the cave sets where the floor was covered with dirt. I was about six feet tall and Ron was about five-eleven, and inconspicuously I began to scrape some of the dirt into a small mound underneath my feet so that I'd stand a little taller. Well, Ron saw what I was doing, and he began to do the same thing! (The first time I'd ever heard of an actor doing this, it was Humphrey Bogart on *Sahara*.) Ron and I kept at it, going up and up, getting taller and taller, until the assistant cameraman said, "Say, I've gotta adjust this camera. Your heads are out of frame!" We were both ambitious, and maybe we were both a little vain, and we were vying to get the best out of the scene, to do the best and look the best.

(Kenneth Tobey tells the same sort of story about a picture of his called *It Came from Beneath the Sea*. Ken was not much taller than his leading lady Faith Domergue, so just before a beach scene shot on a sound stage at Columbia, he piled up some sand and stood on it so that he would look taller than she was. But Ken was standing on sand, not compacted dirt like Ron Randell and I were; he packed the sand as hard as he could, but the sand gave way *while* the scene was being shot. He weighed more than she did, of course, so he sank down to the sound stage floor and she was still up on the sand. By the end of the scene, Ken said, it looked like she was two *feet* taller than he was!)

Margaret Field and I had met on *A Modern Marriage* and later began dating, but by the time we did *3000 A.D.* we had both found other "interests." Hers was Jock Mahoney. "Jocko" was a stuntman-turned-actor who had his own Western TV series, *The Range Rider*; they met earlier that year, when she guested on two *Range Rider* episodes filmed the same week. Jocko came on the set of *3000 A.D.* one day, and I remember that I was struck by what a tall son of a gun he was—he had to be six-four. And when Maggie introduced him to me, she kind of proudly said, "Oh, I want you to meet the man I'm in *love* with." He was a very athletic actor and a good-looking guy who did well in *The Range Rider* and later in another series, *Yancy Derringer*; he and Maggie were later married, and Sally Field (Margaret's daughter from a previous marriage) became Jocko's stepdaughter. Many years later, not long before he died, in fact, I saw Jocko again. He gave me a big bear hug and I said, "How's Maggie?" And he said, "Well, I'm not married to *her* anymore!"

And here's one *more* story, this one concerning Sally Field. The first time I saw Sally was when she was perhaps four years old; Margaret lived in an apartment in Pasadena, and when I'd go there to pick her up for a date, I'd see Sally and her little brother. Years passed, and the next time I saw Sally was when she had her own TV series, *The Flying Nun*. I was acting in a segment of some Western series on the Columbia back lot in Burbank; I saw her and called out to her and said, "Hi! I just wanted to say hello." Which I did. But she wasn't too warm, I found myself doing all the talking and the situation quickly became rather awkward; it wasn't hard to tell that she just didn't want to be bothered. Finally I said, "Well, good to see you. Tell your mother hello," and she started to walk off. Then, when she was about eight or ten feet away, she turned on her heel, glared at me and growled, "I don't *live* with my *mother*!"—and then off she went. And I was left standing in the middle of the Western street, sorry that I had spotted her!

Some fans have told me that they like *3000 A.D.* because the combination of science fiction and a Bible-type story makes it such a "different" movie. But I just can't forget all the disorganization on the set and I tend to remember it as a very unsatisfactory, disappointing experience (especially since it followed *The Man from Planet X*).

Unlike *Planet X*, which was rushed into theaters, *3000 A.D.* sat on a shelf for well over a year before RKO finally released it. The new title that RKO put on it, *Captive Women*, was inappropriate; the combination of the two words created the implication of sexual activity. (The picture didn't *have* any, of course, but that title probably gave it a boost at the box office.) And, years later, 20th Century-Fox made *Beneath the Planet of the Apes* which had basically the same plot as *Captive Women*: Battles in the atomic future between "norms" (Charlton Heston and his human friends), a war-like tribe (the apes) and human mutants living in the rubble of the Manhattan subway system. *Beneath the Planet of the Apes* made a lot of money, so perhaps Pollexfen and Wisberg weren't so far off the beam with *Captive Women* after all.

1 Beginning in 1972, there's been much real-life scientific speculation about a possible tenth planet in *our* solar system. This mystery world has actually been dubbed Planet X.
2 In the late 1970s, I went to see Corwin about making a *Planet X* sequel or possibly another science fiction picture, but he was not particularly interested—he'd just had a bad experience with *Viva Knievel!*, a financial flop. But I met with him briefly, and he still remembered the *Planet X* grosses.

Cigarette in hand (as usual), Clark Gable posed for photos with me on the set of Warners' *Band of Angels*.

A WORKING ACTOR

The life of a "working actor" can be a very precarious existence, but it can also be a very interesting one. So many actors were in the same boat I was in during the 1950s, acting in movies and on TV, hoping to act in more good pictures than fair ones and more fair than bad. Some of us held other jobs on the side. The trick for actors in that position was just to *survive*. As William Schallert once put it, talking about *his* early, struggling years in the business, you'd step from one slowly-sinking stone to another as you crossed the stream of life, and keep hoping for a new stone.

One day you might be acting with Duncan Renaldo or Leo Carrillo in an episode of *The Cisco Kid* and the next day you might be playing a small part opposite Clark Gable or Greer Garson. Or working for someone like Billy Graham. William "One-Shot" Beaudine would direct you one week, Raoul Walsh or Michael Curtiz a week later. They *could* be interesting times. Here is a grab-bag of experiences, high and low, from those busy days in the Hollywood "salt mines."

• • • • • •

Western television series—of which there were many!—were a good source of occasional employment for the actor who knew how to sit a horse, holster a gun or throw a punch. One of the longest-running was *The Lone Ranger* with Clayton Moore. There were other Lone Rangers in the movies, and even another one (John Hart) who briefly replaced Clayton in his own series, but Clayton was the best Lone Ranger there ever was. It was a strange thing, but he looked better *with* the mask than with*out* it. It was not a big mask, it was kind of trim, covering his eyes but *not* covering too much of his nose or his forehead. But when Clayton put that mask on, the charisma really bubbled. He was also a good cowboy: He could handle the guns, ride well and do just about anything else that was required.

When I married Alyce King of the King Sisters in 1956, she was a widow with two small boys (Lex, 12, Ric, 8). I wanted to look good in the eyes of my new boys and so, the next time I was asked by the Jack Wrather Company to act in an episode of *The Lone Ranger*, I took Lex and Ric out to the exterior location in Calabassas and introduced them to Clayton. Clayton was very nice—in fact, he couldn't have been *nicer*—and he gave them each a silver bullet. But as the boys and I started to walk away, the prop man came up to us and he said, "Look, Clayton does this too often, and I'm losing more bullets than I can replace in that gun belt. I'm sorry, but you'll have to give them back to me." I tried to bluff the guy, I told him that Clayton hadn't given them silver bullets, he'd given them something else, but it didn't work; the guy had seen the whole thing. He was polite about it—at first—and then he said, "I've *gotta* have 'em back."

By this time Clayton had gone off, to work in the scene, or to do *something*—he wasn't there to give me support. I said to the prop man, "You can't do that, it'll break their hearts! Clayton just gave 'em to them." Then he started to get pretty tough—and, after all, he was just doing his job. So the boys had to give back their silver bullets. They were disappointed, but Clayton *had* made the gesture and tried to make them happy fans, and the boys were thrilled at meeting him. And of course they were also thrilled about getting the silver bullets—even if they did get to keep them for only a few minutes![1]

I also worked with Duncan Renaldo and Leo Carrillo in their Ziv series *The Cisco Kid*, and those were shot lickety-split: You made one of those half-hour shows in two days. You'd do a take, and unless there was a *very* obvious goof, they'd print it and you'd move on, whether the take was any good or not. It was a syndicated series, shot in color, and one of the most popular "kids' Western" series on the air. And Duncan and Leo weren't exactly spring chickens, either; Duncan was in his 50s and Leo was in his 70s at the time.

I remember Leo putting me on the spot one day: I had some dialogue to deliver to the Cisco Kid (Duncan), and Pancho (Leo) was sort of left out of the dialogue. So Leo came to me and said, "When you say your lines to Cisco, you say, 'And Pancho, too!'" Well, I was a little reluctant to start throwing in dialogue that wasn't in the script—I was afraid I'd get called down by the director. I told Leo, "Well, I will, if the director says so." Leo kind of pouted a little bit, but fortunately he didn't pursue it any further!

142

My main memory of *Wild Bill Hickok* is of one of those "it's a small world"-type stories. That was another daytime Western series, made for kids, and it starred Guy Madison as Hickok and Andy Devine as his sidekick Jingles. (During the '40s, Guy had been at RKO and acted in some pretty good pictures, and now he had his own TV series.) Guy and I got to talking one day about one thing and another, and I happened to mention that I was from Oklahoma. He said, "Oh, you are? I have three daughters and my newest one is still a little baby, and I hired a black lady nurse who's from Oklahoma."

"My gosh," I said, "what's her name?", and to my amazement he answered, "Priney McGregor." Well, Priney was *my* nurse when *I* was a baby! (And a few years later, after my wife Alyce had given birth to our son Cam, she said she had to have somebody "live in" and help, and so through Guy Madison we got Priney. Priney was a big, big lady—she wasn't just fat, she was the *strong* type. She used to call Cam "The Little Reverend.")

I had another one of those "small world" experiences when I did a picture called *Oil Town, USA* in 1952. It was the second feature produced by Billy Graham's production company, and it was designed to be shown in churches in the Bible Belt. The picture starred Colleen Townsend, Paul Power and Georgia Lee, and it also featured Billy Graham as well as the Sons of the Pioneers. (I played Colleen Townsend's romantic interest.) We shot it at KTTV in Hollywood, and during the lunch break one day, I sat next to Billy Graham. When we got to talking, I told him that I was from Oklahoma City and that my grandfather was in the cotton business in a firm called Harris Irby and Vose; in Grandfather's day, that was the second largest cotton brokerage firm in the world. Billy Graham asked me, "Did you ever hear of Anderson Clayton cotton brokerage company?" Yes, I had, because they were the *biggest*. The Andersons of Anderson Clayton lived in Oklahoma City, and Graham told me that his entire tuition for four years at seminary was paid by Mr. Anderson, who lived just a few blocks from where *I* had lived in Oklahoma City.

My other memory of that day is how impressed I was with Billy Graham, the *man*: In talking with him, I found him to be a very "genuine" person. Not self-righteous, not overbearingly religious, but very sincere in his dedication to his calling. And a nice person.

•　　•　　•　　•　　•　　•

In addition to working with stars (big ones and small ones) on the sound stages, you also came in contact with them socially. My sister's husband was Bill Sloan, a producer at KNX radio and the "discoverer" of two people that later became well known, Ira Grossel (Jeff Chandler) and Helen Koford (Terry Moore). One afternoon in 1954, Bill called me and said that Jack Warner, the head of Warner Brothers, was giving a dinner party for John Wayne, on the occasion of his recent marriage. (Pilar Pallette was Wayne's third wife, and she stayed with him to the end.) "This is a spur-of-the-moment thing, I know," Bill said, "but Terry Moore needs a date to go to a big, big party at Jack Warner's. Are you available?" You *bet* I was available.

This was just for "appearances," of course; Terry didn't date, perhaps because she was having her secret relationship with Howard Hughes about that time. I picked up Terry at her home and we drove out to Jack Warner's huge estate in the Beverly Hills area. We arrived *after* the rest of the party had started to eat their dinners, but it really didn't matter because Terry had not been *invited* to dinner! Terry and I went into a rec room in the lower part of the home, which was equipped with a bar, and who was standing there but Dean Martin—*he* had not been invited to the dinner part of the evening, either! (At that time Dean was not as famous as he became later.) So we chitchatted and waited for the dinner to end and the rest of the guests to join us. Among the dinner party was Susan Hayward, Faye Emerson, Robert Taylor, Elizabeth Taylor, Gary Cooper, John Wayne (naturally)—those are just a few. (And, of course, Jack Warner, who kept calling me Mr. *Walker*.) It was a big party with a lot of top stars, and the only *really* big Hollywood party I ever attended. It was lots of fun, seeing these stars close-up and observing that they were just like other people, at least off-screen.

•   •   •   •   •   •

I had the thrill of my life working in *Band of Angels* in 1957 with Clark Gable, because—like so many young actors—I have "hero-worshiped" other actors[2], Gable included. There were a lot of Gable-esque types around at that time, George Montgomery, for instance. (The story goes that, when Gable was in the service, Darryl F. Zanuck saw that Montgomery was a good-looking fellow and he put George in a screening room with some Gable pictures and said, "Try to be like *him*.") Tom Neal was another actor that seemed to be trying to take on the Gable look and the Gable mannerisms. Gable had a lot of admirers, and I certainly was in there with the rest of them.

I was so in awe of Gable that when I got on the set of *Band of Angels* and met him, I couldn't think of anything to say except, "Boy, I've been watchin' you all my life!" I asked him if he would object to having a couple of pictures taken with me (I had already set it up with the still cameraman) and he said he was glad to, and we got several shots. He was a very quiet person off-stage, quieter certainly than he was *on* screen. Gable burned up the celluloid the same way that Jimmy Cagney did, he was very animated, but off-screen he sat in his dressing room between sequences and puffed on a cigarette (which probably helped bring on his early demise!). He'd have a pack of cigarettes on the dressing room table and a pack in his pocket and a cigarette in his hand.

Some actors do as much acting between scenes; they're very "on," telling stories about the business and making sure that they're the center of attention. Not so with Gable. I *did* see him in conversation with one of the extras—he made quite a point of going over into the area where the extras were sitting, waiting to be called. While I was on that set at Warner Brothers, that was perhaps the only time Gable went out of his way to do any socializing.

My part in the picture was a small one: I play a dandy at a New Orleans slave auction, and I convince one of my friends *not* to tangle with Gable, who was playing a master duellist. I was nervous about it, and I noticed when I later saw the movie that my voice was pitched higher than it usually was. I was then 36 or 37 years old and that sort of nervousness about working with a big star *should* have worn off by then. But in Gable's case, it hadn't. They say that when Marilyn Monroe was a kid, she had a picture of Gable on her dressing room table and she had him as her father image, and before she could co-star with him in *The Misfits* (1961), she had to make a big adjustment psychologically. I've also heard that Ava Gardner, when she first worked with Gable, couldn't face him. She had to sing a song to him in a sequence and she couldn't do it because she was so nervous, and they had to ask Gable to get out of camera range so that Ava could do the scene. I had somewhat of the same reaction, although not as acute. Having been raised in the Midwest, I regarded some of these people as almost from another planet—the likes of Gable and Spencer Tracy and Orson Welles and so many other great stars.

Raoul Walsh was the director of *Band of Angels*, and my memory

I played Prince Charming to Greer Garson—an extremely gracious lady on and off screen—in Metro's *Her Twelve Men*.

of Mr. Walsh is that he was the comedian most of the time. At one point Walsh looked off to the extras and said, "Now remember, while we're doing this sequence, that Mr. Gable has to go over and get his bourbon occasionally!"—which was not true at all! Raoul Walsh was kidding, making light of what was going on on the set. He apparently enjoyed playing to the crowd, to the extras.

Another major star with whom I acted was Greer Garson. The picture was *Her Twelve Men* (1954) and I appeared to her in dream sequences, playing different characters—I'd be her movie producer, her escort at a military dress ball, a Cossack officer, etc. I was in four scenes with her (no dialogue), and during the time that we worked together, she was extremely kind and gracious and charming. At first I feared she might have me fired from the part because I looked too young, but she didn't say a word about it. She made me feel like I was on equal footing with her, that I was as important to her in those scenes as if it had been Clark Gable. How very smart of her as an actress, doing that so that I would be up to the job. It made me feel very comfortable. Quite a few years later, I got the opportunity to have a still of the two of us from *Her Twelve Men* autographed by Greer, and on it she wrote, "To Bob Clarke— My, weren't we beautiful then!"—which was very sweet.

•　　•　　•　　•　　•　　•

Jack Webb produced, directed and starred in the most popular police show of the decade, *Dragnet*. He was a great friend of mine professionally, and we also knew each other socially to some extent because he did some recording for my brother-in-law Jim Conkling (Donna King's husband) at Warner Brothers Records. The first times I acted with Jack were on the radio version of *Dragnet*, which I worked on three or four occasions; apparently he liked my work, because when the series moved to TV, I appeared on it frequently. Jack was the sort of person who was loyal to the people he liked. It also helped that Alyce and I were friends of Herman Saunders, associate producer of the TV *Dragnet*. I became acquainted with Herm through Alyce, and socially and professionally Herm and I have been much closer friends over the years than Jack and I ever were; it's been a very nice relationship. When a *Dragnet* role would come up, Jack often asked for me specifically, but on other occasions Herm would throw my name out "for grabs." Between the fact that Jack liked me and the fact that I had Herm in my corner, I guested more times on *Dragnet* than on any other television series. Alyce and I are still very close to Herm Saunders and his wife Kae, two very dear and loyal friends.

Here's some background on Jack Webb that many people may not know: In the mid-'40s Jack did a radio show up in San Francisco called *Pat Novak for Hire*, which was written by a guy I went to high school with, Richard Breen. (Dick Breen was brilliant; he was a junior associate writer with Charles Brackett and Billy Wilder when they did *The Lost Weekend*, and he was on the writing team on a number of movies of that caliber.) Anyway, Dick conceived *Pat Novak for Hire* on radio and Jack was the star. After that, Jack moved to Southern California and he had a rough go of it for awhile. Herm Saunders was playing piano over in a little restaurant-bar called The Bantam Cock on La Cienega, and he was good to Jack—perhaps even loaned him money. So when Jack hit it with *Dragnet*, he pulled in Herm, first as his casting director, and then later made him associate producer. Herm worked for Jack a number of years (he produced Webb's *Adam-12*) and was *very* closely associated with him.

Bill Conrad was another one of the actors that Jack liked, and in a way, Conrad was unique among Webb's friends: Bill Conrad was one of the few actors who could be *himself* when he acted with Jack. As for the rest of us, Jack Webb expected us to act like Jack Webb. When you got on his radio and TV *Dragnet*s, you had to give that monotone reading. He did not want acting, he wanted it straight. Even if it didn't sound good, he wanted it straight. Working for Jack as many times as I did was a great compliment, actually, because if you could please Webb, you could please damn near *anybody*. He was the "Orson Welles" of *Dragnet*. He changed the dialogue on the set, he re-wrote, he directed, he was the star, he was *it*. And at one point, that show had 40,000,000 viewers—it was the biggest dramatic series during the early days of television.

In one TV episode I had a long sequence, about six pages, and there was going to be a single closeup on me. Jack had teleprompters on the set, and he instructed me how the scene should be played: "The teleprompter on the left side is *me*," he said, "and on the other side, it's Ben Alexander. When you read your dialogue to me, look on the left. When you read the dialogue to Ben, look on the right." Jack wanted to do it *quick*, he wanted to do it *now*, and he wanted to see how fast he could make it. He liked for the *Dragnet* episodes to be as good as they could, but he also liked to do 'em in a day and a half. (And he did!)

I had my six pages—a lot of dialogue—and I said to myself, "I'm gonna get some animation, I'm gonna get some change of tone and some inflection. I'm gonna *act*." Well, I got down to about the bottom of the first page and Jack stopped me: "Cut, cut. Wait a minute, wait a minute." He came over and said to me, "Bobby, look, *that's* not it. *You* know I don't want you to act, so—just *don't*. Let's do it again, and you know what I want." He was very nice about it.

We started again and I thought to myself, "Okay, I'll cut it in *half*, and I'll still give it some Bob Clarke." And, by God, he stopped me *again*. He said, "Look, Pally..." (That was his favorite expression, "Pally.") He said, "I can stay here the rest of today." He got kind of salty. "*You* know what I want: Just read it like you were reading a newspaper." I wasn't about to speak up, because I wanted to keep on working for him. He didn't want us to *imitate* him, he just wanted us to read it monotone. So we began a third time and I read it like I was reading an article in the paper, and when it was over, he said, "Terrific! I knew you could do it!"

Jack really controlled the set completely; I noticed that every time I worked for him. One day I said to him, "I feel as if I'm a member of the John Ford stock company." To which he responded with a comment that was very much in the Jack Webb style: He said, "It's only because I want the *best*, Pally."[3]

·   ·   ·   ·   ·   ·

I got kind of ticked off at Angie Dickinson. The both of us were in a segment of *Wagon Train* called "The Clara Duncan Story," where she was the star and I was playing an artist. Angie was a very beautiful lady and a competent actress, but she really got off on the wrong foot with me.

In one sequence, I was working with a well-known Italian character actor named Eduardo Ciannelli, who was playing my father. (Ciannelli had appeared on Broadway back in the 1930s with Burgess Meredith and Margo in a play called *Winterset*; that was one of his claims to fame, along with pictures like *Gunga Din* and *Foreign Correspondent* and so many more.) Angie Dickinson wasn't even *in* the sequence that Ciannelli and I were about to do, and yet she was talking to the director about cutting my dialogue! She said, "Oh, *he* doesn't have to say *this*" and "You can do away with *that*." I thought that was very rude, very uncalled-for—she may have been getting star billing in this episode, but she had no business trying to cut dialogue out of a scene she wasn't even *in*! And I *told* her so—I said, "Look, don't get into this. This is *my* scene"—mine and Eduardo Ciannelli's. Fortunately, the director didn't take Angie's advice too seriously, and Ciannelli and I got to do the scene the way it was written.

Ciannelli was another interesting guy to get to work with. He was so *very* Italian, and he usually played gangsters because he had a face that looked like a Luger pistol. He had a mean, *mean* look and yet off-screen he was anything *but*; he was a very kind, gentle sort of person, trying to make it in the business still. And I reflected as I worked with him, "Boy, here's a guy who was big on Broadway 25, 30 years ago, and now he's relegated to one of the supporting parts..." It's a tough business—always has been, always will be.

●   ●   ●   ●   ●   ●

I played supporting roles in so many 1950s TV series, I long ago lost count, but I never had a series of my own back then. The one time I came close was in 1959, right after I got back from making *Beyond the Time Barrier* in Texas. The series was going to be in the vein of *I Led Three Lives*, the old Ziv show with Richard Carlson; ours was going to be a "female version" starring Coleen Gray and myself, and it was based on the life of Marion Miller, an undercover F.B.I. agent who had infiltrated the Communist party in Los Angeles. I got my co-starring role after an interview with the director, Lew Landers, who remembered me from the Tim Holt Westerns and other things we'd done together; as a matter of fact, Coleen and I went to dinner one evening with the real Marion Miller. We shot the pilot at Ziv with Coleen as the infiltrator, me as her husband and an actor named Berry Kroeger as the heavy, but it didn't sell. To the best of my memory, they never even had a title for it.

The other thing I recall about this proposed series is that the producer was a woman, Alyce Canfield. Alyce had been a very prolific fan magazine writer; she had done several stories on Sally Forrest, she was a fan of Ida Lupino's, and now she was breaking into the business as a producer. About four years later Alyce died a very tragic death: She committed suicide by jumping off an overpass into traffic on the Ventura Freeway in Encino. Poor Alyce was only in her 40s.

●   ●   ●   ●   ●   ●

It was great fun and very rewarding to star in the occasional small picture, but it was also fun for a "working actor" to play supporting roles in the occasional "A" picture and see stars like Alan Ladd, Jimmy Stewart, Victor Mature (and many others) at work.

Back in those days, the people in the crafts—the hairdressing and makeup people, particularly—put forth such an effort to do their job to the very best of their ability, and *not* be responsible for any mistake. Because if a mistake occurred (Heaven forbid), they would be dressed down soundly. When I worked in a picture called *The FBI Story* (1959) with Jimmy Stewart, he was by then wearing a hairpiece. After every rehearsal, and after every take—even if Stewart wasn't on camera!—the hairdresser came up to Stewart and carefully combed the hair of the toupee over Stewart's real hair. Pretty soon, all this fussing around became almost laughable. The director was Mervyn LeRoy, who finally spoke up: "Don't, don't, don't keep on doing that!" Well, that hurt the fellow's feelings, and I felt bad for him, because the guy was only trying to do his job. LeRoy realized that he had been a little harsh and he tried to kid him out of it. Directing a picture can sometimes be like walking a fine line.

When you're directing, one of the people you particularly don't want to say the wrong thing to is the star. My experience with Victor Mature was on an adventure picture called *Timbuktu* (1959), produced by Edward Small. It was perhaps a week's work, and we were on location. Mature's leading lady was a gal I'd once dated, Yvonne DeCarlo.[4] My scene in *Timbuktu* was a gruesome one: I was one of the soldiers who was "buried alive"—buried up to our necks in sand.

The funny thing that happened on *Timbuktu* involved the director, Jacques Tourneur. Jacques had worked at RKO years before, when I was there; he had quite a good reputation, and in his time he did do some big pictures. (*Timbuktu* wasn't one of them!) In one scene the camera was at a high angle, shooting down at Mature in a big pit; and it was almost impossible for his face to be seen by the camera. Vic Mature was kneeling down, digging in the sand for something, and trying to look up toward the camera occasionally, but finally he said to Jacques, "Look, I'm not gonna be seen in this." Jacques responded, "Oh, yes you will. We've got you right in the shot."

Vic said, "But my *face* won't be seen," and Jacques came back with, "Well, *that's* all right." And Mature said, "What do you mean, 'That's all right'?! You don't see my *face*? It's all right that my face isn't going to be seen? Oh, really?" Vic didn't like that one bit and he reacted very sarcastically, and very stubbornly he kept trying to tilt his head up a little bit to get his face in the shot!

I also spent five or six weeks on a World War II picture called *The Deep Six* with Alan Ladd and William Bendix. Again, I had a smallish part, as an officer aboard a Navy destroyer; Don Hayden (*My Little Margie*) was in it, too, playing a same-sized part, along with Ross Bagdasarian (the voice of Alvin and the Chipmunks) and Joey Bishop. But to get the parts, we had to be shorter than a line that they had in the casting office; we were told that we *couldn't* be taller than that line, and we all just *squeaked* under. I was six feet tall, taller than the line, but I managed to do it because I wore my lowest tennis shoes.

The reason for all this was, of course, Alan Ladd, who was *so* short. We worked for three weeks out in the Long Beach Harbor before we came back to the studio and did a scene in a ward room that had been fixed up on a sound stage. I was taken aback to see two-by-twelve planks, four inches off the floor, and right away I knew what they were for: Alan Ladd walked on those planks. The rest of us walked on the floor. Nobody laughed; nobody said a word. Again, you don't want to say—or do—the wrong thing to the star.

•   •   •   •   •   •

In the 1980s, I decided to begin making public appearances with a presentation which I called "The Golden Years of the Movies," talking to audiences about some of the experiences I'd had during the heyday of my Hollywood career—offering personal anecdotes and reminiscences along the lines of some of the stories I've told in this chapter. The response was tremendous, and I kept it up for years. How greatly I appreciated people's interest in what I did, and their eagerness to listen to my observations about the stars I worked with.

Actors all *try*, and to some of them success comes very easily; they kind of just slide along and pretty soon success hits 'em right square in the face. To others, it comes not at all. I landed somewhere in between. But one of the "rewards" of my career is that so many people seem to be interested in delving into my films and researching them (particularly those films in the area of science fiction and horror). I'm flattered by their attention, and by the attention of Western fans, and by the attention of the people who attended my "Golden Years" presentations. As any actor will tell you, it's very satisfying to meet fans who find our anecdotes of great interest, and it gives us a sense of having accomplished something of significance.

1 Years later, when the Jack Wrather Company made a feature film about the Lone Ranger, I thought it was just a shame the way they treated

Clayton. I guess they considered him too old to play the part in 1981, which was probably true, but they also demanded that Clayton not make any personal appearances as the Lone Ranger. He tried to get permission to wear the mask, and they even took *that* away from him, because they felt that was infringing on their copyright. Clayton was a good guy, and it was he who made that series *go*, but that didn't seem to matter much to the executives.

2 As an example of one actor admiring and perhaps emulating another, I recall that there was a time when you could hardly tell the difference between Douglas Fairbanks Jr. and Ronald Colman. Fairbanks obviously was a great fan of Colman, and he began taking on certain Colman-like inflections and mannerisms. When they did *The Prisoner of Zenda* together, Fairbanks didn't seem so much like Colman *then*, but later on, as Fairbanks' career progressed, he began to sound like Ronnie a bit, particularly on radio.

3 I was also in a feature that Webb directed, a comedy with Robert Mitchum, Martha Hyer and Webb called *The Last Time I Saw Archie* (1961). This was Jack's attempt at comedy, and I think it fell on its face. Jack wanted to try his hand at comedy, and *The Last Time I Saw Archie* proved that he was a dramatic actor!

4 Yvonne was a very kindly gal, and not nearly the sex siren *off*-screen that she appeared to be *on*-; she was really kind of a shy and timid personality. My memory tells me that the head stuntman on *Timbuktu* was Bob Morgan, Yvonne's stuntman-husband. A few years later, while making *How the West Was Won*, Bob fell off a train and was run over by several of the flatcars, losing a leg. That tragic accident created years of financial difficulties for them, and Yvonne couldn't afford to be fussy about the roles she picked anymore.

I knew *The Astounding She-Monster* was a bad movie when we made it... and never dreamed it would have a "cult" reputation.

TO "B" OR NOT TO "B"— ADVENTURES IN LOW-BUDGET PICTUREMAKING

Some of my nicest—and worst—experiences have taken place on the sets of low-priced pictures. Basically, I have nothing against movies produced on a shoestring budget; one of my best starring films, *The Man from Planet X*, was made for just over $40,000. I also take some pride in the fact that I starred in what was probably the first-ever TV movie, *Three Musketeers*, even though *its* budget was even smaller than that of *Planet X*. My experiences in low-budget picturemaking even prompted me to economically produce and direct my own feature *The Hideous Sun Demon*, which to this day has so many fans that (other circumstances notwithstanding) I still derive a great deal of satisfaction out of having made it.

Low-budget pictures don't have to be bad pictures; just because a movie was made on the cheap doesn't automatically mean that the actors in it can't be good, that the story can't be imaginative, or that the photography and direction can't be interesting and inventive. But a lot of cheap pictures *are* bad, and there have also been times when working in them is nothing less than a maddening, demoralizing experience. I'd like to forget that I made some of *those* pictures, but for some reason even they seem to have their fans.

Republic had the reputation of being one of the cheapest studios in Hollywood, and I'm sure that notoriety was probably well-deserved, but speaking for myself, I had two pleasant experiences there. My first picture at Republic was *Street Bandits* (1951), a programmer in which I played the lawyer for the head of a slot machine syndicate (Roy Barcroft). Working as Barcroft's high-priced "mouthpiece" enables me to care for my mother and propose to my girl (Penny Edwards), but when it becomes clear that Barcroft hasn't stopped at murder, my conscience becomes my toughest client. Somehow the director R. G. "Bud" Springsteen managed to squeeze a lot of plot into just 54 minutes and the end prod-

uct, I thought, was a more-than-acceptable half-a-double bill. Another nice thing about working in some of these low-priced pictures was that it brought you into contact with a wide and interesting assortment of fellow actors. *Street Bandits* was my one opportunity to work, for instance, with Roy Barcroft, a very agreeable guy. Roy was a journeyman-like actor, a contractee there at Republic who did Westerns, crime dramas, serials—Republic put him in *every*thing, because he was always such a believable heavy. My leading lady Penny Edwards was also very nice to work with; her husband was Ralph Winters, a casting director I'd known at RKO.

Through an interview with producer Sidney Picker, I had another starring part at Republic in a movie with Estelita, *The Fabulous Senorita* (1952). Estelita must have been an important part of Republic's output because, even though her pictures were still Grade B, they had *slightly* higher budgets than the run-of-the-reel Republic programmer. And Estelita herself was surely a talented little gal, and also very funny. I found her to be very, very cooperative, and I admired the way she wanted to be "fun" in the picture. (Sad to say, she died very young of cancer, a dozen or so years after I worked with her.) The plot was just a lot of nonsense, with me as a college instructor who gets mixed up with the pretty Estelita (billed as "The Toast of Pan America") and her wacky family; our shooting title was *Girl from Panama*, and it was directed once again by "Bud" Springsteen. The other interesting thing about working in *The Fabulous Senorita* was encountering the supporting actress who played Estelita's sister. She was practically an unknown then, but Rita Moreno went on to win an Oscar, an Emmy, a Tony, a Grammy and everything in between!

The pictures I did at Republic were each done in about 14 days, as opposed to the four- and five-day shooting schedules I'd contended with in the past (and would contend with *again* in the future); that one extra week is of tremendous benefit. *Street Bandits* and *The Fabulous Senorita* were professionally produced and, despite Republic's well-known reputation for chintziness, I wouldn't place either of them in the same category as some of the low-budget pictures that followed.

More representative of what I'm talking about is a little number I did called *The Body Beautiful*, which was one of those "swimming upstream" experiences that can be so exasperating: We were behind schedule throughout, it ran out of money at one point, the director was hard to

The Body Beautiful **was a low-budget picture made on a fast schedule.**

understand, and the leading lady seemed more interested in her love life than in the movie. The story (again) was a mishmash, this one involving a model photographer (me), his model-girlfriend (Noreen Nash) and his secretary (Susan Morrow); the whole thing was just an excuse for showing models in various stages of dress and undress. Susan Morrow was dating Lex Barker at the time, and they would stay out late, *too* late, every night. She would come to work quite bedraggled, quite *worn*, and by midday she was ready to take a nap! (Susan was the sister of Judith Exner, the gal who later had simultaneous affairs with President Kennedy and Chicago mob boss Sam Giancana; she wrote a whole book about it.) Susan was young enough that her nightly activity didn't show on her too much *facially*, but she'd get in late and be pretty tired during the day, and this may have been part of the reason that things got fouled up toward the end.

Body Beautiful was a low-budget picture being made on a fast schedule (six days, maybe seven), and near the end of production they ran out of money; shooting was held up for a day or so while they rounded up some more financial backing. (The money guy had his daughter in the picture.) The director, Max Nosseck, was a funny little man. Max was Polish and he had the same sort of globe-trotting background as Edgar Ulmer: Max made films in Austria, Germany, Spain and France before settling in Hollywood and specializing in inexpensive pictures here. Max spoke in broken English and it was tough to understand what he was saying. Between that, and everything *else* that went wrong, it's a wonder that the picture ever got finished.[1]

Around this same time I also acted in a pair of modest costume adventures with Anthony Dexter, *Captain John Smith and Pocahontas* (1953) and *The Black Pirates* (1954). Both of them were in color, and although they were economically made, they certainly don't fall into the "down and dirty" class of pictures like *The Body Beautiful* or *The Incredible Petrified World*. Tony Dexter was a stage actor whose film debut in the title role of *Valentino* (in 1951) was accompanied by an avalanche of publicity; the career that followed didn't come anywhere near living up to the initial hype. It was a pleasure to work with Tony, who was not only a very professional actor but also a gentleman.[2]

Captain John Smith and Pocahontas was from the writing-producing team of Jack Pollexfen and Aubrey Wisberg, who at this point were making films for United Artists. Dexter played roving adventurer John Smith, in and out of trouble with privateers and Indians in Colonial Jamestown, Jody Lawrence played Indian princess Pocahontas and Douglass Dumbrille played her father Powhatan. The part I had was a good one: I played John Rolfe, Capt. Smith's loyal friend and fellow adventurer, and I even got the girl (Pocahontas) at the end. Also in the picture was Alan Hale Jr., who I enjoyed working with. He was always good for a lot of jokes off-screen.

I thought *Captain John Smith and Pocahontas* turned out pretty well. It was shot in Bronson Canyon, a location which was often used by film companies because it had the rugged, middle-of-nowhere look pictures like these required (even though it was only ten minutes from Hollywood Boulevard!). There were battle scenes with the white settlers fighting Indians, and (as usual on a Pollexfen-Wisberg picture) we were doing our own stunts. One of the "Indians" was Stuart Randall,

I appeared as John Rolfe and Jody Lawrence played Pocahontus in *Captain John Smith and Pocahontas.*

who played the chief of the Mutate tribe in *Captive Women*. There was a scene where I trying to scale a ladder on the side of a fort and Randall was at the top. We were clashing and I was flailing away with my sword like I was supposed to do, and Randall suddenly became irate because (*he* said) I almost hit him with the sword. I *didn't*, it was just that he didn't want any *real* swordplay going on around him. Of course, accidents *can* happen in a scene like that when things are not planned ahead of time; and I have to admit that *that* particular picture didn't have too much planning go into it. In the action scenes, the directions were, "Okay, go! Climb the ladders! Get up there! Fight!" So Randall's concern was maybe warranted—he was furious! Just then, however, Lew Landers (the director) said *cut*, so we backed off.

Another "side benefit" of working in low-cost pictures is the opportunity for travel that occasionally comes an actor's way. (Of course, he can get to travel while making a *big*-budget picture, too!) I got a trip to El Salvador out of *The Black Pirates*, the other movie I did with Tony Dexter. Here Tony played a pirate who arrives at a Latin American town with his men in search of buried treasure. He discovers that a church has been built over the spot where the treasure is buried, so he tricks the local garrison of soldiers into leaving town. Dexter then takes over the entire village, forcing the people to dig inside the church. When the village priest (Lon Chaney) reveals that he found the gold long ago and used it for charity, Dexter becomes enraged and orders the town burned. But the natives, under my leadership, revolt and battle Dexter and his men. (*The Black Pirates* was co-written by Fred Freiberger, who had a long history of minor-league pictures in the years before he produced TV shows like *The Wild Wild West* and *Star Trek*.)

Two actors in the supporting cast of *The Black Pirates* linger in my memory. One was Lon Chaney Jr., who played the village priest. His real name was Creighton Chaney and he was (of course) the son of the famous silent movie actor Lon Chaney, who starred in such immortal films as *The Hunchback of Notre Dame* and *The Phantom of the Opera*. After his dad died, Creighton tried to break into the picture business, and did, but with very limited success. He was told that if he could bring himself to change his name to Lon Chaney Jr., he would obviously get a lot more attention and a lot more parts. His big break came when he played Lennie in Lewis Milestone's *Of Mice and Men* (1939); Lon pursued that part very conscientiously, and he did a marvelous job. He then went on to star in a number of Universal horror films in the 1940s. But Lon Jr. was attempting to follow in some very large footsteps, and I don't think he ever kidded himself that he was in the same league as his dad. (In fact, I remember that he once referred to himself as "the son of the *good* actor.") When Lon was approached about doing *The Black Pirates*, the producers wanted him to play one of the lead heavies—and he said he'd rather play the *priest*. Because it was such a turnaround as far as casting, he thought that would be a better, more interesting part for him. He was also quite a drinker, which I'm sure that everybody who's interested in his life and career probably knows by now. I don't remember him drinking on the set, but I do recall that one afternoon, as we were riding back in a car to our hotel from some location, he pulled out the jug and said, "Does anybody want a drink?" We all declined, and Chaney had his swig.[3]

Shooting in El Salvador was supposed to take three weeks but we ended up spending six weeks there; it rained every day at noon and we'd have to quit filming and move inside. (Making pictures can be

When Lon Chaney was approached about doing *The Black Pirates*, the producers wanted him to play one of the lead heavies—and he said he'd rather play the priest.

slow, tedious work, as any actor will tell you.) The experience was made worse by a Mexican actor by the name of Alfonso Bedoya. He played character roles in Mexican films for years before he made his American debut in John Huston's *The Treasure of the Sierra Madre* (1948) as the smiling bandit ("We don't need no stinking badges!"). He was excellent in that picture—although, let's face it, he had Huston helping him—because he was a very ugly, formidable film heavy, with teeth that were in great need of replacement. When I encountered him on *The Black Pirates*, I realized quickly that the man was a real s.o.b. He was unkempt, he liked to throw his weight around (not that he had very much to throw), he was drunk every night, and he was very rude in front of the gals on the set. And not only that, at some point he must have had his teeth fixed, because on *The Black Pirates* I noticed that he had "new" teeth, and I thought it really spoiled his look!

• • • • • •

The dates are a little vague in my memory now, but at one point in the early or mid-1950s I, as an actor, made a decision to hold out for better pictures, to stay out of work if necessary and wait for some better opportunities. The success that I'd had with Ida Lupino, and the fact that I'd done a workmanlike job of starring in a number of smallish pictures, gave me the feeling that it wasn't necessary for me to be in *every* low-level picture that was offered me. In order to stick to that plan, I needed other sources of income. One of the things I did was to buy a sideline business, a dry-cleaning store, and I hired a fellow to help me run it.

Someone who was very considerate and helpful around that time was an actor named Robert Shayne. Bob began acting on stage back in the '20s, then moved into pictures and later (of course) into television; he was Inspector Henderson on TV's *Adventures of Superman* with George Reeves. In 1952 Bob and I were at Hal Roach Studios on a segment of some TV series (I think it was a whodunnit). We were having a bite in a small lunchroom there and I said to him, "You've had the experience, what do you *do* at this point in life?" He said, "I'm in the insurance business." I asked him how old he was and he said he was 52. I was 32. He said, "I wish I had done, at your age, what I am finally doing at 52. I'm in the casualty insurance business and it makes a very good backstop, a fill-in for when I don't get the acting jobs." One thing led to another and he said, "Would you be interested in coming out to my office sometime? Maybe I can help you get started." For no money that he received, *ever*, he tutored me in the casualty insurance business and he helped me get my license. (And I could have operated out of his office in Van Nuys, if I'd wanted.) He really extended a helping hand to a 20-years-younger actor, saying, "Here's the way you make it if you don't make it [in acting] as big as the big guys. You have a different business and you make that business work." So I learned the insurance business from Bob Shayne, a good actor and a good man.

•   •   •   •   •   •

When you're not a star, your acting career is liable to hit a "flat spot" at any time. During one such lull, I got myself a new agent, a fellow named Bob Brandeis. Brandeis was the type of guy who just wanted a buck; they called him "The Wholesaler." He hit TV early, before agents were much into it, when actors' salaries were 55, 60, 75 bucks a day. (Today it's $500 minimum.) Bob got Lyle Talbot a regular role on the *Ozzie and Harriet* TV series, and he said to me, "Here, I'll show you what Talbot made last month. 1700 bucks. How much did *you* make?" *He* knew how much—or how little, I should say!—I made in the month prior to that; I'd hit such a low point, I hadn't made *any*-thing. Bob said, "Look, I'm handling Harry Lauter and he's doing the lead in a serial at Republic called *King of the Carnival*. There are parts in there. C'mon, we'll go see Harold Chiles."

Harold was in charge of casting at Republic, and he remembered that I had starred in *Street Bandits* and *The Fabulous Senorita* over there. He said, "Bob, I can't put you in this *serial*!"

"Harold," I said ruefully, "I got no *work*. *I'm* willing to do it."

Harold said, "Well, it just kills me to see you do this."

Bob Brandeis had told me that it wouldn't hurt my career, doing this serial, and as it turned out, he was right, it didn't, because at that point, nobody ever *saw* them! (They went out to the Midwest, or wher-ever it was that they still showed serials in 1955, and even *there*, only kids watched 'em.) *King of the Carnival* was a typical action/mystery type of serial: Harry Lauter was a high-wire acrobat who is asked by a friend in the Treasury Department to be on the lookout for the circus employee who is distributing counterfeit money. Lauter battles the mem-bers of the "funny money" gang for 12 episodes until the head of the gang is unmasked (Bob Shayne, of all people!). *King of the Carnival* was the last serial Republic ever made, and it's probably also the last serial that any serial fan would ever want to see. But I'll always remem-ber that it got my career back on track after an awfully dry spell.

•   •   •   •   •   •

Another horrible experience was starring in a cheapie called *Se-cret File: Hollywood,* which we made years before it came out in 1962. It was directed by a music editor named Rudolph Cusumano, who went

Francine York and I got no help from our "director" on the low-budget *Secret File: Hollywood.*

by the name "Ralph Cushman" in the credits. (In the picture, I played a private eye who has a run of bad luck, forcing him to take a job as a photographer for Francine York's Hollywood "scandal magazine.") *Secret File: Hollywood* was shot on an old sound stage near Pico and Fairfax, on sets that were practically bare, and "Cushman," our "director," didn't know the first thing about directing. He would walk in... sit down in the director's chair... fold his arms... cross his legs... and say, "Okay, let's go." He hadn't said more than *hello* to the actors, much less discussed the scene that was about to be shot! (He didn't even have the script!) We realized that he expected the actors to direct themselves, and so we did: Francine, Syd Mason and I worked our butts off trying to make something out of this, with no guidance from our "director."

The behind-the-scenes people got no help from the guy, either. Ray Dennis Steckler was the cameraman, and he kept warning "Cushman" that the sound boom was too low, that the microphone would be seen on the film, hovering over the heads of the actors. But "Cushman" was determined to act knowledgeable and he told Steckler, "Oh, with the lens we're using, you'll never see it." Of course, the damn boom microphone ended up in most of the shots—along with the tops of the sets, the lights and everything *else* the audience isn't supposed to see! I haven't seen *Secret File: Hollywood* in many years; in fact, I may never have seen it at all. I'm frequently told that it's very funny, and that I should take a look, but I've yet to summon up the courage.

"Cushman" may not have known much of anything about directing, but he was actually a nice-enough fellow. Jerry Warren didn't know much of anything about directing, and he was a screamer. Jerry made a dozen or so exploitation-type movies back in the days when a picture of that sort, no matter how bad, could play at drive-ins and the like. Jerry was in it strictly for the bucks, the public be damned. I'm sometimes asked why I did some of these cheap pictures, and my answer has always been an honest one: That's all that was offered to me at the time. I feel sometimes that if I had used some restraint and *not* done some of the movies I did do—*Secret File: Hollywood*, *The Astounding She-Monster* and the ones I did for Jerry Warren—I would have been better off, career-wise. But Jerry came along when I had just gotten married—in 1956, I married Alyce King of the King Sisters, a widow with two sons from a previous marriage. I now had a family to support, so when a producer would offer me five, six, seven hundred dollars for a week's work, starring in some little picture, my sense of responsibility overrode my concern about what that picture might or might not do to my acting career.

Jerry came out to see me, bringing along the script of *The Incredible Petrified World*, and told me that I'd have to wait to get paid until after the picture was finished. I agreed. I've heard it said that *Incredible Petrified World* was the best film Jerry ever did, and maybe I should be grateful for small favors like that, but it was still a miserable film and a pretty miserable experience. John Carradine got top-billing as the developer of an experimental new diving bell which is lowered into the Caribbean. Aboard are a diving expert (myself), a lady reporter (Phyllis Coates), a scientist (Allen Windsor) and a college student (Sheila Carol). The objective is to break a depth record, which they do, but the *second* thing that gets broken is the cable lowering the bell; the explorers sink to the bottom, where they find that they are within swimming distance of the entrance to some air-filled caves. Searching the caves for a route to

Believe it or not, my later Jerry Warren pictures were even *worse* than *Incredible Petrified World*.

the surface, they find maze-like passages, stock footage of a komodo dragon (shot in broad daylight) and a crazy old hermit with a phony beard and a phonier foreign accent. An erupting volcano causes an avalanche which kills the old hermit. The others escape in a just-arrived rescue bell arranged by Carradine.

Between myself, John Carradine and Phyllis Coates, *Petrified World* had a pretty good cast by Jerry Warren standards, and there were moments (not many) when it even looked a little bit like a real movie. We went out to Colossal Cave in Arizona to shoot the cave scenes; we drove there in cars and we stayed at a very inexpensive motel in the nearby town, and Jerry fed us hamburgers for lunch and dinner—and maybe for breakfast, too! (I shouldn't be hypocritical and poke fun about the hamburgers: When I produced *The Hideous Sun Demon*, *my* crew ate an awful lot of hamburgers, too!) We were out there about three days, with *not* enough crew to do the job. The cameraman lit the scene and operated the camera, and any actor who happened *not* to be in a particular shot held the sound boom. We also did our own makeup, held the clapper board and did everything else that needed doing.

In the credits, it says that Victor Fisher was the director of photography, but most of the time it was actually a cinematographer named Brydon Baker, who was working "on the q.t." Nobody could afford to get caught working outside the unions in those days, that was strictly *verboten* because unions were so strong then, and Brydon was very much at risk in doing this; that's obviously the reason that his name isn't on it. I also remember that the sound man was somebody who had a vendetta against the sound union because they wouldn't let him in, so he owned his own equipment and worked for people like Jerry. The one nice memory I have of those days out at Colossal Cave is that Phyllis Coates and I chatted quite a bit, about the business, generally; she was married then to Norman Tokar, the director. Phyllis was a real good pal and we did our best to make it as professional as we could.

The script was already written before Jerry discovered that he could hire John Carradine to play the inventor of the diving bell. To beef up Carradine's part, Jerry sat up all night hurriedly writing nonsensical "scientific" dialogue. (Don't get me wrong—if Jerry had had more time, it *still* would have been nonsense dialogue!) Again, working in that twilight realm of Grade Z movies has its unexpected pleasures: *Incredible Petrified World* was my first opportunity to act with Carradine, one of Hollywood's great character stars. The disappointing part of it all is that Carradine, like me, and like many others, did so many of these cheap pictures that he got the "label" of being a cheap picture specialist. John Ford had Carradine in *The Grapes of Wrath*, DeMille had him in *The Ten Commandments*, he was in *Jesse James* and *Blood and Sand* and so many other fine pictures—and then he got to the point where he had to make movies like *The Incredible Petrified World*. What impressed me the most about Carradine was how strong his concentration was. One night Jerry stuck him in front of a garage door on Melrose Avenue and right there, in the street, with the traffic going by, and with no fellow actor working *with* him, Carradine did a soliloquy of story points, telling the story on this *Incredible Petrified World*. I stood there and watched as Carradine, completely concentrated on what he was doing, came out with the dialogue, not missing a word, giving a really great performance in the most abject, abnormal, *sub*normal circumstances.[4] It's amazing the way actors of Carradine's stature can rise above their material even in cheap pictures like the ones he did late in life, after his drinking and his alimony problems put his career on the skids.

The thing that really galled me about working for Jerry was that he turned into a Mr. Hyde when he switched the camera on. He'd get emotional, holler at people, holler at *me*—and I'd holler right back at *him*. He'd get obstreperous and the actors would become upset. That's no way to make a movie. Later on, Jerry needed a closeup shot of me coming up out of the underwater cave, so we went out on Mulholland Drive one dark night to get the shot. It had rained, and he had me lying down alongside the highway where there were some rocks and a puddle, me wearing the damn scuba headgear. I hated every minute of it, but (again) I was raising two boys and trying to help support my wife; the money was there, and it seemed to be the thing to do at the time. You never get the feeling on a picture like this that it might lead to better things, as I did on the Ida Lupino pictures, and even on *The Man from Planet X*. Instead, it's the unmistakable feeling of taking a big step backwards.

But, oddly enough, Jerry's wife Bri Murphy (the production supervisor and dialogue director on *Petrified World*) *did* go on to better things. Working with her on *Petrified World* I could see that she was very professional in her attitude and that she worked hard and she had ambition to become a director herself. Later, after she and Jerry split, she *did* direct, and today she's achieved a certain amount of fame and industry respect for being Hollywood's first woman cinematographer; she's been Emmy-nominated many times, and has won at least one or two.

• • • • • •

One positive thing I can say about working in those Jerry Warren pictures is that, because of the fact that John Carradine was in them, I'm able to make the claim that I'm probably the only actor to have worked with each and every one of the major horror film stars: Carradine in the Warren pictures, Karloff and Lugosi at RKO, Lon Chaney Jr. in *The Black Pirates*, and Vincent Price and Peter Lorre in radio. It was on radio's *The Saint* that I worked with Price; after the show, we went over and had a drink at one of the local bistros near NBC. Price was "bicoastal," working on Broadway and also in Hollywood movies, and I recall him bemoaning the fact that it was difficult to bear the expense of two homes (an apartment back East and a house in California). He was an extremely gracious man, with no "star" bullcrap about him. (I later worked with him again in a TV version of *A Christmas Carol* which we shot at Jerry Fairbanks Studio on Sunset Boulevard in 1949; he was the narrator and I played the nephew of Scrooge [Taylor Holmes]. We did the show in one day and it was shot with three 16mm cameras, the same sort of way they shoot TV sitcoms with three *video* cameras now.)

I'm not able to say as much about Peter Lorre, because I wasn't able to talk to him too much. The radio show Lorre and I did together was (I believe) *Suspense*; if it wasn't *Suspense*, it was one of those mystery-drama shows. The thing that struck me about Lorre was how very heavy he had become; it seemed to me that he was almost as big as Sydney Greenstreet (Lorre's co-star in so many fine Warners films)! I don't like to say that Lorre was incommunicative, but that would almost describe it; he was very low-key, and my mental picture is of him sitting there *very* lackadaisically, waiting for rehearsal to begin. Despite the fact that I didn't get much of a chance to talk with him, I found my interest piqued by the fact that here I was, working with one of the big names of the mystery, suspense and horror genre, Peter Lorre.

•   •   •   •   •   •

Three of my low-budget pictures were made by Ronnie Ashcroft, a film editor who went into production in the mid-'50s. None of the three films I made for Ronnie were much good, but it was my association with Ronnie that later led to my decision to produce and direct my own film, *The Hideous Sun Demon*.

My first picture for Ronnie was a 1956 Western called *Outlaw Queen* with bandleader Harry James in the lead. Ronnie found out that Harry wanted to be in a Western; *Outlaw Queen* was made around the same time as a Frank Sinatra Western called *Johnny Concho* and one with Tony Martin called *Quincannon, Frontier Scout*, and I guess Harry figured that if Sinatra and Tony Martin could play cowboys-and-Indians, so could he. I don't know how Ronnie found out about Harry's ambition, but he did; Ronnie approached Harry James at the Palladium one night, Ronnie being the enterprising fellow that he was, and he and Harry quickly came to some sort of an agreement. Right away Ronnie went to work putting a deal together to do the Western. Ronnie had a

Bandleader Harry James took his shot at cowboy stardom in *Outlaw Queen* with Andrea King.

couple of Greek musician-friends, Jim Harakas and Andy Ladas, who put money in the picture. Like a lot of investors, they also wanted to act very badly, so Ronnie gave them both parts in the movie and, yes, they acted very badly.

Poor Ronnie had his hands full as producer. Just prior to making *Outlaw Queen*, he was taught some of the ins and outs of picturemaking by a director named Cy Roth. Ronnie agreed to let Roth direct *Outlaw Queen*, which turned out to be a bad mistake. I was not around for any of this, but according to Ronnie, the cast and crew hated Roth: He rode around with a riding crop like Napoleon, hit a horse in the face with that stick, and immediately began falling behind schedule. Ronnie eventually had to fire Roth (the cast and crew cheered at the announcement), and Herbert Greene came on as Roth's replacement. I already knew Herb, who had worked as a second assistant on *Three Musketeers*, *The*

Man from Planet X and *Tales of Robin Hood*.[5]

Outlaw Queen had a pretty standard story, but Ronnie did round up a couple of "name" actors for the leads (Harry James and Andrea King) and he dressed up the supporting cast with other familiar faces (Kenne Duncan, I. Stanford Jolley, Vince Barnett). He also got his hands on stock footage from a first-class Western called *The Woman of the Town* (1943) and integrated some large-scale scenes from that film into *Outlaw Queen*. I really liked working with Harry James, partly because he was so honest about the fact that he realized he was a better trumpet player than an actor. Here was James, the face on the cover of most of the best Big Band albums, one of the biggest names of the Big Band Era, wanting to be John Wayne! I remember that one day he said to me, "I wish I had a voice like yours," and I thanked him for the compliment. But he was right to be unhappy with the way he sounded: His voice was high-pitched and it didn't go with the man. Harry had a handsome look about him (he was dark and sported a mustache) and he very much wanted to be a Western star, but there didn't seem to be anything he could do about his voice. Harry had no more chance of being the next John Wayne than John Wayne had of playing the trumpet.[6]

My third picture with Ronnie (I'm skipping the second one for now) was *Girl With an Itch* (also known as *Girl on the Highway*) with Kathy Marlowe as an itinerant farm worker who hitchhikes between jobs, and causes trouble with her sexiness wherever she goes. ("Marlowe is a voluptuous blonde, bursting at the seams in the one dress that displays most of her charms throughout the picture," wrote a reviewer for *The Motion Picture Exhibitor*. "This is strictly adult stuff and may cause problems where censorship is a factor.") *Girl With an Itch* was nothing for me as an actor to be proud about, but my thrill in doing that picture was to be working with an actor that I had seen as a kid in *King Kong*, Robert Armstrong. (He played my father, and Kathy Marlowe's presence on our farm causes friction between us.) Armstrong was working as a day player at that point, making perhaps 150 a day, but once again, the "actor's dedication" shone through: He never treated it like it was anything but a job that had to be done with the best that he had to offer. He was very reliable and very professional to work with in the scenes we shared. *Girl With an Itch* was small-budget, but I was happy to be involved in a picture that would allow me to rub elbows with someone who had become such a memorable figure in film archives. (Someone on the set, I forget who, asked Armstrong if he had a percentage on *King Kong,* and he kind of grinned and said, "No. Who had any idea it would do the kind of business that it did?")

Between *Outlaw Queen* and *Girl With an Itch*, I made my second picture for Ronnie, *The Astounding She-Monster* (1958). Ronnie's participation in *Outlaw Queen* had left him almost completely bankrupt—an occupational hazard for shoestring producers—but despite this disastrous development, Ronnie was determined to continue working as an independent producer. He checked around and learned that the call was out among distributors for cheap science fiction pictures, which were then big with teenagers and played profitably at drive-ins and the smaller theaters. A year or so before, Ronnie had worked as sound effects editor on an early AIP picture called *Day the World Ended*, a Roger Corman "after-the-Bomb" cheapie about a group of people trapped inside a small home in a Midwest valley, threatened by atom-mutated creatures lurking in the nearby woods and hills. The premise appealed to Ronnie because a picture of that sort could be done very cheaply; apart from some exterior locations, the whole thing could be shot on one set, which would greatly reduce his cash outlay for studio space. Ronnie planned on making the feature in seven days, budgeted it at $50,000 and gave the film the title *The Naked Invader*. He got part of the money from a local finance company by using his furniture as collateral, and made the decision to direct the film himself.

The "naked invader" is a well-stacked woman from space (Shirley Kilpatrick) who arrives on Earth in a projectile and begins prowling the woods in the San Gabriel Mountains near her landing site. It's a busy night in these woods: A geologist (myself) and his dog are rock-hunting, and a pair of crooks (Kenne Duncan and Ewing Brown) and their "moll" (Jeanne Tatum) are driving through together with the young socialite (Marilyn Harvey) they've just kidnapped. The thing turns into a poor man's—a *very* poor man's!—*Key Largo* when the gangsters move into the geologist's mountain cabin, holding the geologist and the socialite (and the dog) captive. The She-Monster kills one of the gangsters (Brown) and the dog and then proceeds to chase the rest of us in and out of the house over and over again. The second gangster (Duncan) and the moll are killed before the geologist concocts an acid bomb and throws it at the She-Monster, killing her. Beside the spot where her body had completely disintegrated is the She-Monster's hinged locket and (inside it) a message from the Master of the Council of Planets, inviting the people of Earth to join this benevolent intergalactic governing body. The geologist and the socialite realize that they have killed an emissary of good will—and conjecture on what shape the Council's vengeance might take.

As far as I was concerned, *The Astounding She-Monster* was pretty awful, but apparently it entertained the youngsters for whom Ronnie made it and it's still a popular film of its type today. Mostly, I'm sure, because it's fun to laugh at. The actual making of the movie was the *real* comedy, however. As usual on pictures like this, the crew was minimal: One gaffer, his helper, a cameraman and a sound man. Also on the set (a $150-a-day stage at Larchmont Studio in Hollywood) was the writer, a fellow by the name of Frank Hall—who hadn't yet finished the screenplay! The guy was off in a corner re-writing dialogue on the spur of the moment and working like crazy to stay ahead of us.

The girl playing the She-Monster, Shirley Kilpatrick, was a real sex bomb—a well-endowed, beautiful gal who wore a silvery, Spandex-type outfit which accentuated her figure. (I didn't learn until much later that Shirley was a stripper.) To give her an unearthly appearance, Ronnie also gave her pointed eyebrows and he focussed a bright light on her in the outdoor scenes so that she would look like she was glowing with radioactivity. (Later, in the film laboratory, her scenes were also given a shimmery "ripple" effect.) Mostly it was the tight, shiny suit that gave her the look of a weird and yet *appealing* kind of alien—but the first time she moved in the doggone thing, it split right up the back. The outfit was so skin-tight that there was no way to properly repair it, and so what they did was use safety pins to hold it together in the back. That's why, in the movie, she never leaves a scene in any way other than backing away from the camera—it added to the weirdness of the character, but the *real* reason she did that is that, if she turned around, she'd be showing the camera her backside!

One of the big "scare" scenes in the picture was going to be a shot of the She-Monster unexpectedly crashing through a window and into the geologist's cabin. A candy-glass window and frame were made at a cost of one or two hundred dollars, which is a big outlay for a single prop when you're working on the sort of budget Ronnie was. But as some of the guys were trying to get the thing into position, they dropped and broke it. If I had been the producer-director, I'd have said, "Oh, hell, forget it," but Ronnie very resourcefully had them put some of the big-

The fallen *She-Monster* (Shirley Kilpatrick) turned out to be a "good will ambassador" from space in the *Astounding* finale.

ger fragments back into the frame of the window and then had Shirley jump through. Later, when he edited the film, he cut that shot in such a way that it actually worked pretty well. (Ronnie edited the movie in his own living room.)

The cinematographer was a fellow by the name of William Thompson, a real oldtimer who also worked the camera on the now-notorious Ed Wood movies (including the "Worst Film Ever Made," Wood's *Plan 9 from Outer Space*). We shot the cabin interiors at the Larchmont Studio on December 17, 18 and 19, 1956, wrapping up a full day ahead of schedule. A month or so later, we shot cabin exteriors at Frazier National Park and then a day of road and forest scenes in Griffith Park. After the first day of exterior shooting, William Thompson was fired; according to Ronnie, he discovered that a lot of the raw film stock he had bought for the picture was missing and he accused Thompson of stealing it. (It later turned out that Ronnie was right.) Brydon Baker, working once again without credit, was behind the camera when we wrapped the thing up.

Ronnie's wife Loraine "stunt-doubled" Shirley Kilpatrick as the She-Monster in two scenes, rolling down a hill and fighting with a bear. The "bear" was played by Kenne Duncan, who got inside a bear skin Ronnie had either borrowed or bought from a taxidermist. According to Ronnie, while they were shooting that scene, Kenne started coughing inside the bear suit and asked if they could break for a minute. Ronnie told the cameraman to stop and unzipped the bear suit, and Kenne came stumbling out of it smoking a cigarette. He'd actually lit a cigarette when he was inside that thing, and started suffocating from all the smoke! This was my first time working with Kenne Duncan, an old pro who had done years of Westerns and serials, mostly at Republic.

The one "player" in *Astounding She-Monster* that I knew already was the collie dog Egan. Egan belonged to my stepsons Lex and Ricky, and it had been named after Jack Egan, a New York publicist and a friend of Alyce's. The dog was given to Lex and Ric by Alyce and their late father Sydney deAzevedo, and it was one of the boys' last links with him. When Ronnie Ashcroft asked if he could use our dog, I said sure.

Ronnie decided to offer the picture to AIP for distribution, and he showed it to Jim Nicholson and Sam Arkoff at Nicholson's house. After the movie was over, the three of them were in the projection room and Nicholson was rewinding the film. Arkoff, puffing on his trademark cigar, made the offer.

"Well, Ron, I'd like to buy it," Arkoff told Ronnie through a cloud of blue smoke. "You know, *you're* going to tell me that you've got $50,000 into this but I *know* you've only got 40 so we'll give you 60."

Ronnie grinned and told him, "You've just bought a picture."

The cigar nearly fell from Arkoff's mouth. "I never made a deal so quick," he said in a whisper.

What Arkoff didn't know was that the cost of *Astounding She-Monster*—which Ronnie had originally projected at around $50,000—had come to just $18,000.

• • • • • •

The salary that Ronnie paid me on *Astounding She-Monster* was $500 a week, which was about right for a picture of this sort, but Ronnie also promised me a 4 percent share of the money *he* made as producer. I thought that was a nice gesture and I thanked Ronnie, but I was certain that I'd never see a nickel over and above the 500 a week. It wasn't that

176

The Astounding She-Monster **turns into a poor man's—a *very* poor man's!—*Key Largo*. [Photo courtesy Eric Caidin/Hollywood Book & Poster]**

I didn't trust Ronnie, it was the fact that I knew how crooked many distributors were back then; I was sure that Ronnie's "producer's share" would come to nothing and that I'd be getting 4 percent of nothing. But Ronnie was a perspicacious guy and when he got involved with AIP he hired Sam Arkoff's cousin to act as his lawyer on this deal, so he could be sure there'd be no shenanigans. My 4 percent came in the form of a check here, a check there, and soon it exceeded the 500 I'd made as my "straight" salary. Thanks to Ronnie's generosity—and integrity, and honesty—over a period of time I received a total of an additional $3000.

In addition to making a pile of money off *The Astounding She-Monster*, it also got me to thinking. Since I knew how much *I* made off of my 4 percent, it didn't take much multiplication to get a rough idea what Ronnie must have earned. If Ronnie could make that amount of money off of a quick, cheap film like *The Astounding She-Monster*, it sort of stood to reason that a science fiction film with a bit more quality and substance to it ought to make as much. Or more.

That's when *The Hideous Sun Demon* was "born."

1 I also remember that for over 30 years Max's brother Martin ran a private screening room on the Sunset Strip; Howard Hughes used to rent it for as long as six months at a time, and often holed up in there for days. Since Martin also kept a lot of unfinished movies in the vault, the place was kind of a monument to the fact that you could sure go wrong by putting your money in movies!

2 Tony's real name was Walter Fleischmann and his first stage name was Walter Craig—he took the surname "Craig" from an old Ros Russell movie called *Craig's Wife*. It was producer Edward Small who changed the man's name again when Walter starred in *Valentino*. When Walter went to sign his contract, the name on the paper was ANTHONY DEXTER. He said, "I'm not Anthony Dexter," and they said, "You are *now*!"

3 One interesting thing that I later found out about Lon was that he had a strange fear of going hungry. I had a friend who used to go fishing and hunting with Chaney, and this fellow told me that between L.A. and his ranch in San Diego Lon had several freezer-lockers full of frozen food (fish and meat and game) that he had either caught or he'd had butchered and stored, because of this inherent fear of going hungry. But Lon was a fun guy.

4 That reminds me of what happened to Robert Taylor after he left MGM; all he was interested in was making money. Taylor was almost as big as Clark Gable at one point, because MGM kept him in big pictures. But when he left, he went over to Columbia and starred in a TV series, *The Detectives, Starring Robert Taylor*; he even made a picture or two for AIP! And this was a guy I remembered from my youth, seeing him in pictures like *Magnificent Obsession* and *Camille*.

5 Later, when the question of who should receive screen credit for directing *Outlaw Queen* went into Screen Directors Guild arbitration, Ronnie showed the film to directors Rouben Mamoulian and William Berke and they gave Herb Greene the sole screen credit.

6 Harry told me a funny story about how, in the early days of his career, he had a tooth missing in the back of his mouth. Later, after Harry became successful and got into the dough, he went to the dentist and got a false tooth—and then found that suddenly he couldn't play the horn as well! He realized that he had developed the habit of keeping a little pocket of air in that area where the tooth should have been, and that little

The Astounding She-Monster got me thinking. That's when *The Hideous Sun Demon* was born. [Photo courtesy Eric Caidin/Hollywood Book and Poster]

bit of extra air prevented him from losing the pressure on the horn. That habit was so second-nature to him that, in order to properly play the horn again, he had to go back to the dentist and have him take that false tooth out!

180

THE HIDEOUS SUN DEMON

I made a nice piece of change for myself starring in *The Astounding She-Monster*, but *more* important than those paychecks was the fact that the experience gave me an awareness that a very profitable picture of that sort could be made for a very small amount of money. Part of the reason that *She-Monster* made the money it did for Ronnie Ashcroft and me was that, at one very pivotal point, Ronnie just happened to be at the right place at the right time: He went over to the offices of American International Pictures looking to make a deal with Jim Nicholson and Sam Arkoff, the heads of the company. He was sitting in some little outer office, waiting to let them know that he was there, and he could hear one of them on the telephone, talking about how they were going to come out real well on some little producer's picture because of the manner in which they were distributing it. (Then *and* now, at distribution companies large and small, the costs of releasing a picture are often exaggerated while the picture's profits are *under*-reported. It's awfully tough for independent producers to protect themselves from this kind of "creative bookkeeping.") It was when Ronnie overheard that conversation that he made the decision to get Abe Lurie, Sam Arkoff's lawyer-cousin, to represent him.[1]

I knew that producing and directing my own picture meant that, sooner or later, I'd be swimming with sharks, but I had "the fever." If a shoestring picture like *The Astounding She-Monster* could make a pile of money, why wouldn't a picture of my own, made with a bit more of an eye toward quality? I think that even Ronnie Ashcroft would have agreed that *The Hideous Sun Demon* had more substance to it than *The Astounding She-Monster*.

The most important consideration was that my film would be commercially successful. At that time, "commercially successful" usually either meant a Western or a monster picture. I opted for the latter—an honest-to-God "monster sci-fi." My idea was to do a picture that would be a variation on the old Robert Louis Stevenson story *Dr. Jekyll and Mr. Hyde*. To be truthful, I never read Stevenson's story but, when I was 12 years old, I sneaked off from grade school with a friend and we went to see *Dr. Jekyll and Mr. Hyde* with Fredric March and Miriam Hopkins. I didn't tell my Mom because I was afraid she wouldn't let me go. (Of course, she was scared and furious when I got home—furious that I went to the movies, but scared until I got back.) I never forgot that day—or how very impressed I was with that movie. So I started out with this plan: To produce, direct and star in a science fiction monster picture in which I would be playing the Jekyll and Hyde characters.

It was at that point that I got Phil Hiner involved. I had met Phil in Chicago, when I was an inspector for the Civil Service Signal Corps there in 1941 and '42 (during World War II). Phil was a part-time writer then; later he moved out here to the West Coast and worked for an aircraft manufacturer, writing how-to books. Phil's real interest, however, was in writing fiction, so we collaborated on the script, "flip-flopping" Robert Louis Stevenson's basic plot. Instead of having a physician drink a potion that changes him into a monster, our plot had as its main character a scientist who is accidentally exposed to fissionable materials. This upsets his chromosome balance so that he reverts, in the sun's rays, into a reptilian sort of monster.[2] Remembering the old Fredric March film, I gave the character two girlfriends, one serious and loyal, the other a "bad girl" from the wrong side of the tracks. Twisting that story around, I hoped that we could come up with a good, solid plot. (And I think, thanks to Robert Louis Stevenson and the Fredric March movie, that we did!) Phil turned our treatment into a screenplay that had the title "Saurus" (the Latin word for reptile).

Once again I went back to the University of Southern California and I took another screenwriting class under Malvin Wald, trying to get a little feeling for the elements necessary for a picture. While there, I met a number of young fellows who were enrolled in the Cinema Department: Tom Boutross, Robin Kirkman, Vilis Lapenieks and others. They were students, all of them in their early- to mid-20s, and several of them lived together in a run-down apartment house, sharing a two-storey apartment with five or six rooms. (They called the place Cinemanor.) When they all showed a lot of enthusiasm about becoming part of my project, we arranged to have a couple of meetings, the first one at their apartment and the second in a classroom at U.S.C. Robin Kirkman even offered to invest in the movie, which was a big step toward getting into

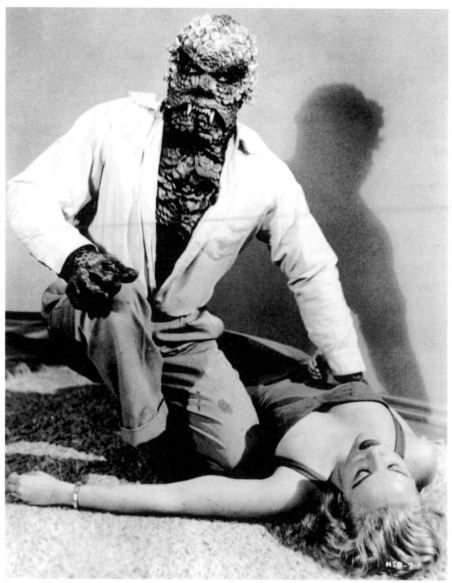

In 1957, the low-budget movie producer's best bet was a Western or a monster movie. I went with the monsters.

production.

Robin turned out to be a very loyal friend through the entire *Sun Demon* experience. Tom Boutross became my co-director and he also edited the film. Vilis Lapenieks photographed, alternating with another couple of fellows, John Morrill and Stan Follis. (We shot on weekends, and sometimes one or more of these guys had other plans. So we always went with whoever was available.) Screen credit for the script went to another U.S.C. student, E. S. Seeley Jr., who was a friend of Robin Kirkman's. Seeley was an esoteric type of fellow, professorial in demeanor, and later on he tried to take more credit for the writing than he deserved. Seeley kept bugging us for more money, more money, and then (to our relief!) he went abroad on some kind of trip, giving us a respite. But he then began writing nasty letters to Robin, threatening us with litigation unless we coughed up additional funds. He was very erratic and quite difficult—a real "character." (And, no, he received no additional moneys.)

After Seeley turned in *his* draft, I still felt that there were rough edges. My very dear friend Beatrice Halstead worked as a secretary for George Murphy, the actor/tap dancer (Murphy had a sideline company that made commercials and industrial films); she was also my business manager. Mrs. Halstead hooked me up with a writer named Doane Hoag, who worked in industrials quite a bit, and Doane did a good job of polishing up the dialogue. When we were trying to come up with a name for our new company, Mrs. Halstead suggested, "Why don't you use Alyce's stage name, 'King'? 'Clarke-King Enterprises'?" That's where the name of the company came from.

Since *Sun Demon* would be non-union, I was a bit restricted in who I could cast, but I thought it would be nice to have another semi-recognizable name in the picture. I tried to hire Andrea King (no relation to my wife), a Warner Brothers contract player of the 1940s. She had acted in Ronnie Ashcroft's *Outlaw Queen* with me and I thought she'd be apt to agree, but Andrea said, "I can't do anything without my agent," and she sort of high-hatted me. (Well... who could blame her?) So I got passed over by Andrea King, and then by an old friend of mine from Oklahoma, Amzie Strickland. Amzie and I went to high school together (different schools, same time), and she later made it big in radio acting in New York in the '40s. I approached Amzie about *Sun Demon*, and she gave the same answer that Andrea did: "I'm sorry, but I can't do anything without talking to Meyer Mishkin [Amzie's agent]." It quickly became pretty obvious, since we were paying 25 bucks a day, that we were going to have to go with unknowns.

We proceeded to get our cast through members of the crew that knew of aspiring actors and actresses around U.S.C. We told them that

Dr. McKenna's second transformation into the scaly Sun Demon.

this was a non-union picture and we had them come out and read. For the "good" and "bad" girls, we got Patricia Manning and Nan Peterson. They were both very sincere in their efforts. Patricia was quite good in the more dramatic role, and Nan had the sex appeal and the obvious physical equipment and looks to be the "bad" gal (and to appeal to the guys). Peter Similuk played the gangster; he had a menacing look and he spoke his lines pretty well. One fellow that didn't come off too well was Robert Garry, who played a scientist. But I ought not to be too

Taking a page from the Fredric March version of *Dr. Jekyll and Mr. Hyde*, we created a "bad girl" character and filled the role with Nan Peterson.

critical, since many of these people weren't professional actors. For instance, the man who played the German doctor was named Fred Pincus, and he made glassware for hardware stores. He had a very obvious accent, and so I asked him, "Do you want to be in this movie?" I figured that if he could just remember and say the words, his accent would make it appear like he was acting! That was the first time he ever acted—and the last! (He wanted to be billed as Fred La Porta, and so that's what we did. I didn't know then why he wanted his name changed, and I don't know now!) Patrick Whyte, who had a fairly sizable part as Dr. Buckell, had played a number of small parts in movies and on TV, and he thought

My niece Xandra Conkling played the little girl who offers to help the fugitive Dr. McKenna.

of himself as an "actor's actor." He helped considerably: He had enthusiasm, he made some good suggestions, and he gave it his best all the time.

For some of the supporting parts, I turned to my in-laws, the King family. Susie, the little girl in the movie, was played by Xandra Conkling, my niece. (She's a grown young lady now, has a husband who works for Hughes Aircraft and has four children.) Her mother, in the film *and* in real life, was Donna King, my wife's sister; she was one of the original King Sisters during the Big Band era. My mother-in-law Pearl Driggs was the elderly lady sitting out on the hospital roof when I first transform into the Sun Demon. (The King Sisters' real name was Driggs, which they changed for obvious reasons—Driggs sounded too much like "dregs." So they took their father's middle name, King, and used that instead.) We used my nephew David Sloan as the young news-boy ("Extra, extra! Read all about it! Weird killer still at large!") Del Courtney, who played the disc jockey, was the fiancé of my sister-in-law Yvonne King; he was an orchestra leader and a deejay in San Francisco. Yet another King Sister, Marilyn, wrote and sang the song "Strange Pursuit" which is heard in the film (mouthed by Nan Peterson). In 1982, when Paramount put together a campy compilation of monster movie clips called *It Came from Hollywood*, they used the scene of Nan singing that song and paid Marilyn $500 for the use of it. I'm also in that scene and so Paramount paid me a few dollars. I can't recall now how much, because it was so minimal, but it wasn't as much as Marilyn got, I remember *that*!

The King family, by the way—the sisters, the kids, Del Courtney, all of them—were wonderful. Everybody pitched in to help, and everybody received a *very* minimal amount of money. Donna's son Chris told me that he was recently in San Jose and he mentioned to some guy there that his uncle was the Sun Demon. Well, the guy practically had a *stroke*! "Really? Your uncle was the *Sun Demon*?? You're kidding! Not really! ...*Really*?" The guy did everything but backflips! (And I wonder if the guy would have been nearly as impressed if, instead of *Hideous Sun Demon*, Chris had dropped the name of the King Family!)

I can't recall precisely when we began production on *Sun Demon*, but it was very close to the time when Alyce gave birth to our son Cam. That puts our starting date at the very end of 1957 or the first part of 1958. We shot only on weekends: We'd have a spot picked for our shooting on a given weekend, we'd rent our lighting, camera and sound equipment on a Friday afternoon and we would therefore get two days of shooting out of a one-day rental. We shot it on twelve weekends over the course of thirteen weeks. (My Dad died on Friday, February 28, 1958, and that weekend we of course did not work.) Believe it or not, we started with $10,000 cash—Robin Kirkman and I each put in $5,000. That must seem ridiculous today but back *then*, making the sort of picture we were making, we felt that we had a shot at making a good, modest science fiction movie.

THE STORY

Dr. Gilbert McKenna (Robert Clarke), a physicist at Atomic Research, Inc., is rushed unconscious to the hospital after a laboratory acci-

188

dent in which he is exposed to a new form of isotope. At the hospital, attending physician Dr. Stern (Robert Garry) confounds Gil's pretty lab assistant/girlfriend Ann Lansing (Patricia Manning) and Gil's mentor Dr. Buckell (Patrick Whyte) by telling them that, despite Gil's prolonged exposure to the dangerous element, he is showing no residual effects.

After a week of tests Gil is allowed to sun himself on the solarium roof. There, before the horrified eyes of an elderly patient (Pearl Driggs), he is temporarily transformed into a scaly, lizard-like monster. Dr. Stern explains to Ann and Dr. Buckell that Gil's exposure to the isotope, combined with the catalyst of sunlight, caused a reversal of the evolutionary process, triggering the brief reversion to the stage of a lizard. Gil must stay out of the sun for the rest of his life.

Gil resigns from his job and takes up residence in Dr. Buckell's deserted country house, beginning a life of brooding solitude. Teetering on the edge of a seaside precipice, he contemplates suicide until the noise of frolicking teenagers on the darkened beach below prompts him to make the most of his strange nocturnal existence. At a nearby bar he flirts with pretty singer Trudy Osborne (Nan Peterson), incurring the anger of her jealous suitor George (Peter Similuk); George starts a brawl and is beaten into unconsciousness by Gil, who flees the bar with Trudy. After a romantic session on the beach, Gil and Trudy fall asleep in the sand, Gil awakening to the first rays of a rising sun. Abandoning Trudy, he races to his car and speeds home, transforming as he drives into the frothing Sun Demon. He rushes into the house and down to the cellar, ducking into a blackened closet to await a return to normalcy. Ann arrives on the scene, pleading with the now-human Gil to consult with a specialist, Dr. Hoffman, who may be able to help him. Wallowing in self-pity, Gil petulantly refuses until Ann is reduced to tears and begs him to see Dr. Hoffman for her sake.

Dr. Hoffman (Fred La Porta) examines Gil and comes to the conclusion that further transformations may increase his skin's sensitivity until only the Sun Demon remains. Ignoring Dr. Hoffman's warning to stay indoors even at night, Gil steals off to the night club to see Trudy. Upset at having been stranded at the beach, she dashes her drink in his face and George and his hoodlum friends haul him outside for a beating. Trudy finally objects when they overdo the job, and after George and his pals are gone she brings the unconscious Gil home to her apartment for medical attention. When George shows up there the following morning,

189

Dick Cassarino, designer of the Sun Demon costume, faced off against his own creation in the oil tank climax.

he misconstrues the situation and leads Gil outside at gunpoint. Exposed to the sunlight, Gil jumps George and transforms in mid-fight into the ferocious Sun Demon. Leaving George's lifeless body draped over the back of a car, the Sun Demon rushes into the woods and eventually arrives home. Resuming his normal appearance within the house, Gil becomes hysterical over his plight until a pounding at the door signals the arrival of the police. Fleeing once more into daylight, Gil rushes to his car and speeds off, accidentally striking a policeman in his maddened escape.

Under the direction of Police Lt. Peterson (Bill White), a dragnet is thrown out over Los Angeles and Gil is forced to take daytime refuge in an oil derrick housing where a little girl, Susie (Xandra Conkling), discovers him and offers to bring him food. Susie's mother (Donna King Conkling) catches the girl stealing cookies, and Susie is forced to tell about the stranger. Alerted, the police move in and Gil flees, collapsing in a railroad yard and transforming into the Sun Demon. After bludgeoning one officer to death with a board, the Sun Demon scales a gas storage tank with a second officer in pursuit. As Ann, Dr. Buckell and Dr. Hoffman gather below and watch with helpless horror, the Sun Demon and the policeman wrestle at the top of the tank, and the policeman fires his revolver point-blank into the creature's heart. Amidst Ann's screams the Demon topples from the top of the tank and plummets to the pavement below. Buckell comforts Ann, murmuring, "The rest of us can only hope that his life was not wasted."

•   •   •   •   •   •

One of the reasons we were able to make *The Hideous Sun Demon* as economically as we did was the fact that we shot on practical locations. (This was something that Roger Corman was known for, and we just followed his lead.) For instance, when we needed a scene in a bar, we just walked into a bar in Santa Monica and asked the owner how much he would charge us to come in there and shoot. The exterior of Dr. McKenna's house was actually a Catholic school; it was an old mansion formerly owned by silent movie star Antonio Moreno. The interiors, however, were shot at a different location, a big old four-storey rooming house on Lafayette Park Avenue. It also had been a mansion in the early days of Los Angeles history, and I'd been in it years before, when part of an episode of *I Led Three Lives* was shot there. When I decided to try to use it in *Sun Demon*, I contacted the lady who ran the place and told her I was interested in renting it for a movie.

"Will you pay me as much as *they* did?" she asked, referring back to the *I Led Three Lives* people.

"Perhaps," I warily replied. "How much was that?"

"Well, *they* paid me $25 a day!"

(Needless to say, that was practically a steal—so much of a bargain, in fact, we actually wrote some extra scenes to be shot in the house, because the price was so right!)

The scene where I transform on the solarium roof was shot atop a hospital on South Hope Street in downtown L.A. It's now called the California Medical Center. We also used its ambulance driveway and a room inside (for the scene where I smashed the mirror). Also downtown was the power plant where we shot scenes of "Atomic Research, Inc."

Using real locations also gave our low-budget picture production values. In other words, the ocean is the ocean, whether it's a small-budget picture or an MGM blockbuster. Shots of me walking along the cliffs were photographed at Bass Rock, and the beach scene with Nan Peterson was shot near Trancas, which is now a very fashionable area. We had sound equipment there for that scene but the roar of the ocean drown out our voices. In post-production, Nan and I had to loop every line.

The oil fields were in the Long Beach area of what had been Signal Hill in the early 1900s. Many of those old wooden derricks still stand and still pump oil. The gas storage tank was located near the Union Station train depot, and it was made available to us through the Southern California Gas Company. It was about 300 feet high, and when I took the dummy of the Sun Demon up to the top to throw it off, my voice (as big and loud as it was) could not be heard by the camera crew down below. We had a very difficult time communicating.

Needless to say, one of the people partly responsible for the popularity of the movie was the fellow who fashioned the Sun Demon mask and costume, Richard Cassarino. Before I found Dick, I first looked up Jack Kevan, the very creative makeup man who made the costume for the Creature from the Black Lagoon. I visited Jack in his Beverly Hills home and told him what I wanted. Jack, however, was used to working for the big studios, and he told me that he'd have to charge me about $5,000. He wasn't overpricing it, but he also wasn't within *my* price range (or even close!). That's when I came upon Dick Cassarino, who was a film buff and a "sometimes-actor." He made a plaster mold of my head and then he fashioned the Sun Demon mask on that. For the scenes in which the Sun Demon was shirtless, I wore the top half of a skin-diving wetsuit covered with scales. The thing was hotter than blue blazes—*so* hot, in fact, that perspiration ran down my body and soaked my pants. I have a still of the Sun Demon, taken after one of the fight scenes, and it looks like I couldn't make it to the men's room!

In addition to creating the Sun Demon mask and costume (which ran us $500), Cassarino also worked as a set designer and he played the policeman who fights with me on the gas storage tank. (We shot all those scenes silent and added sound later.) Dick had a rubber pistol, and there's actually a shot where he fires it and you can see the gun squash up in his hand and the barrel wobble. Dick wasn't the only person working both sides of the camera. Robin Kirkman was our sound recordist and he played the cop that I hit and killed as I raced out of the mansion in the car. Ron Honthaner, our assistant editor, worked on the crew, and he

Tough guy George (Peter Similuk) is about to get the biggest (and *last***) surprise of his life.**

also played a cop. (He was a skinny kid and we had a uniform that fit him; he was the cop that climbed up between the two boxcars.) Ron later went on to work as the assistant to the producer on *Gunsmoke*, and he did well for quite a while. Doug Menville, the boom man, played a different cop.

We also accepted whatever "freebies" we could get. For example, in order for Dr. McKenna to have a flashy car, I struck a bargain with a dealer in the southern part of L.A. who was importing MGs. Our arrangement was that *he* would allow us the use of a car, a sporty little MG convertible, and in return *we* would give him a screen credit. Which we did. I *think*. (I *hope!*)

Because I produced and co-directed the picture, I'm sometimes asked why I also played the Sun Demon, instead of simply hiring a stand-in or a stunt man to take my place in those scenes. I've got a very straight answer: It just never occurred to me! I think that's pretty honest, and rather naive. I could very easily have put somebody else in the costume and nobody would ever have known the difference, and I wouldn't have had to go through all that. It would have been a very obvious and sensible thing to do. But because I was playing Dr. McKenna, I just automatically took on the responsibility of playing the Sun Demon, too. There's not a single shot in that movie where it isn't me inside that outfit.

Tom Boutross, my "co-director," was a tremendous amount of help. He took pains with the picture not only during production but then later, during the editing, when he also treated it with great loving care. In one scene the Sun Demon bursts into the house, frightening his girl-friend. Tom employed a dolly shot: The camera moved in toward the door as the door opened and I entered, "rushing" the camera. That was Tom's "pet shot," and it might be the most memorable shot in the picture. It required a great deal of effort on the part of our semi-amateur crew; they had to lay track on the rough floor in order to make the shot smooth, the guy on focus had to follow-focus with the camera moving, etc. It was a very difficult shot for those guys, who were still learning the business.

Production went smoothly over the course of the twelve weekends and everyone got along nicely. In fact, the one and only time that anyone got a little bit "difficult," that person was *me*. We were shooting the scene on the hospital roof, and I was wearing that hot mask and running around—I was just sweltering. We shot the scene where I jump up out of the wheelchair and run through the doorway, back into the hospital, and I was anxious to move along, to get these scenes finished up so that I could get out of that mask and costume. I looked around and everybody was just standing around, the crew and everybody, chitchatting away. I guess, if anybody ever kinda lost their temper on the picture, at that point *I* did. "Come on, you guys! We gotta break down that setup and go down and shoot in the hospital!" I became upset for a few moments because I was *so* hot and they all seemed so lackadaisical. But, again, I really can't blame them at all; it was more like they were *volunteering* their efforts, because the pay was so negligible—25 bucks a day and all the hamburgers they could eat. (The hamburger idea I got from Jerry Warren!)

My brother Bill Clarke worked as a sales manager at an NBC-affiliate radio station in Amarillo, Texas, and through a friend of his, he offered me the opportunity to go to Amarillo and premiere *The Hideous*

Sun Demon at a drive-in. The manager of the drive-in was a man named Doyle, and Mr. Doyle advertised it heavily. We had a great turnout: For five nights, we packed the drive-in, and we ended up doing $5000 gross business. (The admission then was probably 50 cents.) I was there, along with Nan Peterson, making personal appearances, and we got good publicity.

When Mr. Doyle offered to fly me in his little Piper Cub to Dallas, to show the picture to Universal, I seized the opportunity. It was a hot, hot day, and I had to lug around the 35mm print of *Sun Demon*, eight heavy reels. (When I met with the guys at Universal, one of them said, "We saw you down there, sweatin', bringing those two big cans up the street!") They ran the picture and they gave me an introduction to Universal in California, but to my dismay the people at Universal out here didn't show any substantial interest. I then had an opportunity to show it at Warner Brothers, and I had high hopes that Warners might buy it because I knew they had recently acquired a Roger Corman picture called *Stakeout on Dope Street*. But Warner Brothers passed.

Next I was introduced to Jim Nicholson, the president of American International. I went out to Nicholson's house, where I met his wife Sylvia and their three daughters, and I showed the picture there. Nicholson's daughters liked it, which I thought was a good sign, and Nicholson said, "Show it to Sam Arkoff." I left the print with Arkoff, and he ran it and got back to me. He said he liked it, but he added, "Those jiggling boobs of the gal [Nan Peterson], as she runs down the steps toward the beach—you've got to cut *that*!" (Shows you how far we've come!) Arkoff offered me a flat distribution deal, but I'd already been forewarned by Ronnie Ashcroft that I wouldn't get any money if I made an agreement like that. Too many other producers gave their pictures to companies like AIP and never made a dime—that's a well-known fact. I told Arkoff that I wanted to use *Sun Demon* as a door-opener and produce other pictures, but Arkoff wasn't open to that sort of arrangement. "Oh," he said, "we've got too many producers *now*. But we'll distribute it for you." I said no thanks.

Some time later, I was over on the General Service Studios lot for some reason, maybe to show *Sun Demon* to someone. It was there, in one of the offices, that I ran into Les Guthrie, the very fine production manager with whom I'd worked on *The Man from Planet X*, *Sword of Venus* and other pictures. I told Les what I was up to, and it was Les who

"Made it, Ma! Top of the world!" This shot of the Sun Demon, taken after one of the fight scenes, looks like I couldn't make it to the men's room. The costume was so hot!

told me about a company called Miller Consolidated Pictures. A pair of guys named John Miller and Mike Miller (no relation) had started their own outfit—they wanted to be another Nicholson and Arkoff—and they were getting ready to shoot their first picture, *A Date With Death*, in Roswell, New Mexico. They told me that they'd be needing a companion picture for *A Date With Death*, and I indicated that I might be inter-

My *Date With Death* co-star was Liz Renay, real-life girlfriend of alleged gangland boss Mickey Cohen.

ested in letting them have *Sun Demon* if they'd make me the right kind of deal: I told them I wanted a three-picture contract. They said, "Well, fine—if you don't require any money up front for your *Sun Demon*, we'll release that with our picture as a double bill." They also gave me a part in *A Date With Death*, a job which paid $450 or $500. I was the head of a crime syndicate and Gerald Mohr played a hobo-turned-police chief who gets the goods on me. The leading lady was Liz Renay, the girlfriend of alleged mobster Mickey Cohen.[3]

Through the distribution arm of their company (Pacific International), the Millers released *The Hideous Sun Demon* and *A Date With Death*. (According to the *Sun Demon* poster, THE BLAZE OF THE SUN MADE HIM A MONSTER!) *Sun Demon* didn't get very many reviews, and none of the reviews that it *did* get made it out to be any kind of gem, but they were generally fair to the film and pointed out that it would fulfill the demands of its market. In England it was released under the title *Blood on His Lips* and rated X (*another* sign of changing times!). A British trade publication called *Kinematograph Weekly* said that "Robert Clarke performs vigorously and is effectively photographed as Gilbert alias the lizard man. ...Incidentally, if the hero had signed the pledge and bought himself a decent sun-tan lotion, there'd be no film."

In looking back on my acting in the film, I think I overdid it a little bit—I did too much of a "Kirk Douglas." For example, in the scene where I'm sitting on a divan and I'm very emotional over my situation ("Why should *I* be the one? Why *me*?")—that was perhaps too melodramatic. We did that scene about 14 times before I could bring myself to say, "Okay, that's a take." I kept saying, "Let's do it again"—and again, and *again*—because I had it in my mind that this would be the scene which would prove that I could act. I don't know that it proved anything, except that I could do it 14 times!

Oddly enough, one of the things about *Hideous Sun Demon* that I'm most often complimented on is the background music. I'd like to accept those compliments, but I can't: It all came from the Capitol Record Library. We paid a usage fee and John Seely, a music editor, picked music cues and edited them together. Later, after we did the movie, I would often hear those same cues on TV shows, and I'd say to myself, "Oh! That's from the scene where..."—whatever it was! So it was funny when I would receive letters about *Hideous Sun Demon* which emphasized that the music was so great.

I was once asked to name the scenes in *Hideous Sun Demon* in which I take the most pride. That's a tough question, and I wasn't able to point to any particular ones. But I am proud about two things with regard to *Sun Demon*: *One*, that we had a good story (we followed a *very* good pattern laid down by Robert Louis Stevenson) and, *two*, that the picture has *pace*. That picture never stops. It *moves*. And to this day I have people telling me that it holds up and it's still interesting and it engages their interest as an action/sci-fi/horror film. The hopes I had for it have come to a fruition, even more than I expected, because it now has its own little slot in that genre. I certainly don't mean to imply that I'm comparing it with pictures like *Invasion of the Body Snatchers* or *Forbidden Planet*, science-fiction picture that were super-great. But on the lower level of exploitation, "drive-in"-style sci-fi flicks, *Hideous Sun Demon* has certainly found its place of popularity, partly because it had a little more to it, it had elements that others didn't. This is what the fans tell me and I find that very flattering—particularly since that was *pre-*

cisely one of the things I set out to achieve when we made it. I was also very fortunate to join forces with all of those great guys from the U.S.C. Cinema Department, Tom Boutross and Robin Kirkman and the rest, all of them film nuts dedicated to turning out something good.

The fans tell me we did. I'd like to agree.

1 Ronnie went back into sound effects editing in the 1960s and worked on a lot of television series and movies; he received awards for his work on TV's *Hawaii Five-O* and *Battlestar Galactica* as well as one for the feature *Von Ryan's Express* with Frank Sinatra. He even won an Emmy for sound effects editing *QB VII*. Ronnie was looking to get back into feature production when he passed away in 1988.

2 I even went to the Biology section of the U.S.C. library to do research on the subject; I had heard that the human fetus "evolves" from a one-cell organism to a fish to a reptile before it takes on the characteristics of a mammal. It was simple enough to develop a screenplay where some poor soul finds himself going through that process, *backwards*. The very book in which I did my research is seen in the movie, in an insert shot.

3 I liked what I did in *A Date With Death* but as it turned out, the Millers didn't give me any billing on the posters. They said, "You're the leading actor in *Sun Demon*, and we're not sure we should advertise that you're in *A Date With Death*. We think we should 'play down' the fact that you're in both pictures." That made sense to me, and so I went along with it.

BEYOND THE
TIME BARRIER

My deal with John Miller and Mike Miller of Miller Consolidated Pictures called for me to produce three more movies, so I was on the lookout for scripts to option. My business manager Beatrice Halstead—the same gal who had lined me up with writer Doane Hoag on *Hideous Sun Demon*—put me in touch with a fellow named Arthur C. Pierce, who had written and submitted to her a script called *The Time Barrier*.[1] I met with Arthur and read his script, which I thought had possibilities. Arthur Pierce's great love was writing—he would rather write than anything else—and he sure knew his subjects, mostly science fiction.

I submitted Arthur's script to John Miller, who by that time was already in possession of three other scripts. John submitted all four scripts to some investors that had been lined up in Dallas, Texas, and the Texans thought that *Time Barrier* was the best of the bunch and gave it the go-ahead. (Although I'm sure Art derived inspiration from H. G. Wells' *The Time Machine*, his story was also quite similar to *Captive Women*: "Norms" and "mutates" battling in the devastated world of the future.) A businessman by the name of Robert Madden was the spokesman for the investors, and Madden and his partners came up with the $125,000 to make the picture.

Les Guthrie, the production supervisor on the picture, very appropriately suggested to me that we use Edgar Ulmer as director, and I was certainly in favor of that. Edgar turned out to be a difficult taskmaster for Arthur Pierce, however. I'd found Edgar to be somewhat difficult on *Planet X*, and he was much harder on Art as a writer than he was on me as an actor. He kept asking Art for rewrite after rewrite after rewrite for certain scenes. I kind of stood aside for it, because I respected Edgar and it seemed to me to be important to get as much of his creative input as possible. Art provided the rewrites that Edgar asked for, working at home by candlelight (the power company had shut off his electricity) on his old manual typewriter and trying his level best to get whatever Edgar was after.

One day in the office at General Service Studios, Art turned in the umpteenth rewrite of one particular scene and once again Edgar seemed to be displeased, and he said something that provoked Art. I don't remember Edgar's comment, but it was like lighting a firecracker under Art. Edgar was seated at a desk and Art was sitting in a chair, doodling with a long yellow pencil. Something snapped in this poor, tormented writer's mind: He jumped up out of his chair and leaned across Edgar's desk and broke the yellow pencil in half right in front of Edgar's nose. I think Art would like to have *slugged* Edgar, but the most he could display and still remain a gentleman (which he certainly was) was to break the pencil—which he did. Edgar, of course, was startled, and so was I. I didn't respond, perhaps because I was too surprised, perhaps because I thought that if I got into it, the situation might become even more explosive. Art couldn't do any more than he had done script-wise, and he let it be known by breaking this pencil right in Edgar's face!

It was a very dramatic moment, but later on, one could see the lighter side of it. Art was a conscientious and resourceful sci-fi writer who knew the necessary nomenclature and had done his homework on the technical aspects, but his dialogue wasn't what Edgar was seeking and finally Art got fed up with Edgar's goading. It's funny now to look back on that day and recall the spontaneous reaction it evoked in Art, because it was a harmless outburst and no one was hurt. The incident did seem to bother Edgar a little bit; I remember that later on, Edgar in his heavy Hungarian accent referred to Art as, "This wrrriter who brrreaks his pencil in frrront of my face!" But Edgar's resentment soon passed; he was the type who let everything roll off this back.

As it turned out, *Beyond the Time Barrier* was made at roughly the same time as George Pal's *The Time Machine*, and I've been asked if *Time Barrier* was our attempt to "cut in" on the publicity surrounding *Time Machine* the same way that *The Man from Planet X* "cut in" on *The Thing*. I honestly can't remember, and I think I *would* if that were the case. The funny thing is, when we began casting the movie, one of the actresses who came in to read for the part of Princess Trirene, a girl of the future, was Yvette Mimieux—who later co-starred in *The Time Machine* with Rod Taylor! Yvette was just getting into the swing of things career-wise and she came in to audition. I read with her, and Edgar Ulmer just loved her, but I didn't see her in the part. Her agent was trying to get us to agree to a fat salary—one that was well "beyond our budget barrier"—so we had to pass on Mimieux. I still remember her agent, walking out in disgust, looking back over his shoulder and chiding, "She's gonna be a big star someday, you just wait and see!" And Yvette did go on to make quite a splash in *The Time Machine*, *The Four Horsemen of the Apocalypse* with Glenn Ford and a number of other top films. (And, who knows, maybe if she *had* done *Time Barrier*, she would *not* have been in *The Time Machine*, and she would *not* have had the career that she did. By saying *no* to her, we probably did her the biggest favor of her life!)

Another gal that was in the running was Marjorie Hellen, but before we could sign her, she got a better offer: Paramount signed her up to play Daisy Mae in *Li'l Abner* (1959), and Marjorie—renamed Leslie Parrish—did that picture instead. We ended up going with an unknown, a girl named Darlene Tompkins, and gave her special "AND INTRODUCING" billing.

The other female role in *Time Barrier* was that of Markova, a futuristic *femme fatale*. Les Guthrie said to me one day, "Would you have any objection to Edgar Ulmer's daughter playing that part?", and I said, "No, of course not. It would be a pleasure to have her." Arianne Arden, Edgar and Shirley's daughter, got that role, and she was very cooperative and professional. I thought that she did the part well and that she looked menacing—I believed her as the bad gal and I think audiences generally did, too. Arianne was very pleasant, and to the best of my knowledge she didn't in any way trade on the fact that her father was the director. (And Edgar treated her as he would treat any other actor.) In more recent years, Shirley and Arianne have been quite successful in keeping Edgar Ulmer's name alive via film festivals and other activities.

At first I was not going to play the male lead, they were going to get (they *hoped*) someone with more of a "marquee name." They were looking around and pricing a few actors, and I decided that I wanted *my* name to be in the hopper; I said to John Miller and Les Guthrie, "If you can't get someone whose name is bigger than mine—if you can't afford it in the budget—then I would like to play it." (Edgar went along with that, of course, repaying the favor I'd done him by lining him up as director.) That's how I happened to get the part: Simply because the budget wouldn't allow (say) $10,000 for a "recognizable" name, whoever that might be. I was paid $1000 a week for acting in *Beyond the*

Flying *Beyond The Time Barrier*, Major William Allison rockets from 1961 to the year 2024.

Time Barrier.

THE STORY

The film is set in 1961, two years in the future at the time we made it. Major William Allison (Robert Clarke), an Air Force test pilot, takes off from Sands Air Force Base on a high-speed test flight in the X 80, an experimental aircraft with a special rocket engine. As Allison soars at an unprecedented speed on the edge of outer space, he breaks the time barrier and is transported more than a half-century into the future, to the year 2024.

Allison lands again at the base, unaware that he has passed through a time warp, and he is mystified to find the base deserted and rundown. The world of 2024 is a desolate wasteland; in 1971, lethal cosmic radiation had filtered through Earth's disintegrated ozone layer, endangering its people and forcing an evacuation to Mars. Those left behind—"first-stage mutants"—built their cities underground.

Allison is captured and brought into the subterranean Citadel, where he is regarded as a spy and an enemy by the Supreme (Vladimir Sokoloff) and his burly Captain ("Red" Morgan). The Supreme's mute granddaughter Princess Trirene (Darlene Tompkins), who has telepathic powers, convinces the Supreme that Allison means them no harm. Allison and Trirene are romantically attracted.

A trio of scheming renegade scientists (Stephen Bekassy, John Van Dreelen and Arianne Arden) attempt to persuade Allison to get back to his ship, fly in the opposite direction (thereby reversing the time-travel phenomenon) and find a way to avert the impending cosmic bombardment of 1971. To cover their escape, one of the scientists releases a horde of crazed, radiation-scarred mutants from the Citadel dungeons. In the wild rioting that ensues, Trirene and the three evil scientists are killed. Allison gets to his plane and zooms back through time, arriving back at his air base in 1961—a frail, decrepit old man. Pentagon brass hear his incredible story and promise to prepare for the future.

•   •   •   •   •   •

Since the money for *Beyond the Time Barrier* was coming from Texas, the investors decided that they wanted to the film to be shot there, so that they could have some degree of "control." The scenes at the Air Force base were shot at Carswell Field in Fort Worth; Les Guthrie's father "Pop" Guthrie, our location coordinator, secured that location for us. Carswell Field is still there in Fort Worth. The "wrecked" air base seen in the "future" scenes was located nearby: Les went on a location scouting trip and, about a half-day's drive from Fort Worth, he found this old abandoned World War II Air Force training field, with the buildings in a state of disrepair—just as if it had been made for us! It fit in perfectly with our story.

Most of the film, however, was shot at the old Texas Centennial Fair Grounds in Dallas. Coincidentally, I had visited the Fair Grounds when I was a teenager; the Centennial was held in '36, when I was 16 years old, and I had gone down there on the bus with a couple of buddies. Now here I was, almost a quarter-century later, producing and starring in a movie that was being shot in its long-deserted exhibition halls. The big, barn-like structures looked like warehouses, and somebody had the bright idea that we could use them as sound stages and shoot our "underground" city scenes there. The only problem was that, when you spoke in those large, empty buildings, your voice sounded as though you were in a giant cave or a deep well. The sound man was resourceful, though, and he had the production crew hang a lot of old Air Force surplus parachutes all around to absorb some of the sound.

Our production designer was the great Ernst Fegté, a German-born art director whose movie career went back every bit as far as Edgar Ulmer's did. In pre-production, Fegté had come up with ideas and drawings indicating that the sets for the underground city should have an inverted triangle motif, and Edgar jumped on the idea as being a very good one. Needless to say, I went along with that. Here were two men of great creative talent, Edgar and Fegté, and they *both* liked this concept; I thought to myself, "Great. These two guys have been around the horn more than I have. Let them make this picture as good as possible."

It was nice to have in the cast of *Beyond the Time Barrier* an old actor by the name of Vladimir Sokoloff, playing the Supreme. He was a Russian character actor who was tutored by Stanislavsky at the Moscow Art Theatre and who had worked with Max Reinhardt in Germany. Reinhardt brought Mr. Sokoloff to the U.S. to appear on Broadway in *A Midsummer Night's Dream*, and after that he came to Hollywood and made a number of pictures, most notably *For Whom the Bell Tolls*. I was thrilled to have him in the cast and I thought he added credibility to his sequences; he had a wrinkled, expressive face that was great for the scenes where the Supreme is forlorn about the dim future of his race. We got Sokoloff thanks to Edgar Ulmer, through the Kohner Agency, and for *not* a lot of money, either. (He was only there two days.) A year or two later the poor old guy fell off a horse during the making of *Taras Bulba* and he suffered from that incident until the day he died, which was not too long thereafter.

Darlene Tompkins, who had the non-speaking role of Sokoloff's mute granddaughter, was a conscientious young actress. She had the right, "innocent" look for the part, and although she didn't know sign language, she did an acceptable job of pretending to communicate with hand gestures. (Darlene's mom was also there in Texas, acting as a chaperone, and she was quite nice, too.) In a few scenes I had to carry Darlene, who was not a big gal by any means, but she was just dead weight. (This was after she was killed in the picture, and I was carrying her around.) I was wearing the flight suit, which was hard to move around in, and, oh,

My *Time Barrier* leading lady Darlene Tompkins never saw the movie until a mid-1980s Edgar Ulmer festival at U.C.L.A.

boy, the more I carried her, the heavier she got! Luckily for me, Edgar was the type of director who *didn't* overshoot—he was too mindful of costs.

No offense to "Red" Morgan, but he wasn't right for the role of the Supreme's right-hand man. He had a real distinct Texas accent and he had no business playing a "man of the future," but Les Guthrie said, "We've got to have him as an actor because he's going to program the stunts." Edgar and I agreed to it—with great reservations. I would much rather have gotten a different actor, someone in the class of John Van Dreelen or Stephen Bekassy (our two evil scientists), but it *did* save money to have the stunt coordinator also playing a major role in the picture. And saving money was what Les Guthrie, much to his credit, was always trying to do.

(One more time I want to pass on a bouquet to Les, because he more than anybody else made *Beyond the Time Barrier* work. Even Edgar Ulmer would, I think, agree; he leaned on Les quite heavily. Edgar would say, "Can I do such-and-such, have I got time?"—he would ask Les, and Les would tell him yea or nay. Edgar respected Les and didn't argue, *ever*. Les did the budgeting and he was really what today they would call the "line producer.")

The last scene of the picture called for me to be made-up to look like an incredibly old man. (That, of course, was a steal from *Lost Horizon*, and I'm sure we didn't fool anybody.) I'd suggested to Les that we get Jack Pierce to do the makeup, because Jack was one of the top men in the business. The day we were to do that scene, I had to be in Jack's hotel room by 4:00 that morning in order to be ready on the set at seven or seven-thirty. It was dark when I went from my room to Jack's at the Dallas motel where we were all staying, and I found him already dressed and ready, his makeup table all set up. The way he made me look old was the same way he'd done it for years, with rice paper. Using spirit gum or some other kind of adhesive, he laid rice paper on my face in small pieces, and as they dried, they wrinkled. It took a long time to do my entire face, but he did it with great patience and he certainly did give me the appearance of being an 80- or 90-year-old man.

I considered Jack to be a good friend after having been in his makeup chair on so many different pictures. One which I haven't previously discussed was a movie called *The Valparaiso Story*, which I made just before doing *Captive Women*. We shot that in Valparaiso, Indiana, for the Lutheran Church, and it co-starred Marjorie Lord, Jimmy Lloyd, Margaret Field and Tom Neal. Part of the story was about a basketball team, and at one point poor Jack had to make-up ten basketball players (there were five on each side). A body makeup man Jack was *not*, and I felt it was so degrading for him to be putting leg makeup and arm makeup on all of us. I said, "Oh, come on, let *us* do it, Jack!", but he stuck to the job because he knew his job was makeup. I thought to myself, "They don't know what they're asking of this man, whose reputation, whose skill and craft, is really *not* being properly treated here."

I also remember visiting Jack at his home some years after *Time Barrier*. I was going to go to a masquerade party and I wanted some makeup done, so I called Jack and he said, "Well, come on out to the house." He was living in a nice area in the San Fernando Valley (Van Nuys or Sherman Oaks), and in his home he had photographs of John Boles and Mae Clarke and some of the most beautiful *color* photographs of Karloff as the original Frankenstein Monster. (It was his own idea,

Jack told me in his strange little accent, to shorten the sleeves of the coat that Karloff wore in *Frankenstein* so that Karloff's hands would appear long and claw-like, and so that you could see where the hands had presumably been sewn on at the wrists.)

I've read that Jack was rather bitter about having been dropped by Universal in the mid-1940s, and I do have to admit that, yes, in talking to him, I *also* got that impression. But he was not very expressive verbally, and didn't go into any detail about it. That's what gave me the feeling that he'd been mistreated by Universal, and was not too happy about it. (He also wasn't too happy on the occasions when he had to work with Lon Chaney Jr. Jack was a real stickler for being on time, and Chaney Jr. would always come in late.) Another enduring mental picture I have of Jack is seeing him on the set of *Mr. Ed*, sitting very close to wherever the scene was being shot so that, if they needed him, he could step in in just an instant. Jack was a real perfectionist, an extremely conscientious and dedicated man. By the way, I don't recall seeing Jack making up the mutants in *Beyond the Time Barrier,* but I suppose that he must have, because we had no other makeup man.[2]

I don't remember getting too much direction from Edgar Ulmer on *Time Barrier*; Edgar never was one to delve into a lot of line readings. If it sounded right to him, he'd let you alone. In the film's last scene, where I am seen as the old man, he paid me the one and only compliment I ever got from him. The scene played well, Edgar said, "Cut, print," and then he rubbed his arm as if to rub away the goosebumps and he said to me, in his heavy accent, "That's the first time you've made me feel anything on this picture." He obviously meant to convey that I'd given a good performance in that particular scene, and he meant it as a compliment. But, thinking back on it, it *was* kind of a back-handed one!

Once we wrapped up *Time Barrier*, I came back to Hollywood while Edgar Ulmer and the rest of the crew stayed down in Texas, making a second picture for the Millers called *The Amazing Transparent Man*. I don't know how much *Transparent Man* cost (and I've never seen the picture) but, of the two, *Time Barrier* got the better treatment; we were the first to be produced and we got the most money.

Back in Hollywood, John Miller and Les Guthrie started talking about making a "European version" of *Time Barrier* by getting a shot of Princess Trirene climbing out of a pool bare-breasted. I agreed to let them shoot the scene in the swimming pool in the backyard of our home in North Hollywood, and they hired a girl who was either an actress or a model to stand in for Darlene Tompkins in the scene. (I don't recall whether Darlene refused to do it, or if she wasn't even asked.) The way they shot the scene is humorous as hell now, considering the kind of nudity that is seen in movies today: Les Guthrie being a rather prudish guy, he had the prop guys surround the whole pool with six-foot pieces of plywood so that the neighbors couldn't see what was happening. The girl was going to float on her back *a la* Hedy Lamarr in *Ecstasy*, with all showing. I certainly intended to get a bird's-eye view but Les put up quite a fuss; he wouldn't permit anybody except the cameraman to see her. I don't know whether even *Les* looked! Alyce and I sat in our bedroom and watched TV while they were shooting, so I missed the whole show. Presumably that version is still floating around somewhere, but I've never seen it.

Kroger Babb was the general manager of Miller Consolidated Pictures, and a suggestion that he made concerning the distribution of *Time Barrier* and *The Amazing Transparent Man* turned out to be the undoing of the whole company. Babb was a pioneer of the exploitation film business, an ace huckster/showman who produced his own pictures and then distributed them city by city himself. Years before, he traveled around the country with a film called *Mom and Dad*, which (according to Babb's ballyhoo) depicted a live human birth; after the showing, there'd be books and pamphlets on sale in the theater lobby. The proposal that Babb made to Miller Consolidated, to get them off and running as a distribution company, was straight out of his background as a promotional exhibitor: Babb said the way to kick off the company was to have a gigantic giveaway contest. "Make it a big lottery-type thing," Babb told them. "We'll give away a car or two, all sorts of prizes!"[3]

The Millers went for Babb's idea, and they printed up many thousands of brochures. The plan was to go state by state, starting with a state in the Northwest, Oregon or Washington. But the week that *Time Barrier* and *Transparent Man* opened, that part of the country was hit with the biggest snowstorm that they'd had in years. All of the exploitation money, etc., went for naught—hardly anybody came to the movies. It was a big flop and, practically overnight, Miller Consolidated was on life support. The company had already sent out *Hideous Sun Demon* and *Date With Death*, and I'd even gotten reports of some returns on *Sun Demon*, like $22,000, $23,000, but I hadn't yet received any money. (That

Trying to escape the world of the future.

incoming money was paying for the one hundred *Sun Demon* prints that had been struck; those prints, which cost $25,000, had been charged against my participation.) Well, that failed exploitation campaign suggested by Kroger Babb backfired and triggered the eventual collapse of the company, and there went *Hideous Sun Demon* and *Beyond the Time Barrier* for me. Consolidated Film Laboratories foreclosed liens on *Time Barrier* and *Transparent Man* for lab charges, and then AIP made a deal with Consolidated to take over the distribution of those two pictures. I never received any more than my actor's salary on *Time Barrier*, $1000 a week for two weeks, and I lost quite an amount of money, about $50,000, on *Hideous Sun Demon*.

I've seen *Time Barrier*, of course, and I thought that we did a good job considering our finite resources and a nine- or ten-day schedule. The action that "Red" Morgan choreographed for the finale certainly "hypoed" it, and Ernst Fegté's sets added tremendously to the production values. Adding to the air of "authenticity" that we tried to create was the Air Force stock footage we used in the picture. Locating that

211

was the work of Art Pierce, who knew of an Air Force facility on Lookout Mountain which catalogued and rented out stock footage. Art directed me and Edgar to the place, and right up there at the facility Art and Edgar and I screened footage and selected some that we thought we could use in the movie.

Edgar, as usual, did a hell of a job considering the limitations that he had to work with. A strange and talented man, Edgar; somewhat domineering, the temperamental European, "von Stroheim" type, but he had that miraculous ability to get more on the screen than there was money to put it there! Sometimes he was a real pain in the ass but maybe I was, too, at times. I wanted to increase the quality of *Time Barrier* a few notches above *Hideous Sun Demon*, which was made strictly for the horror market. I thought of *Time Barrier* as science fiction and a bit more "intellectual," but it certainly hasn't come near to being the cult film that *Hideous Sun Demon* has.

And here's an interesting sidelight: About ten years ago, Shirley Ulmer and Arianne were part of an Edgar Ulmer festival out at U.C.L.A., and some of the films that were shown were *Detour*, an Italian-made adventure with Louis Hayward called *Pirates of Capri* and *Beyond the Time Barrier*. It was fairly well attended, and who did I run into there but Darlene Tompkins, whom I hadn't seen since 1959. After the picture was over, out in the lobby, we chatted and she told me, "You know, this is the first time I've seen the picture!"

•   •   •   •   •   •

Am I sorry that I turned producer and made *Hideous Sun Demon* and *Beyond the Time Barrier*, given the disastrous outcome? No, I wouldn't say that I was sorry. If I had *not* done them, I would probably be sorry, and I'd be wishing today that I had put forth the effort. It was an interesting experience. I wish, of course, that it had turned out profitably and that it had led to other things that would have been more mainstream. With Roger Corman, pictures like those were stepping stones to bigger productions. But I took such a terrible financial bath with the bankruptcy on *Sun Demon* and *Time Barrier* that I felt there was no way I could continue as a producer at that point.

But *sorry*? No, never.

1 He got the idea for the title from "the sound barrier," which had recently been broken by Chuck Yeager. I believe it was my idea to add the

word *Beyond*—it gave some action to the title, a little more *oomph*.

2 Art Pierce came down to Texas and worked on the picture as an assistant, and one of the things he did was play one of the mutants. Later, in post-production, I asked John Miller to give Art a job as the assistant to our film cutter Jack Ruggiero, because Art needed the money. Art was always on the lip of poverty; he led a sad life and he didn't have a lot of success, although he did write a number of sci-fi pictures and he even directed a few of them.

3 I remember that the Millers took out a big double-page ad for Miller Consolidated Pictures in *The Hollywood Reporter*, calling themselves "The NEW Company with the old 'PIHSNAMWOHS'!" "PIHSNAMWOHS" was "SHOWMANSHIP" backwards. I wish I had known before I got involved with them that they liked to do things backwards!

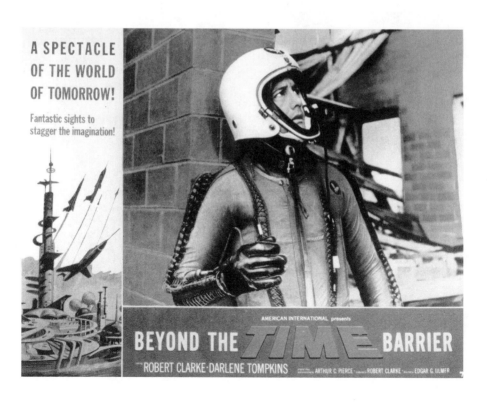

EPILOGUE

I continued to work right on into the 1960s, but at that point it was in TV much more than movies. It was also in the mid-'60s that I began working with my wife and her sisters and their families on TV and on tour as "The King Family."

There wasn't a "King Family" *per se* in 1956 when Alyce and I were married; Maxine, Luise (Mrs. Alvino Rey), Alyce, Donna, Yvonne and Marilyn, working in different combinations throughout the years, were the King Sisters. The King *Family* didn't get started until the 1960s, when the King Sisters made an appearance on *The Hollywood Palace*, an ABC-TV Saturday night series. All six King Sisters came out with their daughters and it was such a hit, the sisters and the seven daughters singing together, they were invited back by Nick Vanoff, the executive producer, for another appearance.

A fund-raising show Yvonne decided to put on for her church in Orinda, California, developed into what was then called the King Family program. It was her idea to use the entire family of husbands, brothers, wives and children (totaling 37). Yvonne obtained a video tape of another benefit show the family gave at Brigham Young University in Utah which she edited and sent out to sell to television. Edgar J. Scherick, ABC vice-president in charge of programming, was so impressed with Yvonne's tape that he scheduled a "King Family Special" which aired on the network August 29, 1964. The overwhelming response of both the public and critics to this TV special resulted in an avalanche of more than 56,000 letters. ABC officials immediately signed the family to do a weekly series. The rest is TV history.

Not being a singer, my role in the series was to occasionally give dramatic readings that had in many cases a tone of sentimentality and warmth. ("Family values," we'd call it today.) That was my place until Yvonne and Del Courtney split up as husband-and-wife. Yvonne and Del had divided emcee duties on the show, and when they divorced, I stepped in and filled the slot vacated by Del, co-emceeing along with

Here I am, third from the right, in the back row, posing with the King Family.

Yvonne. We would talk together, I would introduce one number and then she would introduce the next—we'd mix it up a little bit, and it made for some nice variety in the presentation.

We were on the air in 1965 and 1966—in black-and-white—but then color came in, which presented problems for ABC. ABC only had one color facility out here on the West Coast at the time, and Lawrence Welk got that. That was the reason *The King Family Show* was bounced. We were off for a year or two, then got back on ABC with a half-hour series (executive-produced by Yvonne and Luise) in 1969. After that ran its course, we made holiday specials for syndication—Thanksgiving, Christmas, Valentine's Day, Easter, Mother's Day and so on. These specials kept us busy and kept our name out there so that we were able to do personal appearances during the summer as well. We were still a viable group up until about 1975, when we did our last Christmas special. It was around that time that the King Sisters started thinking about retirement; dates would still occasionally come in for them up until about 1986, when they sang at President Reagan's second inaugural. That was the culmination.

During the last years of the King Family specials, I had my own TV series, *Faith for Today/Westbrook Hospital*. I played Dr. Mason (patterned after Marcus Welby) in this semi-motivational series for the Seventh Day Adventist Church. I was in 50 or 60 of them and each one had a moral: One might be a story of someone being helpful in a family situation, or overcoming an obstacle or some bereavement—they were stories like that, each one having a message of kindness and loving. As the Seventh Day Adventists pointed out, they were directed to the "unchurched" and they were *so* broadly based that, after the Seventh Day Adventists used them, they cut off the head- and tail-end commercials for the Seventh Day Adventist Church and sold them to *other* denominations!

It was after the King Family and *Westbrook Hospital* that I got the idea to become a member of the National Speakers Association and make my "Golden Years of the Movies" presentations. I've made appearances at many civic organizations with the sponsorship of several different financial institutions, among them American Savings and Loan, Independence Bank and the Bank of Encino. (My appearances provided these businesses with an outlet to the surrounding communities.) It turned out to be a very popular public speaking series and I was always booked for several months ahead. It's been tremendous fun, and a definite departure from just being involved in television and/or films as an actor.

It's also been an interesting experience to make the acquaintance of people in the film industry (or its fringes) who as kids were fans of my movies like *Planet X* and *Hideous Sun Demon*. Wade Williams was one of the first fans that came to my attention through personal contact, over 30 years ago. He liked *The Man from Planet X*, and he had even memorized my opening monologue—he was probably that picture's most avid fan! The King Family toured during the summers, when our TV series wasn't in production, and when we traveled through Kansas City, I met Wade for the first time. He has stayed in touch ever since, and at one time he made quite a point of telling me how popular *The Hideous Sun Demon* had become, and that he had observed at conventions a great deal of film-pirating going on, including the illegal copying of *Sun Demon*. Wade said that he wanted to buy it from me and try to stop some of the pirating by renewing the copyright. I wasn't prepared to get into the legal expense of re-copyrighting it, so when he offered me $2000, I sold him the rights and the negative. Since then, in addition to distributing it himself, he briefly sold it to a company (The Twenty Four Horses) which re-titled it *Hideous Sun Demon: The Special Edition* and gave it the old *What's Up, Tiger Lily?* treatment, adding new footage and an all-new soundtrack to turn it into a spoof! (Jay Leno was the voice replacing mine, playing the scientist who in *this* version becomes a monster after ingesting an experimental new "no-sun" suntan lotion.) There was also some new footage shot, and my son Cam acted in the prologue.

In more recent years, Wade paid me commissions for helping him find the people who made two other old films, *The Astounding She-Monster* and *Monster from the Surf*, starring (and directed by) Jon Hall just before Hall took his own life. Wade has also given me the rights to make a *Hideous Sun Demon* sequel if I ever decide to do so, to manufacture *Sun Demon* T-shirts and so on. Wade's a very dedicated collector of memorabilia, a moviemaker in his own right, a very enthusiastic fan and, most importantly to me, a good friend.

I also acted in two direct-to-video features directed by Fred Olen Ray. Like a lot of moviemakers today, Fred is a young fellow who loves the sort of sci-fi movies we made back in the '50s, and now he goes out of his way to cast the old "sci-fi stars" in his movies. I have genuine admiration for Fred because he makes his pictures about as inexpensively as they *can* be made and yet he's such a resourceful moviemaker that they *never* look like the sort of bottom-of-the-barrel stuff I made for directors such as (say) Jerry Warren. My first film for Fred, *Alienator* (1989), a cross between *The Terminator* and *Astounding She-Monster*, featured Ross Hagen, John Phillip Law and Leo Gordon. I wore a robe and a medallion and looked vaguely similar to the Alec Guinness character in *Star Wars*; I played an outer space emissary monitoring activities on a faroff prison planet. In my other movie for Fred, *Haunting Fear* (1990), Brinke Stevens starred as a woman tormented by a recurring dream in which she is buried alive. I played her doctor, whom she suspects was responsible for the death of her father. I appreciate the fact that Fred (and directors like him) are loyal to the older actors.

•   •   •   •   •   •

As I indicated in the very first paragraph of this book, some of my most "memorable" movies are the schlocky ones that *I'd* prefer to forget. I've never tried to make a secret of this fact, and the occasional interviewer will tell me that he can't help getting the feeling that, overall, I'm disappointed in what happened in my career. In many ways, yes. In my early days as an actor, I was riding along on a lot of hopes and dreams and ambitions, boyhood remembrances of the likes of Tom Mix and Fairbanks and Gable and Flynn, and wanting to be as *they* were. I got some chances, but the swashbucklers and the Westerns I did were in the low-budget class, and many of them were very quickly and rather haphazardly done. I proved to my *own* satisfaction that with the proper direction (from, say, Robert Wise, Mark Robson or Ida Lupino) I was a better-than-average actor. I also satisfied myself, while working with Jack Webb, that I could hold my own professionally as a dependable journeyman actor. But I fell into the trap of B-minus productions.

Look what happened, many years ago, to Cesar Romero. He was playing the Cisco Kid in B movies for Fox when studio head Darryl F. Zanuck pulled him out of those and put him into romantic leads opposite actresses like Betty Grable. Romero was able to show what he was capable of, before it was too late, and he became a very popular leading man. Take John Carradine. He was in *so* much junk, more junk than I, but look at some of the better films he did and you'll see that he was a splendid actor. I'm not putting myself on the same plateau, I'm not saying *I* was a splendid actor; what I *am* saying is that in many ways I think I was capable of better than what I got. There have been a lot of roles which I took only because the grocery bill had to be paid.

But some of these B films seem to have created a "cult hero" image for their stars and have given actors like me a place in film history. There's an ongoing, on*grow*ing interest in them, and they "out-popularize" some much better pictures. This has given me the feeling that all was not for naught. Greg Luce, the man behind the "Sinister Cinema" mail-order video company, was one of the first to point out to me that the fans of these B movies are more dedicated than the fans of many bigger-budgeted movies—movies which have faded into obscurity because they *don't* have that cult following. That's made me feel lucky to have done as much as I did. I had dreams and hopes that were not fully realized, and yet I'm glad I gave it my best shot and I'm grateful for the interest that fans have.

I'll never forget something Greg told me: "Because of this cult situation, there are fans that'll remember you longer than some of the actors whose names *you* think are far better. In your slot, *you* are well-remembered." Fifty-five years after hitching a ride to Hollywood, a bit high on expectations and perhaps a bit low on experience, I'm *still* working, *still* meeting fans for the first time, *still* being asked for interviews. In my slot, the fans tell me (and *show* me), I'm still "well-remembered."

What more could I ask for?

With Alyce at Lake Tahoe.

My sons and I pose together as part of the King Family (January, 1996), who were on hand to celebrate the 100th anniversary of Utah entering the Union. Left to right: Ric deAzevedo (director of film services for Warner Bros.; performer on over 55 episodes of *The King Family Show*; performer with Jim Pike and Bob Engemann, original members of The Lettermen, in their new group Reunion); Lex deAzevedo (composer, conductor, arranger, pianist; scored movies such as *Swan Princess* and *Where the Red Fern Grows*; musical director for TV shows such as *The Sonny and Cher Comedy Hour, Dick Van Dyke and Company* and *The Osmonds*); and Cam Clarke (voice-over actor whose animation credits include Leonardo in *Teenage Mutant Ninja Turtles*, Snoopy in *Peanuts* and Die Fledermaus in *The Tick* as well as leads in *Mr. Bogus, Denver the Last Dinosaur, Eek the Cat, Attack of the Killer Tomatoes* and *Dinoriders*).

"Santa" Sun Demon and grandkids (back row left to right): Rebecca, Jennifer, Eric, Rachel, Christian; (bottom row left to right): Sara, Aaron.

The Films of Robert Clarke

The Falcon in Hollywood (RKO, 1944) Produced by Maurice Geraghty; Directed by Gordon Douglas; Screenplay: Gerald Geraghty; Based on the Character Created by Michael Arlen; Photography: Nicholas Musuraca; Musical Director: C. Bakaleinikoff; Editor: Gene Milford

 Cast: Tom Conway (The Falcon), Barbara Hale (Peggy Calahan), Veda Ann Borg (Billie Atkins), John Abbott (Martin S. Dwyer), Sheldon Leonard (Louis Buchanan), Konstantin Shayne (Alec Hoffman), Emory Parnell (Insp. McBride), Frank Jenks (Higgins), Jean Brooks (Roxana Miles), Rita Corday [Paula Corday] (Lilli D'Allio), **Robert Clarke** (Perc Saunders), Walter Soderling, Carl Kent, Chester Clute, Chili Williams, Margie Stewart, Greta Christensen

What a Blonde (RKO, 1945) Produced by Ben Stoloff; Directed by Leslie Goodwins; Screenplay: Charles Roberts; Story: Oscar Brodney; Photography: J. Roy Hunt; Editor: Edward W. Williams

 Cast: Leon Errol (Fowler), Richard Lane (Pomeroy), Michael St. Angel (Andrew), Elaine Riley (Cynthia), Veda Ann Borg (Pat), Lydia Bilbrook (Mrs. Fowler), Clarence Kolb (Mr. Dafoe), Ann Shoemaker (Mrs. Dafoe), Chef Milani (Gugliemi), Emory Parnell (McPherson), Larry Wheat (Watson), Dorothy Vaughan (Annie), Jason Robards (Redmond), **Robert Clarke** (Bit)

The Enchanted Cottage (RKO, 1945) Produced by Harriet Parsons; Directed by John Cromwell; Screenplay: De Witt Bodeen & Herman J. Mankiewicz; Based on the Play by Sir Arthur Wing Pinero; Photography: Ted Tetzlaff; Music: Roy Webb; Editor: Joseph Noriega

 Cast: Dorothy McGuire (Laura), Robert Young (Oliver), Herbert Marshall (John Hillgrave), Mildred Natwick (Abigail Minnett), Spring Byington (Violet Price), Richard Gaines (Frederick), Hillary Brooke (Beatrice), Alec Englander (Danny), Mary Worth (Mrs. Stanton), Josephine Whittell (Canteen Manager), **Robert Clarke** (Marine), Eden Nicholas (Soldier)

The Body Snatcher (RKO, 1945) Executive Producer: Jack J. Gross; Produced by Val Lewton; Directed by Robert Wise; Screenplay: Philip MacDonald & "Carlos Keith" [Val Lewton]; Photography: Robert de Grasse; Music: Roy Webb; Editor: J. R. Whittredge

 Cast: Boris Karloff (John Gray), Bela Lugosi (Joseph), Henry Daniell (Dr. Wolfe MacFarlane), Edith Atwater (Meg Cameron), Russell Wade (Donald Fettes), Rita Corday (Mrs. Marsh), Sharyn Moffett (Georgina Marsh), Donna Lee (Street Singer), **Robert Clarke** (Richardson), Carl Kent, Jack Welch, Larry Wheat, Mary Gordon, Jim

Moran, Ina Constant, Bill Williams

Zombies on Broadway (RKO, 1945) Executive Producer: Sid Rogell; Produced by Ben Stoloff; Directed by Gordon Douglas; Screenplay: Lawrence Kimble; Story: Robert Faber & Charles Newman; Adaptation: Robert E. Kent; Photography: Jack Mackenzie; Music: Roy Webb; Editor: Philip Martin Jr.

Cast: Wally Brown (Jerry Miles), Alan Carney (Mike Strager), Bela Lugosi (Dr. Paul Renault), Anne Jeffreys (Jean La Danse), Sheldon Leonard (Ace Miller), Frank Jenks (Gus), Russell Hopton (Benny), Joseph Vitale (Joseph), Ian Wolfe (Prof. Hopkins), Louis Jean Heydt (Douglas Walker), Darby Jones (Kolaga), Sir Lancelot (Calypso Singer), **Robert Clarke** (Wimpy), Harold Herskind, Emory Parnell, Carl Kent, Martin Wilkins, Nicodemus, Walter Soderling, Virginia Lyndon, Betty Yeaton, Norman Mayes, Bob St. Angelo, Jason Robards, Rosemary La Planche, Bill Williams, Angie Gomez, Dick Botiller, Max Wagner, Rudolph Andrian, Mathew Jones

Back to Bataan (RKO, 1945) Associate Producer: Theron Warth; Produced by Robert Fellows; Directed by Edward Dmytryk; Screenplay: Ben Barzman & Richard Landau; Story: Aeneas MacKenzie & William Gordon; Photography: Nicholas Musuraca; Music Director: C. Bakaleinikoff; Editor: Marston Fay

Cast: John Wayne (Col. Joseph Madden), Anthony Quinn (Capt. Andres Bonifacio), Beulah Bondi (Bertha Barnes), Fely Franquelli (Dalisay Delgado), J. Alex Havier (Sgt. Biernesa), Leonard Strong (Gen. Homma), Richard Loo (Maj. Hasko), Philip Ahn (Col. Kuroki), Ducky Louie (Maximo), Paul Fix (Spindle Jackson), Vladimir Sokoloff (Buenaventura Bello), Abner Biberman (Japanese Captain), Benson Fong (Japanese Announcer), Lawrence Tierney (Lt. Comdr. Waite), John Miljan (Gen. Wainwright), Angel Cruz (Corp. Cruz), Ray Teal (Lt. Col. Roberts), Ken MacDonald (Maj. McKinley), Erville Alderson (Teacher), Bill Williams, **Robert Clarke** (Aides)

Those Endearing Young Charms (RKO, 1945) Executive Producer: Sid Rogell; Produced by Bert Granet; Directed by Lewis Allen; Screenplay: Jerome Chodorov; Based on the Play by Edward Chodorov; Photography: Ted Tetzlaff; Music: Roy Webb; Editor: Roland Gross

Cast: Robert Young (Hank), Laraine Day (Helen), Ann Harding (Mrs. Brandt), Marc Cramer (Capt. Larry Stowe), Anne Jeffreys (Suzanne), Bill Williams (Jerry), Glenn Vernon (Young Sailor), Norma Varden (Haughty Floor Lady), Lawrence Tierney (Ted), Vera Marshe (Dot), Larry Burke (Singer), Edmund Glover, **Robert Clarke** (Operations Officers), Johnny Strong, Paul Brinkman, George Holmes (Pilots)

Radio Stars on Parade (RKO, 1945) Produced by Ben Stoloff; Directed by Leslie Goodwins; Screenplay: Robert E. Kent & Monty Brice; Story: Robert E. Kent; Photography: Harry Walker; Music Director: C. Bakaleinikoff; Art Directors: Albert S. D'Agostino & Walter Keller; Editor: Edward W. Williams

Cast: Wally Brown (Jerry Miles), Alan Carney (Mike Strager), Frances Langford (Sally Baker), Don Wilson (Himself), Tony Romano (Romano), Rufe Davis (Pinky), **Robert Clarke** (Danny), Sheldon Leonard (Maddox), Max Wagner (George), Ralph Peters (Steve), Ralph Edwards & Co., Skinnay Ennis Band, Town Criers, Cappy

223

First Yank Into Tokyo (RKO, 1945) Screenplay & Produced by J. Robert Bren; Directed by Gordon Douglas; Story: J. Robert Bren & Gladys Atwater; Photography: Harry J. Wild; Music: Leigh Harline; Editor: Philip Martin
      Cast: Tom Neal (Maj. Ross), Barbara Hale (Abby Drake), Marc Cramer (Jardine), Richard Loo (Col. Okanura), Keye Luke (Haan-Soo), Leonard Strong (Maj. Nogira), Benson Fong (Capt. Ianabe), Clarence Lung (Maj. Ichibo), Keye Chang (Capt. Sato), Michael St. Angel (Capt. Andrew Kent), Edmund Glover, **Robert Clarke**, Johnny Strong, Eden Nicholas, Jimmy Jordan (Prisoners), Bruce Edwards (Capt. Harris), Selmer Jackson, John Hamilton, Russell Hicks, Beal Wong, Bob Chinn, Chet Vorovan

Man Alive (RKO, 1945) Produced by Robert Fellows; Directed by Ray Enright; Screenplay: Edwin Harvey Blum; Story: Jerry Cady & John Tucker Battle; Photography: Frank Redman; Music: Leigh Harline; Editor: Marvin Coil
      Cast: Pat O'Brien (Speed), Adolphe Menjou (Kismet), Ellen Drew (Connie), Rudy Vallee (Gordon Tolliver), Fortunio Bonanova (Prof. Zorado), Joseph Crehan (Doc Whitney), Jonathan Hale (Osborne), Minna Gombell (Aunt Sophie), Jason Robards (Fletcher), Jack Norton (Willie the Wino), Donn Gift (Messenger Boy), Myrna Dell (Sister), Carl "Alfalfa" Switzer (Ignatius), Gertrude Short (Frowsy Dame), **Robert Clarke** (Cabby), Robert E. Homans (Uncle Barney)

Wanderer of the Wasteland (RKO, 1945) Produced by Herman Schlom; Directed by Edward Killy & Wallace Grissell; Screenplay: Norman Houston; Based on the Novel by Zane Grey; Photography: Harry J. Wild; Music: Paul Sawtell; Music Director: C. Bakaleinikoff; Editor: J. R. Whittredge
      Cast: James Warren (Adam Larey), Richard Martin (Chito Rafferty), Audrey Long (Jean Collinshaw), Robert Barrat (Uncle Collinshaw), **Robert Clarke** (Jay Collinshaw), Harry Woods (Guerd Eliott), Minerva Urecal (Mama Rafferty), Harry D. Brown (Papa Rafferty), Tommy Cook (Chito as a Boy), Harry McKim (Adam as a Boy), Jason Robards (Dealer)

Sing Your Way Home (RKO, 1945) Produced by Bert Granet; Directed by Anthony Mann; Screenplay: William Bowers; Story: Edmund Joseph & Bart Lytton; Photography: Frank Redman; Music Director: C. Bakaleinikoff; Editor: Harry Marker
      Cast: Jack Haley (Steve), Marcy McGuire (Bridget), Glenn Vernon (Jimmy), Anne Jeffreys (Kay), Donna Lee (Terry), Pattie Brill (Dottie), Nancy Marlow (Patsy), James Jordan Jr. (Chuck), Emory Parnell (Captain), David Forrest (Windy), Ed Gargan (Jailer), **Robert Clarke** (Reporter)

A Game of Death (RKO, 1945) Executive Producer: Sid Rogell; Produced by Herman Schlom; Directed by Robert Wise; Screenplay: Norman Houston; Based on the Short Story "The Most Dangerous Game" by Richard Connell; Photography: J. Roy Hunt; Music: C. Bakaleinikoff; Editor: J. R. Whittredge
      Cast: John Loder (Don Rainsford), Audrey Long (Ellen Trowbridge), Edgar Barrier (Eric Kreiger), Russell Wade (Robert Trowbridge), Russell Hicks (Whitney),

Jason Robards (Captain), Gene Stutenroth [Roth] (Pleshke), Noble Johnson (Carib), **Robert Clarke** (Helmsman)

Bedlam (RKO, 1946) Executive Producer: Jack J. Gross; Produced by Val Lewton; Directed by Mark Robson; Screenplay: "Carlos Keith" [Val Lewton] & Mark Robson; Photography: Nicholas Musuraca; Music: Roy Webb; Editor: Lyle Boyer
      Cast: Boris Karloff (Master George Sims), Anna Lee (Nell Bowen), Billy House (Lord Mortimer), Richard Fraser (William Hannay), Glenn Vernon (The Gilded Boy), Ian Wolfe (Sidney Long), Jason Robards (Oliver Todd), Leyland Hodgson (John Wilkes), Joan Newton (Dorothea the Dove), Elizabeth Russell (Mistress Sims), **Robert Clarke** (Dan the Dog), Ellen Corby (Betty), Skelton Knaggs, Victor Holbrook, Larry Wheat, Bruce Edwards, John Meredith, John Beck, John Ince, John Goldsworthy, Polly Bailey, Foster Phinney, Donna Lee, Nan Leslie, Tom Noonan, George Holmes, Jimmy Jordan, Robert Manning, Frankie Dee, Frank Pharr, Harry Harvey, Victor Travers, James Logan, Betty Gillette

The Bamboo Blonde (RKO, 1946) Executive Producer: Sid Rogell; Produced by Herman Schlom; Directed by Anthony Mann; Screenplay: Olive Cooper & Lawrence Kimble; Based on the Story "Chicago Lulu" by Wayne Whittaker; Photography: Frank Redman; Music Director: C. Bakaleinikoff; Editor: Les Milbrook
      Cast: Frances Langford (Louise Anderson), Ralph Edwards (Eddie Clark), Russell Wade (Patrick Ransom, Jr.), Iris Adrian (Montana), Richard Martin (Jim Wilson), Jane Greer (Eileen Sawyer), Glenn Vernon (Shorty Parker), Paul Harvey (Patrick Ransom, Sr.), Regina Wallace (Mrs. Ransom), Jean Brooks (Marsha), Tom Noonan (Art Department), Eddie Acuff, Steve Barclay (MPs), Jason Robards (Col. Graham), Jimmy Jordan (Larry), Robert Manning (Ollie), **Robert Clarke** (Jonesy), Bruce Edwards (Lieutenant), Paul Brinkman (Jackie), Harry Harvey (Airport Clerk), Nan Leslie (Bit on Train), Walter Reed (Montgomery)

Lady Luck (RKO, 1946) Executive Producer: Robert Fellows; Produced by Warren Duff; Directed by Edwin L. Marin; Screenplay: Lynn Root & Frank Fenton; Story: Herbert Clyde Lewis; Photography: Lucien Andriot; Music: Leigh Harline; Editor: Ralph Dawson
      Cast: Robert Young (Scott), Barbara Hale (Mary), Frank Morgan (William Audrey), James Gleason (Sacramento Sam), Don Rice (Eddie), Harry Davenport (Judge Martin), Lloyd Corrigan (Little Joe), Teddy Hart (Little Guy), Joseph Vitale (Happy Johnson), Douglas Morrow (Dan Morgan), **Robert Clarke** (Southern Officer), Larry Wheat (Calm Card Player), Russell Simpson, Major Sam Harris, Carl Faulkner, Forbes Murray, Mary Field, Forrest Taylor, Dick Elliott, Jack Norton, Myrna Dell, Harry Harvey, Eddie Dunn, Lorin Raker, Cosmo Sardo, Nancy Saunders, Frank Dae

Ding Dong Williams (RKO, 1946) Produced by Herman Schlom; Directed by William Berke; Screenplay: Brenda Weisberg & M. Coates Webster; Based on Collier's Magazine Stories by Richard English; Photography: Frank Redman; Editor: Les Millbrook
      Cast: Glenn Vernon (Ding Dong Williams), Marcy McGuire (Angela), Felix

Bressart (Hugo), Anne Jeffreys (Vanessa), James Warren (Steve), William Davidson (Saul), Tom Noonan (Zang), Cliff Nazarro (Zing), Ruth Lee (Laura Cooper), Jason Robards (Kenmore), **Robert Clarke** (Band Leader), Bob Nolan and the Sons of the Pioneers, Richard Kirbel

Step by Step (RKO, 1946) Produced by Sid Rogell; Directed by Phil Rosen; Screenplay: Stuart Palmer; Story: George Callahan; Photography: Frank Redman; Music: Paul Sawtell; Editor: Robert Swink

Cast: Lawrence Tierney (Johnny Christopher), Anne Jeffreys (Evelyn Smith), Lowell Gilmore (Von Dorn), George Cleveland (Simpson), Jason Robards (Bruckner), Myrna Dell (Gretchen), Harry Harvey (Sen. Remmy), Addison Richards (James Blackton), Ray Walker (Jorgenson, F.B.I. Agent), John Hamilton (Capt. Edmunds), James Flavin, Pat Flaherty (Motorcycle Cops), Ralph Dunn (Patrol Car Cop), **Robert Clarke** (Interne)

Sunset Pass (RKO, 1946) Executive Producer: Sid Rogell; Produced by Herman Schlom; Directed by William Berke; Screenplay: Norman Houston; Based on the Novel by Zane Grey; Photography: Frank Redman; Music Director: C. Bakaleinikoff; Editor: Samuel E. Beetley

Cast: James Warren (Rocky), Nan Leslie (Jane), John Laurenz (Chito), Jane Greer (Helen), Robert Barrat (Curtis), Harry Woods (Cinnabar), **Robert Clarke** (Ash), Steve Brodie (Slagle), Harry Harvey (Doab), Slim Balch, Roy Bucko, Steve Stevens, George Plues, Clem Fuller, Bob Dyer, Artie Ortego, Buck Bucko (Posse Men), Carl Faulkner (Passenger), Robert Bray, Dennis Waters (Bank Clerks)

Genius at Work (RKO, 1946) Executive Producer: Sid Rogell; Produced by Herman Schlom; Directed by Leslie Goodwins; Screenplay: Robert E. Kent & Monte Brice; Photography: Robert de Grasse; Music Director: C. Bakaleinikoff; Editor: Marvin Coil

Cast: Wally Brown (Jerry Miles), Alan Carney (Mike Strager), Anne Jeffreys (Ellen Brent), Lionel Atwill (Latimer Marsh), Bela Lugosi (Stone), Marc Cramer (Police Lt. Rick Campbell), Ralph Dunn (Gilley), Jimmy Jordan (Page Boy), Phil Warren (Jennings), Peter Potter, **Robert Clarke** (Announcers), Warren Jackson, Ed Hart, Al Choals (Detectives), Irene Mack, George Holmes, Bonnie Blair, Larry Wheat, Forbes Murray, Kanza Omar, Bob O'Connor, Billy White, Harry Harvey, Eddie Borden, Muriel Kearney

Criminal Court (RKO, 1946) Produced by Martin Mooney; Directed by Robert Wise; Screenplay: Lawrence Kimble; Story: Earl Felton; Photography: Frank Redman; Music: Paul Sawtell; Editor: Robert Swink

Cast: Tom Conway (Steve Banes), Martha O'Driscoll (Georgia Gale), June Clayworth (Joan Mason), Robert Armstrong (Vic Wright), Addison Richards (District Attorney), Pat Gleason (Joe West), Steve Brodie (Frankie), Robert Warwick (Marquette), Phil Warren (Bill Brannegan), Joe Devlin (Brownie), Lee Bonnell (Gil Lambert), **Robert Clarke** (Dance Director)

226

San Quentin (RKO, 1946) Executive Producer: Sid Rogell; Produced by Martin Mooney; Directed by Gordon Douglas; Screenplay: Lawrence Kimble, Arthur A. Ross & Howard J. Green; Photography: Frank Redman; Music: Paul Sawtell; Art Directors: Albert S. D'Agostino & Lucius O. Croxton; Editor: Marvin Coil

      Cast: Lawrence Tierney (Jim Roland), Marian Carr (Betty Richards), Barton MacLane (Nick Taylor), Carol Forman (Ruthie), Richard Powers [Tom Keene] (Schaeffer), Joe Devlin (Broadway), Tony Barrett (Marlowe), Harry Shannon (Warden Kelly), Lee Bonnell (Carzoni), **Robert Clarke** (Tommy North), Raymond Burr (Jeff Torrance), Harry O. Tyler (Pete Moley), Selmer Jackson (Rev. Eckles), Byron Foulger (Mr. Dixon), Paul E. Burns (Fuller), Bobby Barber (Shorty), Fred Graham (Stand-in for Barton MacLane), Lewis E. Lawes (Himself)

The Farmer's Daughter (RKO, 1947) Produced by Dore Schary; Directed by H. C. Potter; Screenplay: Allen Rivkin & Laura Kerr; Based on the Play by Juhni Tervataa; Photography: Milton Krasner; Music: Leigh Harline; Music Director: C. Bakaleinikoff; Editor: Harry Marker

      Cast: Loretta Young (Katrin), Joseph Cotten (Glenn Morley), Ethel Barrymore (Mrs. Morley), Charles Bickford (Clancy), Rose Hobart (Virginia), Rhys Williams (Adolphe), Harry Davenport (Dr. Matthew Sutven), Tom Powers (Nordick), William Harrigan (Ward Hughes), Lex Barker (Olaf), Don Beddoe (Einar), Anna Q. Nilsson (Mrs. Holstrom), Thurston Hall (Wilbert Johnson), Keith Andes (Sven), Harry Shannon (Mr. Holstrom), James Arness (Peter), Cy Kendall (Sweeney), John Gallaudet (Van), William B. Davidson (Eckers), Frank Ferguson (Maatinaan), Charles Lane (Jackson), William Bakewell (Windor), **Robert Clarke** (Assistant Announcer), Carl Kent (Announcer), Jim Pierce (Cop)

Code of the West (RKO, 1947) Produced by Herman Schlom; Directed by William Berke; Screenplay: Norman Houston; Based on the Novel by Zane Grey; Photography: Jack Mackenzie; Music: Paul Sawtell; Editor: Ernie Leadlay

      Cast: James Warren (Bob Wade), Debra Alden (Ruth), John Laurenz (Chito), **Robert Clarke** (Harry), Steve Brodie (Saunders), Rita Lynn (Pepita), Carol Forman (Milly), Harry Woods (Hatfield), Raymond Burr (Carter), Harry Harvey (Stockton), Phil Warren (Wescott), Emmett Lynn (Doc Quinn)

In Room 303 (RKO short, 1947) Produced by George Bilson; Written & Directed by Hal Yates; Editor: Tholen Gladden

      Cast: Leon Errol, Harry Harvey, **Robert Clarke**, Paul Maxey, Gail Davis, Jay Norris, Dick Wessel, Peggy Maley

Thunder Mountain (RKO, 1947) Produced by Herman Schlom; Directed by Lew Landers; Screenplay: Norman Houston; Based on the Novel by Zane Grey; Photography: Jack Mackenzie; Music: Paul Sawtell; Music Director: C. Bakaleinikoff; Editor: Philip Martin

      Cast: Tim Holt (Marvin Hayden), Martha Hyer (Ellen Jorth), Richard Martin (Chito Rafferty), Steve Brodie (Chick Jorth), Richard Powers [Tom Keene] (Johnny Blue), Virginia Owen (Ginger Kelly), Harry Woods (Carson), Jason Robards (James

Gardner), **Robert Clarke** (Lee Jorth), Harry Harvey (Sheriff Bagley), Dick Elliott

Desperate (RKO, 1947) Produced by Michel Kraike; Directed by Anthony Mann; Screenplay: Harry Essex; Additional Dialogue: Martin Rackin; Story: Dorothy Atlas & Anthony Mann; Photography: George E. Diskant; Music: Paul Sawtell; Editor: Marston Fay

     Cast: Steve Brodie (Steve Randall), Audrey Long (Anne Randall), Raymond Burr (Walt Radak), Douglas Fowley (Pete), William Challee (Reynolds), Jason Robards (Ferrari), Freddie Steele (Shorty), Lee Frederick (Joe), Paul E. Burns (Uncle Jan), Ilka Gruning (Aunt Klara), Larry Nunn (Al Radak), Robert Bray (Policeman), Carl Kent (Detective), Carol Forman (Mrs. Roberts), Erville Alderson (Simon Pringle), Teddy Infuhr (Richard), Perc Launders (Manny), Ralf Harolde (Doctor), Kay Christopher (Nurse), Milt Kibbee (Mac), Dick Elliott (Hat Lewis), **Robert Clarke** (Bus Driver),

Under the Tonto Rim (RKO, 1947) Produced by Herman Schlom; Directed by Lew Landers; Screenplay: Norman Houston; Based on the Novel by Zane Grey; Photography: J. Roy Hunt; Music: Paul Sawtell; Music Director: C. Bakaleinikoff; Editor: Lyle Boyer

     Cast: Tim Holt (Brad Canfield), Nan Leslie (Lucy Dennison), Richard Martin (Chito), Richard Powers [Tom Keene] (Dennison), Carol Forman (Juanita), Tony Barrett (Roy Patton), Harry Harvey (Sheriff), Jason Robards (Capt. McClain), Lex Barker (Joe), **Robert Clarke** (Hooker), Jay Norris, Steve Savage, Herman Hack, Bud Osborne, David Sharpe

Dick Tracy Meets Gruesome (RKO, 1947) Produced by Herman Schlom; Directed by John Rawlins; Screenplay: Robertson White & Eric Taylor; Story: William H. Graffis & Robert E. Kent; Based on the Comic Strip by Chester Gould; Photography: Frank Redman; Music: Paul Sawtell; Editor: Elmo Williams

     Cast: Boris Karloff (Gruesome), Ralph Byrd (Dick Tracy), Anne Gwynne (Tess Trueheart), Edward Ashley (L. E. Thal), June Clayworth (Dr. I. M. Learned), Lyle Latell (Pat Patton), Tony Barrett (Melody), Skelton Knaggs (X-Ray), Jim Nolan (Dan Sterne), Joseph Crehan (Chief Brandon), Milton Parsons (Dr. A. Tomic), Lex Barker (Ambulance Driver), Harry Strang (Tim), **Robert Clarke** (Fred [Police Chemist]), Sean McClory (Carney), Robert Bray, Ernie Adams, Jason Robards, Bert Roach

If You Knew Susie (RKO, 1948) Produced by Eddie Cantor; Directed by Gordon Douglas; Screenplay: Warren Wilson & Oscar Brodney; Photography: Frank Redman; Music Director: C. Bakaleinikoff; Editor: Philip Martin

     Cast: Eddie Cantor (Sam Parker), Joan Davis (Susie Parker), Allyn Joslyn (Mike Garrett), Charles Dingle (Mr. Whitley), Phil Brown (Joe Collins), Sheldon Leonard (Steve Garland), Joe Sawyer (Zero Zantini), Douglas Fowley (Marty), Margaret Kerry (Marjorie Parker), Dick Humphreys (Handy Clinton), Howard Freeman (Mr. Clinton), Mabel Paige (Grandma), Sig Ruman (Count Alexis), Fritz Feld (Chez Henri), **Robert Clarke** (Orchestra Leader), Isabel Randolph, Bobby Driscoll, Earle Hodgins, Charles Halton, Jason Robards, Harry Harvey, George Chandler, Don Beddoe, Addison Richards, Ellen Corby, Syd Saylor, Tom Keene, J. Farrell MacDonald

Fighting Father Dunne (RKO, 1948) Produced by Jack J. Gross & Phil L. Ryan; Directed by Ted Tetzlaff; Screenplay: Martin Rackin & Frank Davis; Story: William Rankin; Photography: George E. Diskant; Music: Roy Webb; Editor: Frederic Knudtson

Cast: Pat O'Brien (Father Dunne), Darryl Hickman (Matt Davis), Charles Kemper (Emmett Mulvey), Una O'Connor (Miss O'Rourke), Arthur Shields (Mr. O'Donnell), Harry Shannon (John Lee), Joe Sawyer (Steve Davis), Anna Q. Nilsson (Mrs. Knudson), Donn Gift (Jimmy), Myrna Dell (Paula), Ruth Donnelly (Kate Mulvey), Jim Nolan (Danny Briggs), Billy Cummings (Tony), Billy Gray (Chip), Eric Roberts (Monk), Gene Collins (Lefty), Lester Matthews (Archbishop), Griff Barnett (Governor), **Robert Clarke**, Robert Bray (Priests), Jason Robards, Rudy Whistler, Frank Ferguson

Return of the Bad Men (RKO, 1948) Executive Producer: Jack J. Gross; Produced by Nat Holt; Directed by Ray Enright; Screenplay: Charles O'Neal, Jack Natteford & Luci Ward; Story: Jack Natteford & Luci Ward; Photography: J. Roy Hunt; Music: Paul Sawtell; Editor: Samuel E. Beetley

Cast: Randolph Scott (Vance), Robert Ryan (Sundance Kid), Anne Jeffreys (Cheyenne), George "Gabby" Hayes (John Pettit), Jacqueline White (Madge Allen), Steve Brodie (Cole Younger), Tom Keene (Jim Younger), Robert Bray (John Younger), Lex Barker (Emmett Dalton), Walter Reed (Bob Dalton), Michael Harvey (Grat Dalton), Dean White (Billy the Kid), Robert Armstrong (Wild Bill Doolin), Tom Tyler (Wild Bill Yeager), Lew Harvey (Arkansas Kid), Gary Gray (Johnny), Walter Baldwin (Muley Wilson), Minna Gombell (Emily), **Robert Clarke** (Dave), Jason Robards (Judge Harper), Harry Shannon (Wade Templeton), Forrest Taylor (Farmer)

Beyond Glory (Paramount, 1948) Produced by Robert Fellows; Directed by John Farrow; Screenplay: Jonathan Latimer, Charles Marquis Warren & William W. Haines; Photography: John F. Seitz; Music: Victor Young; Editor: Eda Warren; 82 minutes

Cast: Alan Ladd (Capt. Rocky Gilman), Donna Reed (Ann Daniels), George Macready (Maj. Gen. Bond), George Coulouris (Lew Proctor), Harold Vermilyea (Raymond Denmore Sr.), Henry Travers (Pop Dewing), Luis Van Rooten (Dr. White), Tom Neal (Capt. Harry Daniels), Conrad Janis (Raymond Denmore Jr.), Margaret Field (Cora), Paul Lees (Miller), Dick Hogan (Cadet Sgt. Eddie Loughlin), Audie Murphy (Cadet Thomas), Geraldine Wall (Mrs. Daniels), Charles Evans (Mr. Julian), Russell Wade (A Cadet), Steve Pendleton (Gen. Presscott), Noel Neill (Party Girl), **Robert Clarke**, Kenneth Tobey (Bits)

Ladies of the Chorus (Columbia, 1948) Produced by Harry A. Romm; Directed by Phil Karlson; Screenplay: Harry Sauber & Joseph Carole; Story: Harry Sauber; Photography: Frank Redman; Music Director: Mischa Bakaleinikoff; Editor: Richard Fantl

Cast: Adele Jergens (May Martin), Marilyn Monroe (Peggy Martin), Rand Brooks (Randy Carroll), Nana Bryant (Mrs. Carroll), Eddie Carr (Billy Mackay), Steven Geray (Salisbury), Bill Edwards (Alan Wakefield), Marjorie Hoshelle (Bubbles LaRue), Frank Scannell (Joe), Dave Barry (Hipple), Alan Barry (Hipple, Jr.), Myron Healey (Tom Lawson), Gladys Blake (Flower Shop Girl), **Robert Clarke** (Peter Winthrop),

Almira Sessions, Claire Whitney

The Judge Steps Out (RKO, 1949) Produced by Michel Kraike; Directed by Boris Ingster; Screenplay: Boris Ingster & Alexander Knox; Based on a Story by Boris Ingster; Photography: Robert de Grasse; Music: Leigh Harline; Editor: Les Millbrook
    Cast: Alexander Knox (Judge Bailey), Ann Sothern (Peggy), George Tobias (Mike), Sharyn Moffett (Nan), Florence Bates (Chita), Frieda Inescort (Evelyn Bailey), Myrna Dell (Mrs. Winthrop), Ian Wolfe (Hector Brown), H. B. Warner (Chief Justice Haynes), Martha Hyer (Catherine Bailey), James Warren (John Struthers III), Whitford Kane (Dr. Boyd), Harry Hayden (Judge Davis), Anita Bolster (Martha), **Robert Clarke** (Reporter)

Riders of the Range (RKO, 1950) Produced by Herman Schlom; Directed by Lesley Selander; Screenplay: Norman Houston; Photography: J. Roy Hunt; Music: Paul Sawtell; Music Director: C. Bakaleinikoff; Editor: Robert Swink
    Cast: Tim Holt (Kansas Jones), Richard Martin (Chito), Jacqueline White (Dusty Willis), Reed Hadley (Clint Burroughs), Robert Barrat (Sheriff), Tom Tyler (Ringo Kid), **Robert Clarke** (Harry Willis), William Tannen (Trump Dixon)

Champagne for Caesar (United Artists, 1950) Executive Producer: Harry M. Popkin; Produced by George Moskov; Directed by Richard Whorf; Story & Screenplay: Hans Jacoby & Fred Brady; Photography: Paul Ivano; Music: Dmitri Tiomkin; Editor: Hugh Bennett
    Cast: Ronald Colman (Beauregard Bottomley), Celeste Holm (Flame O'Neil), Vincent Price (Burnbridge Waters), Barbara Britton (Gwenn Bottomley), Art Linkletter (Happy Hogan), Gabriel Heatter, George Fisher (Announcers), Byron Foulger (Gerald), Ellye Marshall (Frosty), Vici Raaf (Waters' Secretary), John Eldredge, Lyle Talbot, George Leigh, John Hart (Executives), Mel Blanc (Caesar's Voice), **Robert Clarke** (Actor in Drive-in Movie)

A Modern Marriage (Monogram, 1950) Produced by David Diamond; Directed by Paul Landres; Screenplay: Sam Roeca & George Wallace Sayre; Photography: William Sickner; Music: Edward J. Kay; Art Director: David Milton; Editor: Philip Cahn
    Cast: Reed Hadley (Dr. Donald Andrews), Margaret Field (Evelyn Brown), **Robert Clarke** (Bill Burke), Nana Bryant (Mrs. Brown), Charles Smith (Jimmy Watson), Dick Elliott (Mr. Burke), Lelah Tyler (Mrs. Burke), Pattee Chapman (Mary), Frank Fenton (Mr. Brown), Edward Keane (Dr. Connors)

Outrage (RKO, 1950) Associate Producer: Malvin Wald; A Collier Young (Filmakers) Production; Directed by Ida Lupino; Screenplay: Collier Young, Malvin Wald & Ida Lupino; Photography: Archie Stout; Production Design: Harry Horner; Music: Paul Sawtell; Editor: Harvey Manger
    Cast: Mala Powers (Ann Walton), Tod Andrews (Ferguson), **Robert Clarke** (Jim Owens), Raymond Bond (Eric Walton), Lilian Hamilton (Mrs. Walton), Rita Lupino (Stella Carter), Hal March (Sgt. Hendrix), Kenneth Patterson (Mr. Harrison), Jerry Paris (Frank Marini), Angela Clarke (Mrs. Harrison), Roy Engel (Sheriff Hanlon), Robin

Camp (Shoeshine Boy), William Challee (Lee Wilkins), Tristram Coffin (Judge McKenzie), Jerry Hausner (Mr. Denker), Bernie Marcus (Dr. Hoffman), Joyce McCluskey (Office Worker), Victor Perrin (Andrew), Beatrice Warde (Marge), Albert Mellen (Scarface)

The Man from Planet X (United Artists, 1951) Written & Produced by Aubrey Wisberg & Jack Pollexfen; Directed by Edgar G. Ulmer; Photography: John L. Russell; Music: Charles Koff; Editor: Fred R. Feitshans Jr.; Assistant Director: Les Guthrie

Cast: **Robert Clarke** (John Lawrence), Margaret Field (Enid Elliot), Raymond Bond (Prof. Elliot), William Schallert (Dr. Mears), Roy Engel (Tommy, the Constable), David Ormont (Inspector), Gilbert Fallman (Dr. Blane), George Davis (Geordie), Tom Daly, June Jeffery

Hard, Fast and Beautiful (RKO, 1951) Associate Producer: Norman Cook; Produced by Collier Young; Directed by Ida Lupino; Screenplay: Martha Wilkerson; Based on the Novel "Mother of a Champion" by John R. Tunis; Photography: Archie Stout; Music: Roy Webb; Editor: William Ziegler

Cast: Claire Trevor (Milly Farley), Sally Forrest (Florence Farley), Carleton G. Young (Fletcher Locke), **Robert Clarke** (Gordon McKay), Kenneth Patterson (Will Farley), Marcella Cisney (Miss Martin), Joseph Kearns (J. R. Carpenter), William Hudson (Interne), George Fisher (Announcer), Arthur Little Jr. (Commentator), Bert Whitley (Young Official), Edwin Reimers (Announcer), Ida Lupino, Robert Ryan (Cameos)

Casa Manana (Monogram, 1951) Produced by Lindsley Parsons; Directed by Jean Yarbrough; Screenplay: Bill Raynor; Photography: William Sickner; Editor: Ace Herman

Cast: **Robert Clarke** (Larry), Virginia Welles (Linda), Robert Karnes (Horace), Tony Roux (Pedro), Carol Brewster (Honey), Paul Maxey (Maury), Jean Richey (Marge), Rio Brothers, Eddie Le Baron Orchestra, Spade Cooley, Yadira Jiminez, Zarco & D'Lores, Mercer Brothers, Armando & Lita, Betty & Beverly, Olga Perez, Davis & Johnson

Pistol Harvest (RKO, 1951) Produced by Herman Schlom; Directed by Lesley Selander; Screenplay: Norman Houston; Photography: J. Roy Hunt; Music: Paul Sawtell; Director: C. Bakaleinikoff; Editor: Douglas Biggs

Cast: Tim Holt (Tim Holt), Richard Martin (Chito), Joan Dixon (Felice), Guy Edward Hearn (Terry Moran), Mauritz Hugo (Elias Norton), **Robert Clarke** (Jack Green), William (Billy) Griffith (Prouty), Bob Wilke (Andy Baylor), Joan Freeman (Felice as a Girl), Harper Carter (Johnny), Herrick Herrick (Capt. Rand), Lee Phelps

Street Bandits (Republic, 1951) Produced by William Lackey; Directed by R. G. Springsteen; Screenplay: Milton Raison; Photography: John MacBurnie; Music: Stanley Wilson; Editor: Arthur Roberts

Cast: Penny Edwards (Mildred Anderson), **Robert Clarke** (Fred Palmer), Ross Ford (Tom Reagan), Roy Barcroft (Monk Walter), John Eldredge (L. T. Mitchell),

Helen Wallace (Mrs. Martha Palmer), Arthur Walsh (Arnold Black), Harry Hayden (William Carrington), Emmett Vogan (Brownell), Jane Adams (Jane Phillips), Charles Wagenheim, Richard Bartlett, Norman Field, Robert Long, Dick Cogan

The Valparaiso Story (Roland Reed Productions, 1951) Produced by Roland Reed; Directed by Frank Strayer; Makeup: Jack P. Pierce
　　　Cast: **Robert Clarke**, Marjorie Lord, Jimmy Lloyd, Margaret Field, Tom Neal, Clark Howat

Tales of Robin Hood (Lippert, 1951) Produced by Hal Roach Jr.; Directed by James Tinling; Story & Screenplay: Le Roy H. Zehren; Photography: George Robinson; Music: Leon Klatzkin; Editor: Richard Currier; Assistant Director: Lester Guthrie
　　　Cast: **Robert Clarke** (Robin Hood), Mary Hatcher (Maid Marian), Paul Cavanagh (Sir Gui de Clairmont), Wade Crosby (Little John), Whit Bissell (Will Stutely), Ben Welden (Friar Tuck), Robert Bice (Will Scarlet), Keith Richards (Sir Alan de Beaulieu), Bruce Lester (Alan A. Dale), Tiny Stowe (Sheriff of Nottingham), Lester Matthews (Sir Hugh Fitzwalter), John Vosper (Earl of Chester), Norman Bishop (Much), Margia Dean (Betty), Lorin Raker (Landlord), George Slocum (Captain of the Guards), John Doucette (Wilfred), John Harmon (Robber), Matt McHugh (Guard), David Stollery (Robin as a Boy)

The Fabulous Senorita (Republic, 1952) Produced by Sidney Picker; Directed by R. G. Springsteen; Screenplay: Charles E. Roberts & Jack Townley; Story: Charles R. Marion & Jack Townley; Photography: Jack Marta; Music: Stanley Wilson; Editor: Tony Martinelli
　　　Cast: Estelita (Estelita Rodriguez), **Robert Clarke** (Jerry Taylor), Nestor Paiva (Senor Rodriguez), Marvin Kaplan (Clifford), Rita Moreno (Manuela), Leon Belasco (Senor Gonzales), Tito Renaldo (Pedro), Tom Powers (Mr. Delaney), Emory Parnell (Dean Bradshaw), Olin Howlin (Justice of the Peace), Vito Scotti (Esteban Gonzales), Martin Garralaga (Police Capt. Garcia), Nita Del Rey, David Sharpe, Dale Van Sickel

Captive Women (RKO, 1952) Associate Producer: Albert Zugsmith; Written & Produced by Aubrey Wisberg & Jack Pollexfen; Directed by Stuart Gilmore; Photography: Paul Ivano; Music: Charles Koff; Editor: Fred R. Feitshans Jr.
　　　Cast: **Robert Clarke** (Rob), Margaret Field (Ruth), Gloria Saunders (Catherine), Ron Randell (Riddon), Stuart Randall (Gordon), Robert Bice (Bram), William Schallert (Carver), Paula Dorety, Chili Williams (Captives), Eric Colmar (Sabron), Douglas Evans (Jason), Marshall Bradford (Councillor), Leah [Lia] Waggner (Mutate), George Bruggeman (Norm Hunter), John Close (Up-River Man)

Sword of Venus (RKO, 1953) Associate Producer: Albert Zugsmith; Written & Produced by Aubrey Wisberg & Jack Pollexfen; Directed by Harold Daniels; Photography: John L. Russell; Music: Charles Koff; Editor: W. Donn Hayes
　　　Cast: **Robert Clarke** (Robert Dantes), Catherine McLeod (Claire), Dan O'Herlihy (Danglars), William Schallert (Valmont), Marjorie Stapp (Duchess de

Villefort), Merritt Stone (Fernand), Renne de Marco (Suzette), Eric Colmar (Jean Goriot), Stuart Randall (Hugo), Marshall Bradford (Physician), Ken Terrell (Coachman), Jack Reitzen (Innkeeper), Donald Brodie (Jailer), Gerald Oliver Smith (Sir Norman Blandish), Wilson Benge (Butler), Al Hill (Sailor on Beach), Eddie Parker, Sol Gorss (Servants in Swordfight)

Blades of the Musketeers (Howco, 1953) (Theatrical release of the TV movie *Three Musketeers*) Produced by Hal Roach Jr.; Directed by Budd Boetticher; Screenplay: Roy Hamilton; Based on the Novel by Alexandre Dumas; Photography: Benjamin Kline; Editor: Herb Smith

      Cast: **Robert Clarke** (D'Artagnan), John Hubbard (Athos), Mel Archer (Porthos), Keith Richards (Aramis), Paul Cavanagh (Prime Minister Richelieu), Don Beddoe (King Louis XIII), Marjorie Lord (Queen Anne), Lyn Thomas (Constance Bonacieux), Kristine Miller (Lady DeWinter), Charles Lang (Duke of Buckingham), Pete Mamakos (Rochefort), Hank Patterson (Fisherman), James Craven, Byron Foulger

Captain John Smith and Pocahontas (United Artists, 1953) Presented by Reliance Pictures; Written & Produced by Aubrey Wisberg & Jack Pollexfen; Directed by Lew Landers; Photography: Ellis Carter; Music: Albert Glasser; Editor: Fred R. Feitshans Jr.

      Cast: Anthony Dexter (Capt. John Smith), Jody Lawrence (Pocahontas), Alan Hale Jr. (Fleming), **Robert Clarke** (John Rolfe), Stuart Randall (Opechanco), James Seay (Wingfield), Philip Van Zandt (Davis), Shepard Menken (Nantaquas), Douglass Dumbrille (Powhatan), Anthony Eustrel (King James), Henry Rowland (Turnbull), Eric Colmar (Kemp), Joan Nixon (Lacuma), Franchesca di Scaffa, William Cottrell

Oil Town, USA (Great Commission Films, 1953) Screenwriter, Producer & Director: Dick Ross; Musical Director: Tim Spencer

      Cast: Colleen Townsend, Paul Power, Georgia Lee, **Robert Clarke**, Redd Harper, Cindy Walker, Billy Graham, The Sons of the Pioneers, Ralph Ward

The Body Beautiful (Phoenix, 1953) A Sam Kubetz Production; Produced & Directed by Max Nosseck; Screenplay: Nat Tanchuck & Arnold Philips

      Cast: Susan Morrow, **Robert Clarke**, Noreen Nash, Paul Guilfoyle, O. Z. Whitehead, June Smaney, Dolores Fuller

The Black Pirates (Lippert, 1954) Produced by Robert L. Lippert; Directed by Allen Miner; Screenplay: Fred Freiberger & Al C. Ward; Based on the Story "El Torbellino" by Johnston McCulley; Photography: Gil Warrenton; Music: Antonio Dias-Conde; Editor: Carl L. Pierson

      Cast: Anthony Dexter (Dargo), Martha Roth (Juanita), Lon Chaney Jr. (Felipe), **Robert Clarke** (Manuel), Victor Manuel Mendoza (Castro), Alfonso Bedoya (Garza), Toni Gerry (Carlotta), Eddy Dutko (Little Dog)

Her Twelve Men (MGM, 1954) Produced by John Houseman; Directed by Robert Z. Leonard; Screenplay: William Roberts & Laura Z. Hobson; Story: Louise Baker;

Photography: Joseph Ruttenberg; Music: Bronislau Kaper; Editor: George Boemler

Cast: Greer Garson (Jan Stewart), Robert Ryan (Joe Hargrave), Barry Sullivan (Richard Y. Oliver, Sr.), Richard Haydn (Dr. Avord Barrett), Barbara Lawrence (Barbara Dunning), James Arness (Ralph Munsey), Rex Thompson (Homer Curtis), Tim Considine (Richard Y. Oliver, Jr.), David Stollery (Jeff Carlin), Frances Bergen (Sylvia Carlin), Ian Wolfe (Roger Frane), Donald MacDonald (Bobby Lennox), **Robert Clarke** (Prince), Dale Hartleben, Ivan Triesault, Stuffy Singer, Peter Votrian, Peter Roman, Kate Lawson, Vernon Rich, Peter Adams, Sandy Descher, John Dodsworth, Phyllis Stanley, Edgar Dearing, Ron Rondell

The Benny Goodman Story (Universal, 1955) Produced by Aaron Rosenberg; Screenplay & Directed by Valentine Davies; Photography: William Daniels; Music: Joseph Gershenson, Henry Mancini, Sol Yaged, Alan Harding & Harold Brown; Editor: Russell Schoengarth

Cast: Steve Allen (Benny Goodman), Donna Reed (Alice Hammond), Berta Gersten (Mom Goodman), Herbert Anderson (John Hammond), Robert F. Simon (Pop Goodman), Sammy Davis, Sr. (Fletcher Henderson), Dick Winslow (Gil Rodin), Barry Truex (Benny Goodman at 16), David Kasday (Benny Goodman at 10), Hy Averback (Willard Alexander), Wilton Graff (Mr. Hammond), Shep Menken (Harry Goodman), Louise Lorimer (Mrs. Hammond), Harry James, Martha Tilton, Gene Krupa, Lionel Hampton, Ziggy Elman, Ben Pollack, Teddy Wilson, Edward "Kid" Ory, Benny Goodman (Themselves), **Robert Clarke** (Roger Gillespie), Cynthia Patrick

King of the Carnival (Republic serial, 1955) Associate Producer & Director: Franklin Adreon; Screenplay: Ronald Davidson; Photography: Bud Thackery; Music: R. Dale Butts; Editor: Joseph Harrison; 12 chapters

Cast: Harry Lauter (Bert King), Fran Bennett (June Edwards), Keith Richards (Daley), Robert Shayne (Jess Carter), Gregory Gay (Zorn), Rick Vallin (Art Kerr), **Robert Clarke** (Jim Hayes), Terry Frost (Travis), Mauritz Hugo (Sam), Lee Roberts (Hank), Chris Mitchell (Bill), Stuart Whitman (Mac), Tom Steele (Matt Winston), George DeNormand (Garth), Bill Scully (Burton), Tom McDonough (Hal), Bert LeBaron, Eddie Parker (Riggers)

Outlaw Queen (Globe Releasing Corp., 1956) Produced by Ronnie Ashcroft; Directed by Herbert Greene; Screenplay: Pete La Roche; 70 minutes

Cast: Andrea King (Christina), Harry James (Rick Mason), **Robert Clarke** (John Andrews), Jim Harakas (Jim), Andy Ladas (Andy), Kenne Duncan (Sheriff), I. Stanford Jolley (Conway), William Murphy (Brandon), Vince Barnett (Gambler), Hal Peary (Bartender), John Heldring (Bank Manager)

Band of Angels (Warners, 1957) Directed by Raoul Walsh; Screenplay: John Twist, Ivan Goff & Ben Roberts; Based on the Novel by Robert Penn Warren; Photography: Lucien Ballard; Music: Max Steiner; Editor: Folmar Blangsted

Cast: Clark Gable (Hamish Bond), Yvonne De Carlo (Amantha Starr), Sidney Poitier (Rau-Ru), Efrem Zimbalist Jr. (Ethan Sears), Rex Reason (Seth Parton), Patric

Knowles (Charles de Marigny), Andrea King (Miss Idell), Torin Thatcher (Capt. Canavan), William Forrest (Aaron Starr), Raymond Bailey (Mr. Stuart), Ray Teal (Mr. Calloway), Carolle Drake (Michele), Russell Evans (Jimmee), Marshall Bradford (Gen. Butler), Juanita Moore (Budge), Roy Barcroft (Gillespie), **Robert Clarke** (Friend), Bob Steele, Zon Murray (Privates), Ann Doran (Mrs. Morton), William Schallert (Lieutenant), Charles Horvath (Soldier)

My Man Godfrey (Universal, 1957) Produced by Ross Hunter; Directed by Henry Koster; New Screenplay: Everett Freeman, Peter Berneis & William Bowers; Based on the Novel by Eric Hatch and the Screenplay by Morris Ryskind & Eric Hatch; Photography: William Daniels; Music: Frank Skinner; Editor: Milton Carruth
      Cast: June Allyson (Irene Bullock), David Niven (Godfrey), Jessie Royce Landis (Angelica Bullock), Robert Keith (Alexander Bullock), Eva Gabor (Francesca), Jay Robinson (Vincent), Martha Hyer (Cordelia Bullock), Jeff Donnell (Molly), Herbert Anderson (Hubert), Eric Sinclair (Brent), Dabbs Greer (Lt. O'Connor), **Robert Clarke** (George), William Hudson (Howard), Richard Deacon (Farnsworth), Robert Foulk (Motor Cop), Fred Coby, Jack Mather, Voltaire Perkins

The Helen Morgan Story (Warners, 1957) Produced by Martin Rackin; Directed by Michael Curtiz; Screenplay: Oscar Saul, Dean Reisner, Stephen Longstreet & Nelson Gidding; Photography: Ted McCord; Art Director: John Beckman; Editor: Frank Bracht
      Cast: Ann Blyth (Helen Morgan), Paul Newman (Larry Maddux), Richard Carlson (Russell Wade), Gene Evans (Whitey Krause), Alan King (Ben Weaver), Cara Williams (Dolly), Virginia Vincent (Sue), Walter Woolf King (Ziegfeld), Dorothy Green (Mrs. Wade), Ed Platt (Haggerty), Warren Douglas (Mark Hellinger), Sammy White (Sammy), Peggy De Castro, Cherie De Castro, Babette De Castro (Singers), Jimmy McHugh, Rudy Vallee, Walter Winchell (Themselves), **Robert Clarke** (Guest), Herb Vigran, Tito Vuolo, Joe Besser, Walter Reed, Paul Bryar, Iris Adrian

The Deep Six (Warners, 1958) Produced by Martin Rackin; Directed by Rudolph Maté; Screenplay: John Twist, Harry Brown & Martin Rackin; Based on the Novel by Martin Dibner; Photography: John Seitz; Music: David Buttolph; Editor: Roland Gross
      Cast: Alan Ladd (Alec Austen), Dianne Foster (Susan Cahill), William Bendix (Frenchy Shapiro), Keenan Wynn (Lt. Comdr. Edge), James Whitmore (Comdr. Meredith), Efrem Zimbalist Jr. (Lt. Blanchard), Joey Bishop (Ski Krakowski), Barbara Eiler (Clair Innes), Ross Bagdasarian (Slobodjian), Jeanette Nolan (Mrs. Austen), Walter Reed (Paul Clemson), Peter Hansen (Lt. Dooley), Richard Crane (Lt. [jg] Swanson), Morris Miller (Collins), Perry Lopez (Al Mendoza), Warren Douglas (Pilot), Nestor Paiva (Pappa Tatos), **Robert Clarke** (Ens. David Clough), Paul Picerni (Merchant Marine), Ann Doran (Elsie), Jerry Mathers (Steve)

The Astounding She-Monster (AIP, 1958) Produced & Directed by Ronnie Ashcroft; Story & Screenplay: Frank Hall; Photography: William C. Thompson; Music: Guenther Kauer

Cast: **Robert Clarke** (Dick Cutler), Kenne Duncan (Nat Burdell), Marilyn Harvey (Margaret Chaffee), Jeanne Tatum (Esther Malone), Shirley Kilpatrick (The She-Monster), Ewing Brown (Brad Conley), Loraine Ashcroft (Shirley Kilpatrick's Double), Scott Douglas (Pre-Credits Narrator), Al Avalon (Other Narration)

A Date With Death (Pacific International, 1959) Produced by William S. Edwards; Directed by Harold Daniels; Screenplay: Robert C. Dennis
    Cast: Gerald Mohr (Mike Mason), Liz Renay (Paula Warren), Harry Lauter (George Caddell), Stephanie Farnay (Edith Dale), Ed Erwin (Art Joslin), **Robert Clarke** (Joe Emanuel), Boyd "Red" Morgan (Urbano), Lew Markman (Potter), Tony Redman (Mayor Langlie), Frank Bellew (Weylin), William Purdy (Huber), Ray Dearholt (Sam), Melford Lehrman (Bender)

The Hideous Sun Demon (Pacific International, 1959) Associate Producer: Robin C. Kirkman; Produced by **Robert Clarke**; Directed by **Robert Clarke** & Tom Boutross; Screenplay: E. S. Seeley Jr.; Additional Dialogue: Doane Hoag; Original Idea: **Robert Clarke** & Phil Hiner; Photography: John Morrill, Vilis Lapenieks & Stan Follis; Production Manager: Robin C. Kirkman; Music: John Seely; Editor: Tom Boutross
    Cast: **Robert Clarke** (Dr. Gilbert McKenna), Patricia Manning (Ann Lansing), Nan Peterson (Trudy Osborne), Patrick Whyte (Dr. Frederick Buckell), Fred La Porta (Dr. Jacob Hoffman), Peter Similuk (George), Bill Hampton [Bill White] (Police Lieutenant), Robert Garry (Dr. Stern), Donna King Conkling (Susie's Mother), Xandra Conkling (Susie), Del Courtney (Radio Announcer), Pearl Driggs (Woman on Hospital Roof), David Sloan (Newsboy), Cass Richards [Richard Cassarino], Robin Kirkman, Ron Honthaner, Doug Menville (Cops), Marilyn King (Singing Voice of Nan Peterson), Darryl Westbrook, Helen Joseph, Fran Leighton, Bob Hafner, Bill Currie, John Murphy, Tony Hilder, Chuck Newell

Girl With an Itch (Howco, 1959) A Don-Tru [Don & Leonard Jones & Truman Hendrix] Production; Executive Producers: R. Crane & Don Jones; Produced & Directed by Ronnie Ashcroft; Screenplay: Peter Perry, Jr., E. Shayer Heath & J. M. Kude; Based on the Story "Girl on the Highway" by Ralph S. Whitting; Photography: Brydon Baker; Music: Guenther Kauer; Sound: Dale Knight
    Cast: Kathy Marlowe, Robert Armstrong, **Robert Clarke** (Ory), Scott Douglass, Patti Gallager, Sarah Padden, Clem Bevans, Dick Crane, Peter Perry Jr., Carleton Crane, Merle Peters, Sandra Giles

The FBI Story (Warners, 1959) Produced & Directed by Mervyn LeRoy; Screenplay: Richard L. Breen & John Twist; Based on the Book by Don Whitehead; Photography: Joseph Biroc; Music: Max Steiner; Editor: Philip W. Anderson
    Cast: James Stewart (Chip Hardesty), Vera Miles (Lucy Hardesty), Murray Hamilton (Sam Crandall), Larry Pennell (George Crandall), Nick Adams (Jack Graham), Diane Jergens (Jennie as an Adult), Jean Willes (Anna Sage), Joyce Taylor (Anne as an Adult), Victor Millan (Mario), Parley Baer (Harry Dakins), Fay Roope (McCutcheon), Robert Gist (Medicine Salesman), Buzz Martin (Mike as an Adult), Ann Doran (Mrs. Ballard), Forrest Taylor (Wedding Minister), Scott Peters (Dillinger),

William Phipps (Baby Face Nelson), **Robert Clarke** (FBI Man), Luana Anders (Mrs. Graham), Terry Frost (Craig), Roy Thinnes, Judd Holdren (Guests at Party)

Cash McCall (Warners, 1959) Produced by Henry Blanke; Directed by Joseph Pevney; Screenplay: Lenore Coffee, Marion Hargrove; Based on a Novel by Cameron Hawley; Photography: George Folsey; Music: Max Steiner; Editor: Philip W. Anderson
      Cast: James Garner (Cash McCall), Natalie Wood (Lory Austen), Nina Foch (Maude Kennard), Dean Jagger (Grant Austen), E. G. Marshall (Winston Conway), Henry Jones (Gil Clark), Otto Kruger (Will Atherson), Roland Winters (Gen. Danvers), Edward C. Platt (Harrison Glenn), Edgar Stehli (Mr. Pierce), Linda Watkins (Miriam Austen), Parley Baer (Harvey Bannon), Dabbs Greer, Olan Soule, **Robert Clarke**, Walter Coy

Timbuktu (United Artists, 1959) Produced by Edward Small; Directed by Jacques Tourneur; Screenplay: Anthony Veiller & Paul Dudley; Photography: Maury Gertsman; Music: Gerald Fried; Editor: Grant Whytock
      Cast: Victor Mature (Mike Conway), Yvonne De Carlo (Natalie Dufort), George Dolenz (Capt. Dufort), John Dehner (Emir), Marcia Henderson (Jeanne Marat), James Foxx (Lt. Marat), Leonard Mudie (Mohamet Adani), Paul Wexler (Suleiman), **Robert Clarke** (Capt. Girard), Willard Sage (Maj. Leroux), Mark Dana (Capt. Rimbaud), Larry Perron (Dagana), Steve Darrell (Nazir), Larry Chance (Ahmed), Allan Pinson (Sgt. Trooper)

Beyond the Time Barrier (AIP, 1960) Executive Producers: John Miller & Robert L. Madden; Produced by **Robert Clarke**; Directed by Edgar G. Ulmer; Story & Screenplay: Arthur C. Pierce; Photography: Meredith M. Nicholson; Music Composed & Conducted by Darrell Calker; Editor: Jack Ruggiero; Makeup: Jack P. Pierce
      Cast: **Robert Clarke** (Maj. William Allison), Darlene Tompkins (Princess Trirene), Arianne Arden (Markova), Vladimir Sokoloff (The Supreme), Stephen Bekassy (Karl Kruse), John van Dreelen (Dr. Bourman), Boyd "Red" Morgan (The Captain), Ken Knox (Col. Martin), Don Flournoy, Tom Ravick, Arthur C. Pierce (Mutants), Neil Fletcher (Air Force Chief of Staff), Jack Herman (Dr. Richman), William Shepard (Gen. York), James Altgens (Secretary Lloyd Patterson), John Loughney (Gen. LaMont), Russell Marker (Col. Curtis)

The Incredible Petrified World (Governor Films, 1960) Produced & Directed by Jerry Warren; Screenplay: John W. Steiner; Photography: Brydon Baker; Music Director: Josef Zimanich; Editors: James R. Sweeney & Harold V. McKenzie
      Cast: John Carradine (Dr. Millard Wyman), **Robert Clarke** (Craig Randall), Phyllis Coates (Dale Marshall), Allen Windsor (Paul Whitmore), Sheila Noonan [Carol] (Lauri Talbot), George Skaff (J. R. Matheny), Maurice Bernard (Ingol), Joe Maierhauser (Jim Wyman), Lloyd Nelson (Wilson), Harry Raven (Captain), Jack Haffner (Reporter), Jerry Warren (Plane Passenger), Milt Collion, Robert Carroll, Lowell Hopkins

The Last Time I Saw Archie (United Artists, 1961) Produced & Directed by Jack Webb; Screenplay: William Bowers; Photography: Joseph MacDonald; Music: Frank

Comstock; Editor: Robert Leeds

Cast: Robert Mitchum (Archie Hall), Jack Webb (Bill Bowers), Martha Hyer (Peggy Kramer), France Nuyen (Cindy), Joe Flynn (Pvt. Russell Drexel), James Lydon (Pvt. Billy Simpson), Del Moore (Pvt. Frank Ostrow), Louis Nye (Pvt. Sam Beacham), Richard Arlen (Col. Martin), Don Knotts (Capt. Little), Robert Strauss (Master Sgt. Stanley Erlenheim), Harvey Lembeck (Sgt. Malcolm Greenbriar), Claudia Barrett (Lola), Theona Bryant (Daphne), Elaine Davis (Carole), James Mitchum (Corporal), **Robert Clarke** (Officer-Aide), Nancy Kulp (Secretary Willoughby), Don Drysdale (Soldier at Mess Hall), Howard McNear (General)

Secret File: Hollywood (Crown, 1962) Produced by Rudolph Cusumano & James Dyer; Directed by "Ralph Cushman" [Rudolph Cusumano]; Story & Screenplay: Jack Lewis; Photography: Gregory Sandor; Music: Manuel Francisco; Assistant Director: Gene Pollock; Editor: James Dyer

Cast: **Robert Clarke** (Maxwell Carter), Francine York (Nan Torr), Syd Mason ("Hap" Grogan), Maralou Gray (Gay Shelton), John Warburton (James Cameron), Bill White, William Justine, Martha Mason, Barbara Skyler, Kathy Potter, Eleanor Ames, John Shaner, Diane Strom, Selime Najjar, Shirley Chandler, Maya Del Mar

Terror of the Bloodhunters (Associated Distributors Productions, 1962) Produced & Directed by Jerry Warren; Screenplay: "Jaques Lecotier" [Jerry Warren]; Photography: Bill William; Music Director: "Erich Bromberg" [Jerry Warren]; Production Assistant: Chuck Niles; Gaffer: Phil Howard; Wardrobe: Stan Larson

Cast: **Robert Clarke** (Steven Duval), Robert Christopher (Whorf), Dorothy Haney (Marlene), William White (Dione), Steve Conte (Cabot), Niles Andrus (Commandant), Herbert Clarke (Muller), Mike Concannon (Lt. Veardo), Darrold Westbrook (Jacobe), Alberto Soria (Officer), Charles Niles (Estes)

The Lively Set (Universal, 1964) Produced by William Alland; Directed by Jack Arnold; Screenplay: Mel Goldberg & William Wood; Story: Mel Goldberg & William Alland; Photography: Carl Guthrie; Music Supervisor: Joseph Gershenson; Editor: Archie Marshek

Cast: James Darren (Casey Owens), Pamela Tiffin (Eadie Manning), Doug McClure (Chuck Manning), Joanie Somers (Doreen Grey), Marilyn Maxwell (Marge Owens), Charles Drake (Paul Manning), Carole Wells (Mona), Greg Morris (Bit), Peter Mann (Stanford Rogers), Russ Conway (Dave Moody), Frances Robinson (Celeste Manning), Ross Elliott (Ernie Owens), Martin Blaine (Prof. Collins), **Robert Clarke** (Doctor)

The Restless Ones (World Wide, 1965) Produced & Directed by Dick Ross; Screenplay: James F. Collier; Photography: Ernest Haller; Music: Ralph Carmichael; Art Director: Stan Jolley; Editor: Eugene Pendleton

Cast: Georgia Lee (Mrs. Winton), Robert Sampson (Mr. Winton), Johnny Crawford (David Winton), Kim Darby (April), Jean Engstrom (April's Mother), Billy Graham (Himself), Jerome Courtland, Lurene Tuttler, Don O'Rourke, Rick Murray, Bob Random, Patrick Moore, Joe Eilers, Timothy Sims, I. Stanford Jolley, Burt Douglas, Kay Cousins, **Robert Clarke**, Pam McMyler, Marlene Ludwig, Rick Kelman, Paula Baird, David Wright

Zebra in the Kitchen (MGM, 1965) Produced & Directed by Ivan Tors; Screenplay: Art Arthur; Story: Elgin Ciampi; Photography: Lamar Boren; Music: Warren Barket; Editor: Warren Adams

Cast: Jay North (Chris Carlyle), Martin Milner (Dr. Del Hartwood), Andy Devine (Branch Hawksbill), Joyce Meadows (Isobel Moon), Jim Davis (Adam Carlyle), Dorothy Green (Anne Carlyle), Karen Green (Wilma Carlyle), Vaughn Taylor (Councilman), John Milford (Sgt. Freebee), Tris Coffin (Councilman Lawrence), **Robert Clarke** (Mr. Lionel), Percy Helton (Mr. Richardson), Robert Lowery (Preston Heston), Doodles Weaver (Nearsighted Man), Jon Lormer (Judge), Vince Barnett (Man in Man-Hole), Phil Arnold (Man in Tub), Marshall Thompson (Shaving Man), Eddie Quillan

INDEX

Other Books Available from
Midnight Marquee Press

Midnight Marquee Actors Series: BELA LUGOSI **edited by Gary J. and Susan Svehla**

18 well-known authors analyze over 30 films of the legendary Bela Lugosi.

"A must. I insist you readers order it right now!" *Cult Movies*

"The book is well-conceived and intelligently organized... what's even better is that the authors bring fresh perspectives to Lugosi's films by successfully placing each movie into the context of Bela's career and into the context of Hollywood of the time." *Filmfax*

"This book is what books on specific actors should be, good reads." *Monster Scene*

Softbound, 320 pages, 6"x9", $20.00

The Rise and Fall of the Horror Film **by Dr. David Soren**

Detailed analyses of major directors, trends, and representative horror/fantasy films. Topics include foreign horror films, Carl Dreyer, F.W. Murnau, Paul Leni, Jean Cocteau, Fritz Lang, Universal, Lewton, Nuclear Horrors, Hammer, Dario Argento, etc.

"...you may think you're in for pretentious pontification, but Soren never bores as he examines the influence of painting and architecture on serious filmmakers in the fantasy area." *Fangoria*

Softbound, 112 pages, 6"x9", $10.00

Guilty Pleasures of the Horror Film **edited by Gary J. and Susan Svehla**

Some of today's foremost film writers look at their personal "guilty pleasure"... films generally thought of as bad. Included are: *Indestructible Man, The Brain that Wouldn't Die, Frankenstein Conquers the World, Two Faces of Dr. Jekyll, Robot Monster, King Kong (1976), Horror Island, Unknown Island, The Flesh Eaters, She Creature, Omega Man, Juggernaut, Supernatural, Rodan, Giant Gila Mosnter, Voodoo Man, Dune, Private Parts*, more.

Softbound, 320 pages. 6"x9", $20.00

To purchase books or to be placed on our mailing list, write: Midnight Marquee Press, Inc., 9721 Britinay Lane, Baltimore, MD 21234 (Phone: 410-665-1198; Fax 410-665-9207). Please include $3.00 shipping for one book, $1.00 for each additional book (same order). (Canada $5.00, $1.50 for each additional book.) MD residents please include 5% sales tax. Visa and Mastercard accepted.